MONEY

MONEY

Roy Harrod

MACMILLAN
ST MARTIN'S PRESS

First published 1969 by
MACMILLAN AND CO LTD
Little Essex Street London WC2
and also at Bombay Calcutta and Madras
Macmillan South Africa (Publishers) Pty Ltd Johannesburg
The Macmillan Company of Australia Pty Ltd Melbourne
The Macmillan Company of Canada Ltd Toronto
St Martin's Press Inc New York
Gill and Macmillan Ltd Dublin

Library of Congress catalog card no. 72–85481

Printed in Great Britain by
RICHARD CLAY (THE CHAUCER PRESS), LTD
Bungay, Suffolk

CONTENTS

PREFACE

IN this volume I have sought to translate into book form the contents of a course of lectures that I have delivered in Oxford University for more than forty years. It need hardly be said that these lectures have been subject to continuing revision in the light of current events, and I am not sure whether any of the original texture remains. Further additions have of course been made since my last delivery of these lectures in 1967.

Much of the book had already been put into shape by then, but by no means all of it. I may claim to have had bad luck in the time I chose for getting the volume into its final form. In a textbook one seeks to make the reader aware, both of the general theory of the subject, and also of the abiding shape of certain institutions, as distinct from merely ephemeral adaptations of them. My date of retirement from Oxford was 30 September 1967. Since then, in hardly more than a year, we have had the acceptance at Rio de Janeiro of a system of Special Drawing Rights, the institution of a two-tier valuation of gold, a number of important arrangements to consolidate the position of sterling and an acute currency crisis, centred upon Europe, in November 1968, the outcome of which is not certain. These decisions and changes may be thought not to be of transitional significance only, but to have altered what may be regarded as the permanent landmarks of our monetary institutions. But this is not yet certain. I did not want to delay the publication of my book, and no one could say how much delay would be needed before we could be sure that the new institutional arrangements would be lasting features of the monetary scene. I have recorded the main events that have occurred before going to press.

The volume is intended for use by University students at graduate or undergraduate level and by others who wish to gain greater insight into monetary questions. It aims primarily at a formulation of general principles. But it is interlaced with a good deal of historical matter. It is not possible to understand the principles of money in depth without some knowledge of how it has evolved to its present condition. What is money?

It is not like a physical substance, such as gold, in regard to which we believe that we can specify with precision its properties, as they will be for all time, by laboratory analysis. Money is a social phenomenon, and many of its current features depend on what people think it is or ought to be. And this in turn depends, through the progressive building up of established traditions, on important problems and crises that have arisen in the past and on decisions that have been made, for good or ill, by authorities in key positions.

Certain things can be said about money considered as an abstract concept based on certain definitions. Any such pure theory of money, divorced from its historical evolution, is bound to be rather thin. A theory of money that could be useful for current day-to-day interpretations and decisions should be much richer than this, and made so by reference to history.

The order of the book is perhaps unusual. I have begun by describing forms of money, which have lasted for long and will continue into the future, like coins, bank-notes, bank deposits and foreign exchange markets. It seemed to me needful that the reader should have knowledge of what money has been and continues to be in the concrete, so to speak, before embarking him on a purely theoretical discussion. I then proceeded to a theoretical exposition. Finally, in the later sections I have come away from abstract theory and back to institutions, in order to describe those of more recent origin. It seemed to me that in this final phase the reader would gain from some knowledge of pure theory. And so we have the sequence – institutions that have endured over a considerable time, pure theory, modern institutions.

I hope that this volume may be regarded as a worthwhile textbook beyond my own country. In this connection I ought, perhaps, to apologise for the rather frequent references to sterling. I hope that this does not seem to imply a parochial view. The references are particularly prominent in the earlier chapters. The justification for this is that sterling was of predominant importance as a currency before 1914, and that many of the classical debates, decisions and practical precepts, in regard to money, related to sterling in the first instance. What emerged from them was often translated into arrangements for the dollar and for other currencies.

In 1925 I offered a course of eight lectures on the Federal Reserve System, in the University of Oxford. This created a little surprise, as even reasonably well-educated Englishmen at that date were not quite sure what the title referred to. I gave a similar course once every two years until the Second World War, endeavouring to keep it up to date by reference to the publications of the System and to books about it. I have also since 1930 made recurrent contacts with the Board of Governors of the Federal Reserve in Washington and with the Federal Reserve Bank in New York, and I am deeply grateful for the consideration and kindness that has been shown me over so many years. I hope accordingly that a potential American reader will not think that an Englishman cannot know much about the monetary matters that especially concern him.

It is usual in a Preface to add expressions of indebtedness. To do this in my case would entail a narrative of my whole thinking life as an economist, and that would hardly be appropriate in this place!

But I shall express gratitude to my wife for her help in the arduous task of making an Index.

And I would also thank the Rockefeller Foundation for having given me the facility of staying in its beautiful Villa Serbelloni for a period of work on revision and rewriting.

R. F. H.

PART ONE

Forms of Money

1

COINS[1]

1. Introductory

IT is perhaps not necessary to dwell on the traditional definition of money as being a medium of exchange, a measure of
value, a medium for deferred payments and a store of value.
Many primitive societies, including the feudal régimes of the
middle ages, have conducted most of their exchanges without
the intermediation of money. In medieval times, for instance,
rents were paid in labour or in kind; thus landlords obtained
what they wanted by the direct service of their tenants and the
tenants produced most of what they needed for themselves.
The advantage of having money as an intermediary in a
society in which the division of labour is carried to an advanced
stage is obvious. If the producer can sell his product to those
who need it most and buy what he requires from a different
set of people, namely, those best able to produce the things
that satisfy his needs, welfare will clearly be increased. Barter,
the direct exchange of commodities for commodities, lingers on
in backward societies, and even in certain international transactions. An efficient international monetary system has not yet
been extended to all parts of the world.

The use of money as a measure of value arises naturally from
its use as a medium of exchange. By its use in the latter capacity
most people acquire some sense of the purchasing power of
money in general and are thus able to form a rough judgement,
on the occasion of each exchange, about whether they are
getting a good bargain as buyers and sellers. In order to get this
advantage under a barter system, they would have to acquire
a rough knowledge of the purchasing power of all the different
commodities, about the markets for many of which they may
have no direct knowledge.

[1] Some standard books on the subject are: R. Ruding, *Annals of the Coinage of
Great Britain*, 3 vols (3rd edn, 1840); W. A. Shaw, *History of Currency, 1252–1894*
(1895); A. E. I. Feaveryear, *The Pound Sterling: a history of English money* (1931).

From its use as a measure of value flows the practical maxim that money ought to have a constant value, however constancy may be defined. One would think that this would be a most elementary objective of policy. It is a strange fact that after so many centuries of experience in so many countries man has not yet succeeded in providing for himself a money with a stable value. It may be laid down that a primary objective of the science of money should be to yield such practical maxims as might serve to make it possible for a society so desiring to have a money of stable value. It is a mistake to think that failures have been due only to the perversities or mischief of the governmental authorities. An effort of greater understanding is still needed.

The functioning of money as a store of value has been somewhat neglected in classical monetary theory. More recently it was brought into great prominence by Keynes's doctrines about what he called 'liquidity preference'.

These four functions are normally performed by a single medium, except in times of serious disorder. For instance, in the period of great inflation in Germany after the First World War paper marks continued to be handed around, and thus served as the medium of exchange, while in many transactions price quotations were made in terms of the dollar which thus served as a measure of value; the amount of dollars agreed upon was related to the quantity of marks handed over by reference to the daily (or hourly!) quotation for the mark in terms of dollars in the foreign exchange market.

2. The Precious Metals

We may begin our study by referring to the principles of the coinage. Through most of recorded history coins have been used as the exclusive, or almost exclusive, monetary medium. For most of the time the coins, or anyhow the principal coins, were made of one or other of the precious metals, gold and silver.

It is traditionally stated that these commodities were chosen for use as money on the ground of their having in eminent degree the following four important qualities. It is clearly necessary that, if a medium is to be used as money, it should be homogeneous. Otherwise, bargains expressed in money will be of uncertain content. Secondly, the medium should be malleable, so that a given block of the substance in question can be divided into precisely equal parts. The third traditional quality is that of durability. This is clearly needed for the function of a store of value, but a substantial measure of durability is also needed for the simple role of medium of exchange. There is a further point about durability. If the substance is durable in high degree, the stock outstanding at a given time is likely to be large in proportion to current production, and this tends to make for stability of value, since value will not be so much affected by vagaries in current production.

Finally, there is the quality of portability. This means that the value of a unit, whether expressed in weight or extension, should be high.

Croesus, King of Lydia (560–546 B.C.), first had the idea of issuing what we now call coins, both of gold and of silver, namely, pieces of the precious metals of standard size and weight. A superscription was placed on each piece, in order that the user might be able readily to identify that what he was being offered was indeed a piece of metal of the prescribed weight. Lydia was conquered by Persia, which had large resources in the precious metals. Coins rapidly gained circulation throughout the Mediterranean, partly through the trading activities of the Phoenicians.

It was needful to give names to the various pieces. In one famous case, the pound, the name given was nothing other than the name of the weight itself. In the issue of William the Conqueror the 'pound' was quite simply a pound of silver. This was the 'tower' pound, slightly different from the troy pound, the former being the weight of a piece of metal in the Tower of London. A pound was naturally too heavy for ordinary circulation; this consisted at the time of silver pennies, these each being an aliquot part, $\frac{1}{240}$, of a pound of silver. It is a remarkable thing that for more than two centuries the British monetary unit suffered no depreciation at all. How different from our modern conditions of perennial inflation! This was doubtless helped by the fact, already mentioned, that money was used in a limited number of transactions only. In the following period there was progressive debasement, and in the time of Queen Elizabeth I the pound (money) contained only about 4 oz of silver.

The names of coins have a connection with the concept that was eventually evolved of 'legal tender'. One individual might want to make a bargain or contract with another individual to pay so much money in exchange for goods or services rendered. He would express the bargain in terms of the names of the coins. He could then legally discharge his obligation by tendering coins having the names in question. It would be more convenient to refer to coins by their names, these being recognised in law, than to express a bargain in terms of such and such a weight of one of the precious metals. It was up to the authorities to ensure that there were in circulation pieces of metal answering to the recognised names.

This system is also connected with the concept of a 'standard'. This refers to the amount of precious metal supposed to be embodied in the named coins. So long as the legal weight of the named coins remained the same, the standard remained the same. If the quantity of metal officially contained in a coin was reduced, then the standard was said to be debased.

It is next necessary to explain certain principles relating to the maintenance of a good coinage.

3. Wear and Tear (Gresham's Law)

The precious metals of their nature are durable. But even so, they may suffer some erosion. For instance, the superscription may become somewhat blurred. Over many ages this natural process was from time to time reinforced by the artificial one of 'sweating'. Fraudulent persons could get some metal off the coins without making them appear so bad that they could legitimately be refused in payment. Before the invention of milling in the seventeenth century, coins were also often clipped on their edges.

There seems to have been a tendency for this process to accelerate in certain periods, just as in modern times an inflation that has for a while been only moderate may suddenly degenerate into a galloping inflation. When the coinage became worn, counterfeiting was facilitated. This counterfeiting played a primary part in monetary developments until quite recent times. The counterfeiters could pass lightweight coins into circulation without this being readily noticed if the main coinage was in bad condition. And so the moment would come, sometimes rather quickly, when the Government felt that it had to do something about the matter.

At this point Gresham's Law came into play, a law well understood for centuries before Sir Thomas Gresham, but named after him for reasons which will be explained. The law states that 'bad money drives out good'. If the authorities issue new coins into a circulation that has become somewhat worn, the new coins will at once disappear, whether into hoarding or for foreign payment, so that matters will not have been mended. Thus the coins in actual circulation would continue to get worse and worse. The only device that the authorities could think of was to reduce the standard amount of metal in a coin of given name, say the penny, so that the new coins were of lighter weight than the old worn coins. Either could be used to discharge debt. Thus it was the new coins that were the 'bad' money relatively to the old, and the new coins thus drove the old out of circulation. That was what was wanted. As the new coins were sharply marked, the process of erosion by sweating, etc., would be halted for the time being. But this result was only achieved by reducing the standard value of the coin, otherwise known as debasement. This reduction of value was not, it may be believed, usually effected from perversity or mischievousness, but was the only known device for countering Gresham's Law and keeping the coinage in reasonably good shape.

In England this process was terminated by the personal intervention of Queen Elizabeth I, a very great woman. Debasement might, of course, also be effected, not from the virtuous motive described above but to bring some profit to the sovereign. He might issue lighter-weight coins which would temporarily retain the purchasing power of the old coins and thereby help the Government to cover its running expenses, before the inevitable inflationary consequences of such a debased issue served to raise prices. I believe that our first monarch to do this, anyhow to any great extent, was Henry

VIII. But by the time that Queen Elizabeth I came to the throne, the coinage in circulation was already in disorder owing to the processes above described. Queen Elizabeth desired a new issue. Her adviser, Sir Thomas Gresham, pointed out that in the event of a new issue there would have to be a reduction in the standard content of the coins owing to the operation of the well-known law which, owing, presumably, to the lucid way in which Sir Thomas Gresham described it to Queen Elizabeth, has since been known as 'Gresham's Law'. But Queen Elizabeth was not willing to follow in her father's footsteps and authorise a further debasement of the standard content of the coins, and told Sir Thomas Gresham that there must be no such debasement. Doubtless he again stressed Gresham's Law. Queen Elizabeth said that in that case all the old coins must be collected and brought in to the mint so that they could no longer drive out the new coins. We may well believe that Sir Thomas Gresham expostulated that this was 'administratively impossible'. But Queen Elizabeth insisted that it should be done. And it was done. Edicts were issued ordering that those not complying with the Queen's orders should be 'hanged, drawn and quartered'.

This recoinage constituted a new chapter in currency history. There was no further debasement of the pound, apart from a small adjustment in 1601 (about 2%), until 1931.[1] Who will arise to check our modern-type debasement? The penalties would not need to be so severe!

There were similar recoinages, under William III, of which Macaulay has given a classic description, and under George III. But then the system changed again. By the Act of 1774 it was laid down that coins should be legal tender 'by weight as well as by tale' (tale = counting). This may seem reactionary. It deprived users of the convenience conveyed by the super-

---

[1] The *silver* content of the shilling, and therefore the silver value of the pound (= 20 shillings), remained the same from 1601 to 1816, when Britain officially went over to the gold standard, but without any debasement (see below, p. 17). Thereafter the gold value of the sovereign (= one pound) remained the same, in theory and practice, from 1816 until 1931. There was thus unbroken continuity in the value of the pound, apart from two periods of major war, from 1601 to 1931. But between 1601 and 1717 the *gold* value of the pound had been reduced by 34·6%. This was owing to changes in the legal parity between gold and silver (see p. 14), which Britain had to make in that period, in order to keep more or less in line with the changing parities in other countries.

scription on the coin, by which coins having the superscription had legally to be accepted in discharge of debt; there had formerly been no question of having to weigh them every time they passed from hand to hand in exchange, to make sure that they were of the right weight. The Act of 1774 deprived the public of this convenience. But circumstances were somewhat different. In the middle ages, and later, coins might go out into remote parts of the country and circulate there for decades, or even centuries, without ever coming into the hands of the authorities. But by 1774 private banks were dotted all over England. In the ordinary course of trade coins were repeatedly coming into and out of these banks. What actually happened was, not that the coins were weighed every time they changed hands, but that they were weighed every time they came across the counter of a bank, which was sufficiently often. After 1774 the various banks set up little weighing machines on their counters, which they have to this day. The authorities allowed a fine latitude, by which they would replace coins marginally below standard. Coins substantially below ceased to be legal tender.

This system obviated the need for further global recoinages.

4. Right to Melt or Export ('Convertibility')

Maintenance of the condition of the coins in accordance with their standard content was not sufficient to keep a circulation in good condition. There also had to be what, in relation to a note issue, we commonly call 'convertibility'. Indeed, there had to be a two-way convertibility, but we may begin with convertibility in the sense in which it is ordinarily used. It could happen, as a result of the business cycle or other developments, that the number of coins in circulation became redundant to present need. Or it might happen that a country had an adverse balance of payments. In the latter case there would be a balance of people wishing to swap their coins for a medium acceptable in foreign payment, such as gold or silver or the coins of another country.

If the coins were in good condition, one might infer that it was impossible for them to fall below their legal value, since they contained in themselves the amount of gold (or silver) that constituted their legal value. One would only have to melt them or to export them for melting abroad; or indeed, a foreign customer might be content not to melt them but to hold them as a reserve, just as foreigners now hold dollars or sterling. Thus the value of the coin was underpinned at its legal level through the agency of its intrinsic content.

For this system to work perfectly, however, it was needful that people should have the legal right to melt or export the coins. But it was just this right that governments in earlier days were not inclined to allow.

For many ages countries had laws against melting and export-ing. When the precious metals came into Spain in great abundance from the new world, the Spaniards rejoiced, and instituted strict laws prohibiting exportation from Spain. What was the use of having acquired these great treasures if they were merely to be dissipated among other countries of Europe?

The right to melt or export may be regarded as the equivalent of what we call 'convertibility' in the case of notes. If there were laws against melting and exportation and these could be enforced, then, in the event of the supply of coins becoming redundant, they could fall to a discount, just as redundant notes can fall to a discount if they are not convertible into the metal that they are supposed to represent.

Laws against melting and exportation are not, however, easy to enforce, since it is extremely difficult to prevent sur-reptitious melting and smuggling; coins in redundant supply might, however, go to a moderate discount to cover the cost and legal risk.

It was accordingly a step forward when in 1661 England allowed the free export of gold. The authorities may have been somewhat influenced by the arguments of Thomas Mun who explained, albeit still in the mercantilist tradition, that the right way to accumulate treasure was to have a favourable balance of trade, that free trade in the precious metals was a good way of attracting trade, and that the legal prohibitions against export were of no avail. It may well be that this en-lightened policy of allowing the free export of gold was one of the causes of the rapid growth of London as a centre of entrepôt trade and finance in the following centuries.

5. Reverse Convertibility ('Seigniorage')

The idea of the metallic standard was that the pieces in circulation should be of a specific gold (or silver) value, as laid down in the statute, neither more nor less; thereby owners of the coins could exchange them for gold (or silver) at a fixed rate, or with other currencies of a gold (or silver) standard at a fixed rate. Whether this is a helpful system in relation to the desideratum of stable money is another question, to be discussed later. That was what was conceived to be the best way of achieving the objective of stability in former times.

The right of exportation safeguarded coins against becoming depreciated in terms of gold. And, as we have seen, full value coins could not in effect get very much depreciated, even if there was no such right, because of the possibility of smuggling.

But it was not desirable that they should become appreciated either. That was a possibility. Here were these coins with their finely worked superscriptions. Why might they not become appreciated as rare and beautiful objects, as against their gold (or silver) content, just as old, or even new, British sovereigns are today?

This could only be prevented by the right of citizens to have gold (or silver) bullion minted in unlimited quantities. If the coins showed any tendency to rise in value above their gold content, it would pay the individual, given the right of mintage, to bring gold bars to the mint and have them turned into coins. Unlimited mintage was the necessary complement to the right to melt and export, if the coins were to maintain a stable value in terms of the precious metal.

Minting has a cost. Authorities have often charged this cost against those who brought in gold (or silver) bars, so that someone exchanging gold bars for gold coins got somewhat less value in terms of gold. If the charge was correctly equated to the cost of mintage, it was called brassage; but the issuing authority might have the idea of making a higher charge, in order to make some profit. If he did this, the charge was called seigniorage (*droit de seigneur*). The French were still charging 8% in the eighteenth century. One might think of this as a harmless form of taxation, but it is unsound from a currency point of view. A currency subject to seigniorage is liable to fluctuate against other currencies (and bullion), and this is precisely what was not desired. It could fluctuate between the lower level constituted by what could be obtained by melting the coin and a higher level equal to the content of the coin plus seigniorage. Coinages subject to seigniorage did not stand at the higher level all the time. If they did, this would be no great evil. They fluctuated between the top level and the bottom level, in accordance with the phases of the business cycle and the balance of payments of the country concerned. From the point of view of having a stable currency, seigniorage may accordingly be pronounced a bad thing; and to a lesser degree brassage also.

The charge for minting was abandoned by England in 1666, another important step forward. But a slight charge still remained. If we take the period after 1717, an ounce of 22-carat gold was minted into £3 17s 10½d, but someone tendering an ounce of gold only got £3 17s 6d. In 1829 this difference was reduced, and the tenderer of gold bars could get £3 17s 9d for an ounce of 22-carat gold. This charge was said to be made, not to cover the cost of minting, but to cover the interest during the time taken for the minting. The idea may occur that this was unworthy. Why, having taken the heroic step of abandoning all seigniorage and brassage, retain this paltry 1½d as an interest charge? Why not come clean and give the tenderer of bullion £3 17s 10½d?

On this point the authorities were in the right. This difference of 1½d made possible the retention and expansion of a gold bullion market in London. Had the price been absolutely fixed, both ways, at £3 17s 10½d, no gold bullion market could have existed. The consequences would have been most inconvenient. Everyone with gold in hand would simply have taken it to the mint and had it coined, while anyone needing gold for remittance abroad or other purposes could have reconverted the coins into bullion. There would have been a vast amount of quite unnecessary minting, which the authorities would be doing without any charge. But with the bullion market in existence, the mass of buying and selling could be conducted in that market without the gold being minted at all; only the residue would be taken for minting, namely, when the price in the market was tending to fall below the £3 17s 9d limit.

This difference between the buying and selling price of gold is the gold coinage analogue of the limits now allowed above and below the gold parities of currencies in the International Monetary Fund. Those margins render the functioning of foreign exchange markets possible.

If the authorities do not allow unlimited mintage, the value of their currencies may become divorced from that of the precious metal they embody. For instance, when India 'closed the mints' to silver in 1893, the value of the rupee began rising progressively over the value of its silver content.

6. Bimetallism

We have so far discussed the three main topics relevant to the maintenance of a gold (or silver) standard coinage system, namely: (1) the need to keep the existing circulation in good condition, (2) the need for the right to melt or export and (3) the need for the right of unlimited mintage (with a minimum charge). The implication has been that a given country has decided to have a gold or silver standard and has provided the population with a series of coins of given names, the coins in each set in the series being of the same weight. If a country uses one metal only, it is said to be on a monometallic standard. But many countries during the last six centuries have for much of the time been on a bimetallic standard.

This was a paradoxical arrangement, but it worked very well. Country A names certain coins and states what their gold content is. It names other coins and states what their silver content is. And it also states – and here is the paradox – what the value of the gold standard coins are in terms of the silver standard coins. For instance, for a certain period the guinea was a gold standard coin while the shilling was a silver standard coin, each of specified weight in gold and silver respectively, and it was also stated that 20s – later 21s – went to make up a guinea. Debts could be paid in golden guineas or silver shillings alternatively.

The need for bimetallism arose from the requirement, already discussed, of portability. In the Dark Ages and early Middle Ages there was no active gold circulation. This was because nations were poor and because the amount of trans-actions in money was limited. Silver, with its lower value, was the more convenient metal to carry around. But when larger transactions became more frequent, silver was found to be too bulky. Florence coined the golden florin in 1252. In the next century many nations adopted gold coinages alongside their silver coinages. The bimetallic system remained in being in some countries until 1873.

During all this period there were free markets in gold and silver where the forces of supply and demand operated. The remarkable thing is that the relative valuation of silver in terms of gold conformed to what the monetary authorities in the various countries ordained, and not the other way round. There was a gradual declension in the official valuation of silver, particularly in the seventeenth century. Starting with about 12 units of silver to one of gold, the system ended up (the U.S.A.) with a ratio of 16 units of silver to one of gold. This is a very small change over more than six centuries. It is in striking contrast with the rapid fall of silver to 30 to 1 in the quarter-century after the bimetallic system was given up.

The reason for this stability is what is known as the 'com-pensatory action' of the bimetallic system. If there was at any time a rise in gold production while silver production remained stagnant, there would be a tendency for gold to fall in open markets relatively to silver. As soon as this tendency set in, it would be profitable to have gold minted and take silver out of the circulation, since the official mint parity between the two metals would remain unchanged. Thus gold would be absorbed into circulation and silver disgorged, and this was sufficient to offset variations in production and leave the relative values of the metals in free markets unimpaired. This is related to the fact, already mentioned, that in the case of the precious metals the amount of stock in circulation is large relatively to annual production. Consequently, a small change of the mix of metals in circulation would be sufficient to counterweigh quite a large change in the mix of current production.

The stability of the relative value of gold to silver over the centuries shows that the system worked fairly well. It was not perfect. The gradual rise in the value of gold indicated that there were periods when the compensatory action was not quite sufficient to ensure that enough gold remained in circulation. Furthermore, there was not complete co-operation between different countries, any more than there is at present. There were slight differences between the ratios established by the various mints. This might lead to a pull of one of the metals out of country A into country B and force A, or possibly B, to adjust the official mint parity.

England, like many other relatively advanced countries, was on a bimetallic standard for several centuries. The original standard was, as has been described, silver. The principal circulation consisted of silver pennies. Shillings were introduced in the beginning of the sixteenth century and crowns and half-crowns later. The first significant gold coinage was in the mid fourteenth century, consisting of gold florins, named after the Florentine florins. It is not needful to give a catalogue of coins. There were among others nobles, angels, sovereigns and guineas. The guinea issued in 1661 in connection with African trade became especially popular. Throughout there were some disorders owing to the bad condition of the coinage between successive debasements or recoinages as well as to the irregularities of the bimetallic system itself. For some years in the period following the great recoinage described by Macaulay England had a freely floating exchange rate between gold and silver, the guinea fluctuating around 22s or 23s. In this short period it may be said to have been on a monometallic silver standard; but that was a very brief phase.

It is possible to have much argument about when England went over from the bimetallic standard to the gold standard. It is very common in monetary matters to find haziness and imprecision in regard to the steps of evolution. That remains true today. When, for instance, precisely did the supreme power in world monetary affairs pass, perhaps only temporarily, out of the hands of the International Monetary Fund into the hands of the 'Group of Ten'? There are five important dates in the transition from bimetallism to gold monometallism by England, which stretch over more than a century.

1717. The currency was, as usual, in some disorder and Sir Isaac Newton, the famous astronomer, then Master of the Mint, decided to devote his mind to this subject. He established that 1 oz of silver ($\frac{111}{120}$) fine should be coined into 5s 2d, and 1 oz

of 22-carat gold ($\frac{110}{120}$ fine) should be coined into £3 17s 10½d.
This gave a ratio of approximately 15·2 to 1. This was substantially less favourable to silver than the French ratio of
14½ to 1 and it seems likely that in the ordinary way there would
have been an efflux, subject to transport costs, of silver to
France. But the silver coins in England were in bad condition
and this retained them in circulation. Some have liked to say,
owing to the bad state of the silver coinage, that England was
really on the gold standard in the remaining part of the
eighteenth century. This view is perhaps not tenable.

Newton did not intend to take the country off the bimetallic
standard. On the contrary, he thought that he was putting that
standard on a sound basis. His great brain did not succeed in
doing this, but it is surely going too far to say that England had
abandoned the bimetallic standard at this time. Had the
French ratio been altered, as it was destined to be in 1785, it
should probably have decided to have a silver recoinage.
It might even have altered the ratio, had the state of affairs
got too bad.

1774. This date has already been mentioned with reference
to the recoinage and the new principle that the coins would be
legal tender 'by weight as well as by tale'. This principle was
applied to gold coins and to silver coins in amount in excess of
£25. Since the silver coinage was below weight at this time,
this in effect meant making the silver coins that actually
existed legal tender up to £25 only. Some would regard this as
the crucial date, since coins that are legal tender only up to a
limited amount cannot be regarded as part of the standard.
As against this, the silver coins remained legal tender up to
unlimited amounts, if in good condition. There was nothing
in the Act to suggest that there could never be a silver recoinage,
which would bring the coins up to their standard weight. This
decision remained to be taken.

1798. In 1797 England temporarily went off a metallic standard altogether; bank-notes became inconvertible and depreciated, but at first only slightly. Meanwhile the French Finance
Minister, Calonne, had altered the ratio to 15½ to 1. French
finances were in a disturbed condition at this time and this
may have been a manoeuvre to get some profit out of minting.
This could have given the British trouble. Very soon after that,

however, the French Revolution broke out and the French went over to paper money, which soon became highly inflated. In 1796, however, there was a return to a metallic standard under the influence of Napoleon, and with the new ratio it is quite possible that some silver would have come to England for minting – its ratio being fractionally more favourable to silver, despite the slight depreciation of the paper pound.

Accordingly, in 1798, it closed the mint to silver. This is the classic step that is supposed to betoken departure from a standard, as when the Latin Union closed their mints to silver in 1873 and India in 1893. But it is not certain that such action should be given its full significance when a country is not on a metallic standard at all, but has, temporarily, an inconvertible paper currency. This closing of the mint might simply be regarded as a war-time expedient, like the suspension of convertibility itself.

1816. This should probably be taken as the date when England decided to come on to the gold standard. That was the intention of the Act passed under the influence of the first Lord Liverpool. The British did not actually come on to the gold standard in that year, as the notes remained inconvertible until 1821. The Act laid down that 1 oz of silver when tendered should be minted into 5s 6d, but that the tenderer of an ounce should get 5s 2d only. It was thought that levying this seigniorage on silver even without limiting the right to have it minted, while gold continued to be minted without seigniorage, would suffice to make the silver coins subsidiary. But it is by no means certain that it would have done so permanently. This part of the Act was never put into operation.

1821. This marks the real inception of a full gold standard in England. The bank-notes were made convertible once more. Furthermore, the provision for the minting of silver on demand was never put into operation. That was the crucial point in the establishment of the full gold standard. Was this omission due to an administrative oversight? That would be very characteristic of monetary history. The inception of a full gold standard by England was, of course, destined to have profound effects for a century and more.

Thereafter the silver coins in the British system became what are called 'token' coins.

7. Token Coins

A token coin is usually said to have three characteristics: (1) the value of the metal that the coin contains is less than the value of the coin when used as money; (2) the coin is legal tender up to limited amounts only; (3) owners of bullion cannot have it minted, as of right, if they wish. It has been seen how the British silver coinage came to acquire these three characteristics through the combined effect of successive measures.

The use of the expression 'token coins' has not always been unambiguous. It is not quite certain that the second characteristic referred to above is necessary for a coin to be a token coin. For instance, Indian rupees after 1893, the silver content of which was less than their monetary value, and which were not mintable in unlimited quantities on the presentation of silver bullion, were sometimes called token coins, although they were legal tender in unlimited quantities. If we want to distinguish coins which have all the three characteristics listed, as distinct from those that have the first and third only, we may call them subsidiary coins. Since there must be *some* instrument of payment which can be tendered in unlimited quantities, those which may be tendered in limited quantities only may be regarded as subsidiary.

8. The Demise of Bimetallism

In 1821 Germany and most countries to the east were on a silver standard, but the countries that later became known as the Latin Union (France, Italy, Switzerland, Holland and Belgium) were on a bimetallic standard, as was also the United States of America. For the last-mentioned William Hamilton was responsible and he expressed indebtedness to Isaac Newton's researches. Beautiful gold and silver coins were minted and they are to be found in museums. They never had much circulation. In 1834 President Jackson established a new ratio of 16 to 1. This was unduly favourable to gold, and silver coins could not have been minted under it. For all this period the United States currency was very irregular and foreign coins mostly did service for small change. For big denominations, notes were in ample supply, so that neither the official gold nor silver coins circulated. But for most, although not for all, of the period the notes were convertible into metal at the official rating.

In 1852, with a view to getting some order into the lower denominations, what were called 'trade dollars' were issued. These had smaller silver content than was prescribed by Hamilton, and were in effect token coins. But the Hamilton silver dollar remained on the statute book, and could at any time have come into circulation if the supply of silver rose or there was an adjustment in gold–silver parities in other countries; it remained an underlying support to the value of silver.

The abundant discoveries of gold in California and Australia in the middle of the century tended to put pressure on the bimetallic countries, in the sense that silver tended to be drained out of their circulations. This was beginning to prove an inconvenience. In 1865 the Latin Union countries co-operated to issue a 5-franc piece, also of sub-standard content.

It may have been a pity that they did not have more patience, for at the self-same time that they issued this coin, silver began to pour out of the mines of Nevada and became a relatively more abundant metal, and this token coinage would in a year or two have proved quite unnecessary.

The demise of bimetallism came in 1873. Silver was tending to push gold out of circulation in the bimetallic countries. This was for two reasons: (1) there was the high silver production of Nevada, with gold production in California and Australia tailing off; (2) after the Franco-Prussian war Germany decided to go over from a silver standard to a gold standard, thus absorbing gold and disgorging silver. The pure silver standard was doubtless proving inconvenient. Germany may have chosen gold, rather than bimetallism, owing to the example of Britain, which was a pre-eminent commercial and financial nation at that time. The operation was facilitated by indemnity payments coming from France.

The super-abundance of silver due to these two causes finally made the Latin Union countries decide to close their mints to silver in 1873. But there remained the United States. This country was at the time on an inconvertible paper currency (greenbacks). Some busybody decided to take the Hamilton silver dollar off the statute book in 1873. The 'trade dollar' continued to be in circulation. The history books do not recall if the independent actions of the Latin Union and the United States had any connection. It is probable that their coincidence in a single year was fortuitous. Between them they put an end to the bimetallic system.

They did not, however, put an end to the discussion of it. The gold value of silver began to fall fairly rapidly. When the United States returned to a metallic standard in 1879 and it appeared that the mints were no longer open to silver, there was considerable consternation. It seems that many were taken unawares by the effects of the little-discussed elimination of the Hamilton silver dollar in 1873. Probably few appreciated that it was the existence in *law* of the Hamilton silver dollar (which, however, had hardly ever circulated) that sustained the price of silver, while the trade dollars, which everyone knew, were of no avail for this purpose.

A great agitation arose in the United States, culminating in the Presidential campaign of Bryan, which was nearly successful. The famous expression was used: 'America is being crucified on a cross of gold.' This agitation for a restoration of silver may have been partly actuated by silver interests, but there were deeper reasons, and there was considerable agitation for a restoration of silver in other countries also. A series of international conferences were held, the last in 1892, but, like many more recent international conferences about monetary questions, they were of no avail.

Three of the 'deeper reasons' may be mentioned:

1. The bimetallic standard had the convenience of establishing a fixed rate of exchange between countries on a pure gold standard and countries on a pure silver standard. There still remained a number of countries in the latter category. The British were particularly worried by this problem, especially in relation to trade with India (silver standard) and to investment

there, which was then running at a high level. Alfred Marshall's contributions[1] to these discussions, in the form of evidence before successive Royal Commissions, may be deemed his finest work and were the basis of much subsequent monetary doctrine, such as the 'purchasing power parity theory'.

2. The quarter-century following 1873 was a period of falling world prices. Gold alone, the production of which was not running at a high level, now had to do a large part of the work that gold and silver had jointly done before. It was held that the falling prices were responsible for the trade depression, which was evident in many quarters.

3. The more abstract theorists claimed that there was likely to be a greater stability of prices – and stability was a matter of as much concern then as it has been subsequently – if the amount of money supply was a function of two independent variables, namely gold production and silver production, than if it was a function of one variable only. I have not succeeded in getting mathematical colleagues to give a satisfactory formulation of this proposition; it was widely believed.

In the course of his evidence Alfred Marshall proposed a scheme, which would redeem the second and third advantages of bimetallism, without, however, securing the first also. That he did not attempt to retrieve the first was probably owing to undue anxieties about the practical difficulties of operating the bimetallic system. He did not have enough of the historic perspective of six centuries which might have caused him to throw aside these anxieties. Furthermore, if a return to bimetallism had actually been agreed upon in the international conferences, presumably Britain and Germany would have added themselves to the number of those subscribing to bimetallism, and these two countries along with the United States and the Latin Union would certainly have been sufficient to maintain bimetallism as a workable international system.

Marshall's plan was that the standard should consist, not of a certain weight of gold, not of a certain weight of silver, not of a certain weight of gold *or* a certain weight of silver, but of a certain weight of gold *plus* a certain weight of silver. This would have brought back silver into active use to supplement

---

[1] Official Papers of Alfred Marshall, Nos. 1, 2 and 4.

the exiguous supplies of gold, and thus achieved the objective listed as (2) above. It would also have had the advantage of yielding a more stable standard, if the proposition referred to in (3) above is correct. But the value of 1 oz of gold in terms of 1 oz of silver would under his scheme have been allowed to fluctuate freely, and thus the problem of fluctuating exchange rates between monometallic silver countries and monometallic gold countries or between Marshall system currencies and the rest would not have been obviated. Marshall called his scheme symmetallism.

It may be mentioned that the American Congressman, Mr Gorham, put forward a similar scheme during the debates on President Jackson's reform (1834). One may think of symmetallism as a first step towards a system in which a currency would have stable purchasing power, not in terms of one or more precious metals but in terms of a basketful of commodities, while these commodities were left perfectly free to fluctuate in value against each other.

In 1893 the Indian mints were closed to silver. The monetary value of the rupee rose above the level of its silver content, and the rupee became for the time being a currency without metallic attachment. Once again we come to an event for which it is impossible to give a precise date, since what happened in the first instance has to be interpreted in terms of administrative decisions, which are not always precisely defined, still less published. The year 1900 is probably the best date to give for the adoption by India of the gold standard. More strictly, perhaps, it should be called a gold exchange standard, an expression that has come into popular use lately without its meaning being at all clearly defined. The rupee was convertible into sterling, and sterling was convertible into gold, so that the rupee was itself indirectly convertible into gold.[1]

The silver rupee had a value of 2s so long as a bimetallic system was in operation (viz. up to 1873). It was fixed at 1s 4d when the gold standard was introduced, having thus had a debasement in terms of gold. It may be thought that the Indians were well served by this arrangement. Prices fell considerably in this quarter-century in the gold standard world,

[1] For the Indian system, see especially J. M. Keynes, *Indian Currency and Finance* (1913).

with the depressive effects already noticed, while in this period, when the rupee fell from 2*s* to 1*s* 4*d*, prices in India were fairly stable.

The agitation in favour of bimetallism faded out towards the close of the century. This was owing to the application of the cyanide process in South Africa which led to large gold production there. For a brief period until 1914, the international money supply was adequate. Some might say that it was more than adequate, since prices began rising.

2

NOTES AND BANK DEPOSITS

1. Notes

A MAN may deposit some gold (or silver) in a bank and receive a certificate that he has done so, which also constitutes a promise by the bank to repay him his gold on demand. He may then use this certificate as money. He may give it to someone to whom he has to discharge a debt. 'Look, here is this promise by the famous bank X to pay me in gold; if I give it to you, it will pay *you* the gold.' We may call these certificates bank-notes. They may be a convenient substitute for gold, both for carrying about, especially in large denominations, and for sending through the post.

In a system in which the bank went no farther than this – perhaps there never has been such a system in practice – the quantity of notes in circulation would be precisely equal to the quantity of gold deposited with the bank. Professor Cannan has called this a 'cloakroom' system of banking. The tickets issued by a cloakroom are equal in number to the coats hanging in it.

If the system of using notes, rather than metal, in circulation proves convenient, the bank may perceive that it is unlikely that all the notes will be brought in on a given day with a request for repayment of the gold, which was previously deposited. Accordingly, it has the idea that it can lend out some of the gold that it has in hand. Indeed, it must do this if it is to earn any interest and thus pay its way. So having arranged a loan with a client, it will propose to hand over to him some of its gold. But a client may say, 'Oh no, I do not want that gold; I should much prefer some of those nice notes that you issue.' The bank is only too willing to pay him out notes rather than gold. And since the client presumably wants to put the borrowed money to use, these notes go into circulation. When the loan is repaid, notes go out of circulation, just as they do if and when the original depositors of gold wish to withdraw their gold.

At any one time the quantity of notes in circulation will be equal to the quantity of gold deposited in the bank plus the quantity of loans, still outstanding, made by the bank. This is the fundamental principle governing the amount of the money supply, which applies also in the case of bank deposits, as we shall see presently. There may be a slight modification to this, in cases where the earnings of a bank from interest, etc., are not equal to the expenses that it incurs and has to pay out plus interest and dividends to stock-holders.

When the Bank of England was founded (1694), it was authorised to issue notes. The purpose of its foundation by worthy men of repute was to lend money to William III, since the Stuart monarchs, who preceded him, had acquired rather a bad reputation in their monetary dealings. In the eighteenth century in England there were Bank of England notes in circulation as well as notes issued by a number of private banks, owned by individuals or partners. Companies were at that time not allowed to do banking business. The motivation behind this law was probably the same as that to which expression was given in a different way in the United States by the prohibition of branch banking. The idea was that if a corporate bank with a high-sounding name established itself in a small town, the population might be beguiled into lending money to an unsound institution. If banks had by law to be private partnerships, then the integrity and credit-worthiness of their owners would probably be known to most people. This provision did not, however, prevent a number of bank failures in the eighteenth century. The Bank of England notes and the private bank notes circulated side by side and the private banks might hold part of their reserves in the form of Bank of England notes.

2. The Quantity Theory of Money
(Bullion Committee Report, 1810)[1]

In 1797 the Bank of England was on the verge of bankruptcy. The basic cause of this unfortunate development was the war

[1] 'The Report of the Bullion Committee (1810)', reprinted in E. Cannan's *The Paper Pound* (1920); *The Report of the Committee on the Resumption of Cash Payments* (*1819*); D. Ricardo, *Collected Poems*, vols 3 and 4, edited by P. Sraffa (alternatively,

against France. As in more modern times, wars have been apt to be accompanied by inflationary processes. It was believed, hopefully, anyhow in official circles, that the war was likely to be quickly terminated, and that therefore it would be an unnecessary hardship to impose taxation to cover its cost. The income tax was introduced only in 1801. Loans were issued to the public, but the Bank of England also lent to the Government, thus increasing the money supply. There were difficulties also on the side of the balance of payments, mainly owing to substantial subsidies by Britain to encourage allies to maintain their war-like efforts against France.

It has already been noted that immediately on the outbreak of the French Revolution, the French went over to a paper currency (Assignats and Mandats Territoriaux) which soon became grossly inflated. In 1796 the Directory insisted on restoring the metallic circulation. Sir Ralph Hawtrey has stressed the point that the demand for the metals for minting purposes in France caused a drain upon the metallic reserves of the Bank of England.

Whatever the cause, the reserves were in fact depleted, and the Bank of England approached the point when it would be unable to convert its notes into gold. The Bank Restriction Act was passed in February 1797 forbidding the Bank of England to convert any more notes into gold. This euphemistic mode of enactment bears the distinct hall-mark of traditional monetary verbiage throughout the ages. It was as though the Bank of England was longing to convert its notes into gold, but an unkind government was denying it the right to do so. The form of words was devised to maintain 'confidence' in the Bank. When the Bank of England notes ceased to be convertible into gold, they began to lose value in terms of gold.

This is not a history of money. But certain historic events should be understood because they gave rise to the formulation of principles that have been embedded in the theory of monetary policy. The Bank Restriction Act led in due course to the report of the Bullion Committee (1810) (see below), which is the classical exposition of the 'quantity theory of money'.

in *Economic Essays* (1966), edited by E. C. K. Gonner); Professor Foxwell's introduction to Andreades's *History of the Bank of England* (1966); R. G. Hawtrey, *Currency and Credit* (1919), 3rd edition, ch. 18.

It is one of the most important documents in the literature of money. It came in due course to be accepted, not only by academic economists but also by the administrators of British monetary policy, as the basic text for more than a century. And by consequence it had influence far beyond Britain.

It is a common practice to refer to the formulation by Irving Fisher in his *Purchasing Power of Money* as a source for the quantity theory. Fisher's book was in fact a classroom text, to be commended for its clear expositions, but published at the end, rather than at the beginning, of the period, in which the 'quantity theory' was supposed to be the most important principle relating to money. Of course, the Bullion Committee did not invent the quantity theory. Traces of it may be found in writers dating back for centuries before that. But it brought the theory into relation with practical issues. What is perhaps of especial importance is that the depreciation of the pound-note, which it had to consider, was a moderate one only. Anyone could see that wild inflations, such as occurred with the French issue of assignets, were disorderly. With a depreciation that is moderate only, the matter is more subtle.

The depreciation of the pound after the passage of the Bank Restriction Act was signalised by the rise in the price of gold bullion as expressed in sterling and by the fall of the pound sterling in the foreign exchange markets of other countries. At first the depreciation was only slight. We have already seen that it was sufficiently small in 1798 for people to fear that the Calonne bimetallic ratio might cause silver to be brought into England for minting.

It took rather a serious turn for the worse in 1809. This was connected with a big expansion of trade, due partly to the opening up of South America and partly to a relaxation in Napoleon's grip upon his Continental System for debarring British goods from the continent, owing to his preoccupation with the campaigns in Austria and Spain.

Ricardo wrote letters to the *Morning Chronicle* in 1809 and later followed these up by a series of pamphlets on the currency question. The letters attracted attention and led to the appointment of a Select Committee to inquire into the cause of the high price of gold bullion, to consider the state of the circulating medium and of the foreign exchanges (the 'Bullion Committee').

The two central doctrines of the Bullion Committee were: (1) that the value of notes used as currency depends on the quantity issued, and (2) that the quantity of notes will be automatically regulated so as to maintain their value at par, if the notes are always convertible into gold. This requirement, in relation to the maintenance of the value of a note issue, is analogous to the right to melt or export coins in relation to the maintenance of the value of a coinage. In the case of the coins, the price of gold bullion expressed in terms of the coins can never rise in the market above the parity because, if it did, the holders of the coins would refuse to buy bullion in the market and simply melt or export the coins and get bullion at par that way. If the right to melt or export is not allowed, none the less the coins, if in good condition, will not fall very far owing to the possibility of smuggling. In the case of convertible notes, the price of bullion can never rise in the market in terms of notes, since, if it did, holders of the notes would take them to the authorities and get them converted into gold, at par.

The Bank of England refused to accept these doctrines at the time. They held that the value of a note depended upon its backing. They contended that all the notes that they had issued were backed either by government securities or sound bills of exchange, that they had never had any defaults on any of the bills that they had discounted and that consequently it was absurd to say that the notes were depreciated, since they were 100% backed by assets of unquestioned soundness. When it was pointed out that the price of gold bullion had in fact risen, they contended that it was not that the notes had depreciated but that gold had appreciated, taking the view that the latter was due to Napoleon having hoarded gold in his war-chests and thus rendered it unnaturally scarce.

The last-mentioned contention is clearly open to a terminological rebuttal. We may say that, in relation to a gold standard, we *define* a depreciation of notes as a fall in their value in terms of gold, so that the high price of gold bullion was conclusive evidence of depreciation; this could be reinforced by reference to the fall of sterling in terms of other currencies in the foreign exchange markets, and by the fact that the price of gold had not risen in terms of other currencies still convertible.

One might not be content with this view of the matter. The only way of going behind the formal rebuttal is to refer to the value of gold in terms of commodities. Actually, gold had fallen in this period rather considerably. As regards Napoleon, the facts were the exact opposite of those alleged; he had seized on hoards of gold and put them into circulation to pay for his expenses. Thus more gold had come into circulation and its value had fallen in terms of goods, although not quite so much as sterling had. There was no sense in which gold could have been said to have appreciated.

Parliament refused for the time being to accept the findings of the Bullion Committee. A series of resolutions denying its main doctrines were proposed by Vansittart and passed by the House of Commons (May 1811). It *can* be argued that in doing this Parliament showed good sense. This point has been put by Professor Foxwell in his introduction to Andreades's *History of the Bank of England.* To have adhered strictly to gold standard rules and resumed convertibility in two years from 1810, as desired by the Bullion Committee, might have had an adverse effect on the war effort. Some inflation may be useful in wartime. The country gentlemen in Parliament may have instinctively felt this. In such circumstances they may have thought it expedient to agree with the Bank of England attitude, rather than first to endorse the theory of the Bullion Committee, and then say that they were not going to accept its consequences, on the ground that a little bit of inflation, as we now call it, would be good for the war effort. This phenomenon of rejecting the plain truth in favour of saying something that will have a better effect on confidence occurs over and over again in monetary history.

Even the Bank Directors may have half agreed with the Bullion Committee. They certainly began to exercise a more restrained credit policy. It is difficult to judge how far a certain amount of unemployment, which then came on, was due to the more restrained policy of the Bank and how far to a tightening up by Napoleon of his Continental System in 1810. The Luddite riots by machine breakers took place in 1811. In those days the rank and file of workers did not know as much about how a deflationary policy could cause unemployment as they do now. They blamed the machinery instead.

Sterling recovered strongly after the defeat of Napoleon in 1814 and again after Waterloo. Prices fell in consequence of the cessation of war-time activities. It was during this period that the Gold Standard Act (1816), already mentioned, was passed, and it was generally assumed that full convertibility would be restored very soon. The Bank began buying gold in preparation for a restored gold standard. Ricardo scolded them for this, holding, correctly, that the purchase of an asset by a central bank was inflationary; a better preparation for a return to convertibility would be for them to *sell* gold and thus reduce the quantity of the note issue.

3. Ricardo's Further Views

Things did not turn out as expected. The pound began to depreciate again. This was doubtless due to a strong boom that developed. Peace increased the tempo of the industrial revolution. The renewed depreciation upset people, including the Parliamentarians. It was all very well to tolerate some disorders and use anodyne words while the war was on. It was quite a different matter for a depreciation to be allowed to occur in peace-time.

A new committee was appointed, this time including Ricardo, on the Resumption of Cash Payments. It reaffirmed the doctrines of the Bullion Committee and Parliament was now ready to endorse these. The only special point of interest about the second committee is that it went into the question of the velocity of circulation more thoroughly than the Bullion Committee, although that also discussed it. It was pointed out to the committee that the course of prices was not fully correlated with the variations in the amounts of notes issued year by year. The discussion of the velocity of circulation substantiates the claim that the 'quantity theory' was fully dealt with by these committees. The second committee still held that convertibility was a necessary and *sufficient* remedy for any tendency towards an over-issue of notes. If prices rose because the velocity of circulation was rising, notes would be tendered for conversion and the increased purchasing power due to the higher velocity of circulation would be fully offset by the reduction in the quantity of notes consequent upon their conversion.

A final word may be said about Ricardo's views on the situation. There were suggestions that a restoration of the old gold standard might cause hardship owing to the consequent fall of prices as expressed in sterling. Ricardo was not averse to a devaluation in principle, but held that the actual depreciation of the pound was not sufficiently serious to justify such a measure.

But at the same time he gave a warning. For him the great danger was not in the fall of prices due to the restoration of the old gold value of sterling but a fall in prices that might be due to the higher value of gold itself, owing to its greater scarcity in relation to expanding world trade. And this is how things actually worked out. Commodity prices as expressed in gold fell heavily and there was great hardship in consequence, especially among small farmers. Many had expanded production during the war and borrowed in order to do so, when food prices were high. When prices collapsed, many of those who had survived the great enclosures of the eighteenth century had to pack up.

To avoid this evil, which he foresaw, Ricardo proposed that Britain should not return to the use of gold coins but adopt what is now called a gold bullion standard. He thought that Britain should continue with the note circulation, as the principal monetary medium, but make the notes convertible into gold bullion, in amounts not less than 60 oz. He argued that this would be a powerful weapon for preventing the fall of prices that was liable to be caused by the increasing scarcity of gold itself. His point was exactly the same as that made by the Genoa Conference (1922) after the next war of comparable magnitude to the Napoleonic Wars, namely the First World War. The Genoa proposal for a gold bullion standard was widely adopted, but Ricardo's proposal was not adopted at the time. It might have contributed to easing the fall of prices and the hardships that followed therefrom.

Under the influence of the Cash Payments Committee, Bank of England notes were made fully convertible once more in 1821.

4. Bank Deposits

The client of a bank might say: 'Look, I do not want those notes of yours; they will only get stolen. Can't we just leave it that I am in credit with you for so much, and can draw upon you as and when I need to?' A credit of this character may be called a deposit. Eventually, to meet the requirement of such a client, the cheque-book was devised. A cheque-book may be thought of as tantamount to a bundle of notes, each divisible by a pair of scissors into small parts of various sizes. Payments could be made by this method otherwise than in round sums only. A claim in this form could not be so easily stolen as a bundle of notes, and it has the additional advantage that the whole amount does not have to be withdrawn from the bank at the outset, and that the bank might possibly allow interest on what was temporarily left on deposit.

Apart from these questions of convenience, a client is in the same basic position in relation to his bank, whether he has $£X$ of his bank's notes or $£X$ on deposit at his bank, on which he is entitled to draw. When he has to make a payment, if the person he pays would accept a bank-note of bank A, he would also, presumably, be willing to accept a cheque drawn on bank A.

In principle all payments might be made by cheque. Let us temporarily suppose this were done, forgetting for the moment about notes.

The total quantity of deposits at the bank will be equal to the gold (or silver) paid in plus the sum total of loans of different kinds made by the bank and not yet repaid to it. Loans made by the bank include the purchase by it of securities, such as bills or bonds. Thus under this system the sum total of deposits outstanding with the public is governed in precisely the same way as would be the sum total of notes outstanding, if notes only and not cheque-books were used. It is to be noted, and this is quite central to the whole matter, that individuals cannot add to the sum total of deposits outstanding at the bank by being more thrifty, unless their thrift leads them to acquire precious metals acceptable to the bank as money. If an individual has no dealing with the precious metals and his thrift consists in making his income exceed his expenditure, the amount of cheques paid to him by other individuals will exceed the amount of cheques that he pays to other individuals. This means that the other individuals, taken as a group, must draw down their own deposits at the bank in order to make their collective payments to the individual in question exceed their receipts from him. The increase of the deposit of one man is exactly reflected by the decline in the deposit of somebody else, so that there is no net increase in deposits. There can be an increase only if someone pays gold into the bank, or if the bank extends its lending operations.

It might be thought that at this point we must bring notes back into the picture, since an individual might increase his deposit by paying in some notes, rather than at the expense of someone else's deposit. Well then, we simply have to enlarge the horizon. The bank's liabilities are of two kinds, namely deposits and notes outstanding. The sum total of these liabilities is equal to the gold paid into it and not withdrawn plus the net outstanding loans that it has made, including its purchase of securities. The two components of these liabilities may go up or down relatively to one another, to meet the convenience of individuals. If the note liabilities go down, the deposit liabilities will go up; and conversely. The sum total remains the same, unless the bank increases its loans or has a net intake of gold.

One may ask why gold (or silver) has a special place. It is because these commodities are the only ones in which the bank is willing to deal. If a client brought some tin and asked the bank to increase his deposit by the amount of the value of the tin, the bank would refuse on the ground that it did not deal in tin.

If the client brought some securities to the counter, the bank might conceivably be willing to buy them, although normally the bank's purchase of securities is undertaken on its own initiative, not on that of its client, except possibly in the case of bills. Such a purchase would indeed involve an increase of deposits. But this comes under the formula that deposits can and must be increased if the bank makes a net purchase of securities (including bills).

In this connection there is a well-known aphorism that 'bank loans create deposits'. If A passes a cheque to B, this normally reduces A's deposit and increases B's, the sum total of deposits remaining the same as before. But if A's deposit is initially zero and A persuades the bank to lend him the where-withal to pay B, then the sum total of deposits is increased, B's deposit being up by the amount of the cheque paid to him, and A's deposit remaining the same as before, viz. zero.

It is next needful to go over to the two-tier system of banking, which now obtains in most countries, consisting of a central bank and a number of commercial banks.[1] We first concentrate on the central bank. This bank receives gold and lends. (In this 'lending' we include, as always in the case of banks, the purchase of securities.) These processes cause deposits at the central bank to come into existence and/or notes to be issued by it. The deposits will normally be held, for the most part, by commercial banks, or, as we may call them, non-central banks. These commercial banks will also hold notes, known as till money. (Vault cash is the American name.) But some of the notes issued by the central bank also go into circulation among the general public. Thus the net gold acquired by the central bank plus the loans made by it (including the purchase of securities) add up to a sum which is equal to A, the deposits of the non-central banks with it, plus B, notes in the tills of the non-central banks, plus C, notes in the hands of the public. For the time being, we may include the organs of government as part of the 'public'; the ways in which governments deal with their cash in hand differ from country to country. Each commercial bank regards its share of A plus B as its 'cash'. A is readily convertible into B, and conversely, to suit the convenience of the bank.

Gold may flow into the central bank directly from the hands of a member (X) of the non-bank public. In principle X could retain a deposit at the central bank of amount equal to the gold paid in by him. More usually in most systems the central bank will pay him by cheque (or, possibly, by notes if he needs them). X will then pay the cheque into his own bank (Y); this gives Y a deposit of like amount at the central bank.

[1] It has been usual for central banks to hold the nation's gold stocks and this is assumed, for simplicity, in the following analysis. In 1934 the Federal Reserve System handed over its gold to the United States Treasury in exchange for gold certificates; this makes no difference to the analysis. The somewhat more complicated British system, by which the Exchange Equalisation Account began (1932) to hold part and later (1939) all of the gold stock, will be dealt with in due course.

Thus the final position is that the central bank will have extra gold of a certain amount, bank Y will have an extra deposit at the central bank of that amount, which it can convert into notes if it wishes, and X will have an extra deposit at bank Y of that amount, which he can proceed to circulate to others or encash for notes. If X, instead of selling his gold to the central bank, pays it into his own bank, which will normally pass it on to the central bank, the same result ensues.

If the central bank 'lends' by the open market purchase of securities (bills or bonds), the seller of the securities (X), or the broker operating on his behalf, will have a central bank cheque in hand, which he will deposit at his bank (Y). Again the same result ensues – an increased deposit (or note) liability by the central bank, an increased asset in the hands of bank Y in the form of an increase in its deposit at the central bank (or an increase of central bank notes in its vault), and an increased deposit in the name of X at bank Y.

In the United Kingdom and the United States the central bank (Bank of England; Federal Reserve System) does by far the greater part of its lending by 'open market operations'. In the United Kingdom the Bank of England does not normally make loans directly to commercial banks. It does make loans to the Discount Houses (see below), but usually only for brief periods. The Federal Reserve Banks lend for substantially longer periods to the member banks of the system. But even then the amount of direct lending done in this way is small by comparison with the amount of 'lending' done by way of 'open market operations' (purchases of bills and bonds) which are effected through the established market in such securities.

The upshot of this is that, if the central bank has an increase of assets, whether through a gold inflow or its own increase of 'lending' (including the purchase of bills or bonds), some commercial bank will have an increase of assets of equal amount, in the form of claims on the central bank (deposits at it or notes issued by it) and an increase of deposit liabilities of equal amount to its customers. (In a system in which commercial banks issue their own notes, now becoming rare, some of this increase in liabilities may be constituted by an increase in their own notes outstanding.)

So far the result of a gold inflow or an increase of central bank 'lending' is that the commercial banks have an increase in their central bank assets (their deposits at the central bank or central bank notes in hand) and an increase of equal amount in their deposit (or, possibly, note) liabilities. They will then feel free to undertake an increase of lending on their own account.

At present the British commercial banks work regularly to the rule – subject to an exception to be mentioned in a later chapter – that their cash holding must be equal to 8% of their total deposit liabilities. They also have gradually come to work to a rule of having at least a certain minimum proportion of their assets in liquid form ('liquidity ratio'). This will be discussed later.

The member banks of the Federal Reserve System are subject to a legal requirement (see below) that their reserves in the form of deposits at their Federal Reserve Bank plus vault cash shall not fall below a certain prescribed ratio of their deposit liabilities. The principal difference between the United Kingdom and the United States systems is that the British commercial banks work fairly rigidly to the 8% ratio, lending out anything that they have in excess, while the American banks sometimes let their ratio of cash to liabilities rise above the legally prescribed ratio, holding what are known as 'excess reserves'.

We may now revert to the initial position, *before* the effect of lending by the commercial banks is taken into account, in which the gold holding plus lending by the central bank equals $A + B + C$; if the notes in the hands of the non-bank public = C, the commercial banks will have deposits at the central bank plus vault cash = $A + B$ and also deposit liabilities to their customers of $A + B$. Thus their deposit liabilities will be covered to the extent of 100% by claims on the central bank. We may compare their collective position with that of a single bank which has received gold but not begun to lend. The commercial banks as a collection are clearly in a position to do much lending, if they are content to have no more than 8% of their deposit liabilities in the form of claims on the central bank.

The individual bank, taken in isolation, can lend only a proportion of its share of $A + B$, say approximately 92% of it if it is working to an 8% ratio. But this lending, provided that it does not increase the notes wanted by the public, will add to the share of $A + B$ held by some other commercial bank. After a particular bank X has lent 92% of its share of $A + B$, the other banks will have additional claims on the central bank, which are commonly called their 'cash', equal to 92% of the initial share of bank X in $A + B$. (This must be modified to the extent that some of the lending by bank X may come back to itself in the form of additional deposits. Some person M who borrows from bank X may use the facility obtained to pay a cheque to N, who also keeps his account at bank X.) When banks Y, Z, etc., proceed to lend 92% of their cash, other banks will gain a corresponding amount of cash.

Thus the banks, as a collection, can lend much more than 92% of $A + B$. If they lent 92% only, their total deposit liabilities would be 1·92 times their cash, viz. the original $A + B$ together with 92% of $A + B$ 'created' by their own lendings. But if they are satisfied with having a cash ratio of 8% only, they can, as a collection, lend approximately eleven times $A + B$. After that their deposit liabilities, taken as a collection, will be about twelve times $A + B$ and that is what they work towards. Of course, they must keep step with each other. If the banks other than X did not lend at all, then bank X would be rigidly confined to lending 92% of its share of $A + B$ only. Similarly in the intermediate ranges. In the end, as a collection, they must lend about eleven times their cash if they are to finish with not more than an 8% cash ratio.

This has been subject to the assumption that the lending does not cause the public to seek to draw out notes from their banks. But it will in fact do so.

It may be convenient to schematise this matter. Let us call the total deposit liabilities of the commercial banks D.

$$A + B + C = \text{net gold holding} + \text{net outstanding loans of the central bank}$$
$$D = 12\tfrac{1}{2} \ (\text{gold plus lending of central bank minus } C)$$

The ratio of D to C is settled by the convenience of the outside public. This is not a stable ratio, but varies from time to time. Let us suppose that at a given time D is $2\tfrac{1}{2}C$.

Then
$$D = \tfrac{25}{12} \ (\text{gold} + \text{lending of central bank})$$
$$D + C = \tfrac{35}{12} \ (\text{gold} + \text{lending of central bank})$$

$D + C$ is sometimes called the 'money supply'. Given that the cash ratio, referred to above (in the British case, 8%), is stable, and given that the convenience of the public in the mix of deposits and notes held by it is stable, the money supply is governed by the net gold holding + the lending of the central bank. In regard to its gold holding the central bank may be, anyhow temporarily, in a passive position, this depending on the country's balance of payments. But, as it is in control of its lending, it has the power to fix the money supply where it wants to be; e.g. it can offset an inflow of gold by a sale of securities of equal amount. If the convenience of the public as regards the mix of its holding of notes and deposits at the banks varies, the central bank can vary its lending accordingly, so as to keep the total money supply where it wants it to be. Alternatively, it can vary its lending so as to keep the total quantity of deposits at commercial banks at the level that it desires.

In countries in which banks do not work to a rigid cash ratio, the problem of the central bank is a little more complicated, but its commanding position remains.

5. Peel's Bank Act (1844)

Most economists and others thought that, once convertibility had been firmly established in England in 1821, the currency system would work smoothly. It was accordingly disappointing when a series of crises occurred, notably in 1825, 1836 and 1839. What was the Bank of England doing? These crises appeared to be caused by the over-issue of notes with consequent inflationary tendencies. Bank of England spokesmen defended themselves as having conducted the business of the Bank prudently. The idea arose that this was not so, that the sanction of convertibility was not sufficient to prevent the Bank making temporary over-issues leading to crises and that the Bank of England would have to be further fettered.

Two contending schools of thought arose, one known as the Currency School, which was led by Overstone and Torrens, the other known as the Banking School, which was led by Tooke and Fullarton.

One way of approaching this controversy, which was somewhat tangled, is to ask the question, much asked at the time, what each school meant by the word 'money'. The Currency School held that money consisted of coins and notes. The Banking School held that money consisted of coins only, and that notes were mere 'promises to pay'. Incidentally, Bank of England notes were made legal tender only as late as 1833. There was an episode during the inconvertible period which only a legal mind could distinguish from giving a legal tender status to notes during the remainder of that period. When Lord King requested his tenants to pay their rent in gold coin, an Act was passed making it temporarily illegal to refuse to accept notes in discharge of debt. The formal establishment of the status of legal tender for notes in 1833 might seem to give the Currency School a point.

Our first instinct would be to favour the Currency School in this controversy. It was surely unrealistic to refuse to regard notes that were in active use as a medium of exchange as money, and something of a quibble to insist that they were only promises to pay money. But at a deeper level our sympathies now are surely with the Banking School. What they held was that it was superficial to diagnose the causes of recurrent boom and bust as being recurrent over-issues of notes. They held that these over-issues, if such they were, were part of a wider phenomenon, namely an undue expansion of currency *and* credit. The Currency School held that if only the Bank of England were put in a strait-jacket as regards the note issue, and forbidden by law to make recurrent over-issues, all would go smoothly forward. The Banking School held that this did not go to the root of the matter, and that all would not necessarily go forward smoothly. When the Banking School refused to allow notes to be money, it was because they did not want to draw a line between notes on the one side and other credit instruments on the other. Terminologically we should have more sympathy with them if they had said, not 'Notes are not money' but 'Notes are indeed money, but so also are bank deposits'. But at that date no one had gone as far as to be able to think of bank deposits as 'money'. Now we do so regularly.

We still have our present-day terminological difficulties. In much learned writing the word money is extended to apply to all deposits at the regular deposit banks. But in many official statistics, such as those provided by International Financial Statistics (International Monetary Fund), only current accounts (demand deposits) are counted as part of the money supply and deposit accounts (time deposits) are excluded. This is indeed more than a terminological question, just as was the issue at stake between the Currency and Banking Schools. We reach quite different assessments of the requirements of what is called 'monetary policy', according to whether we think its ends will best be served by securing a steady (or anti-cyclical) increase in demand deposits only or in total deposits.

Thus we cannot blame the Banking School for having at that date refused to call bank deposits money, and we may even sympathise with their refusal to call notes money, because, if they had agreed to do so, they would have drawn the line between money and non-money where they did not think that it ought to be drawn. It is possible that in a wider concept of money, if they had been willing to allow this, they might even have wanted to include bills of exchange, which were in active circulation in those days as means of settling ordinary transactions. (What about 'Euro-currencies' in these days?)

Peel's Bank Act (1844) represented the temporary triumph of the Currency School. The Act divided the Bank of England into two departments, the Issue Department and the Banking Department. The division still exists and is important, but its significance is somewhat different from what it was in those days. The Issue Department was authorised to issue £14 million worth of notes backed by Government Securities, and it was laid down that all notes in addition to £14 million must be backed by gold to 100%. At the same time it was laid down that the private banks were not to increase their note issues and that, if any of them became joint stock companies or amalgamated, they must cease to issue notes, and that two-thirds of their previous right of issue would be transferred to the Bank of England and added to the fiduciary section of its issues. By this process of transfer, the fiduciary issue of the Issue Department gradually rose to £19,750,000 at the end of the First World War.

The Banking Department was to conduct the deposit and

lending business of the Bank of England. The triumph of the Currency School doctrine was most strikingly signalised in the words used by Peel in his speech, in which he explained to the Bank of England that it could feel perfectly free in its Banking Department to conduct business on the lines of ordinary banks and in competition with them. The currency question having been settled by the rigid and automatic restriction on the Issue Department, all could be expected to go forward smoothly. The Bank of England need not think it had any further or discretionary duties in managing the monetary system in the public interest.

6. Reaction Against the Act

But after the Act was passed, crises did not cease to occur. On the contrary, there were very severe crises in 1847, the culmination of the railway boom, in 1857 and in 1866. It was evident that a reappraisal was needed. The most important thinker in this process of reappraisal was Walter Bagehot, the editor of *The Economist* newspaper, whose sustained pro-paganda eventually caused official acceptance of a different point of view about the duties of the Bank of England.

We have seen that in the eighteenth century many banks held part of their reserves in the form of Bank of England notes; in due course they began to hold part of them in the form simply of deposits at the Bank of England. It was the duty of the Banking Department to look after these deposits. Peel's Bank Act itself, by its very restrictive limitation on the note issue, served to encourage the use of cheques instead of notes. Meanwhile, despite the wishes of Ricardo, the greater part of the smaller denomination currency in circulation consisted of gold coins. Bank-notes were not issued in denominations under £5 (worth not far short of 100 dollars of today).

Bagehot in substance took over the doctrines of the Banking School. He held that it was the duty of the Banking Depart-ment to watch the state of credit very carefully and use restraint in its lending when business conditions were becoming what we now call 'over-heated'. It is, of course, a mistake to suppose that anti-cyclical monetary policy began only in fairly recent times. It was advocated by Bagehot and was officially accepted as correct in Britain in the later part of the nineteenth century.

Bagehot also defined the functions of the bank as 'lender of last resort'. At that time this function was specifically thought of in relation to the crises. These occurred at the point of the culmination of a boom and ushered in a period of recession. Prices of securities and commodities fell suddenly and severely. The consequence was that many firms which were doing perfectly sound business found themselves in acute embarrassment. If they had liabilities pending, they might find themselves unable to meet them because the value of their assets had dropped calamitously. In these conditions no one was willing to lend money, because if anyone was lucky enough to be the owner of some spare liquidity, he would hold on to it to meet pending obligations. Consequently no one was able to borrow money, however excellent his assets might be. The whole situation froze up. Bankruptcies were multitudinous. It was in these circumstances that Bagehot held that the Bank of England should lend freely – albeit at a penal bank rate, as high as it chose to put it. If no one else was willing to lend, the Bank of England should lend without limit of quantity against any sound assets, by whomsoever submitted. Then, when people knew that there was at least one person still willing to lend, namely the Bank of England itself, the situation unfroze. Others became willing to lend also, since they knew that, if they had sound assets, they could recoup themselves at the Bank of England. It is to be noted that no serious domestic monetary crisis occurred in Britain after 1866.

7. Reserve Requirements

We have seen that Peel's Bank Act divided the bank into two departments, the Issue Department and the Banking Department, that the Issue Department was allowed to issue £14,000 million worth of notes against government securities, and that every note in addition to this amount had to be backed 100% by gold.

Peel's system is known as that of a fixed maximum fiduciary issue. The trouble with the system, which is common to other systems that have a gold requirement in relation to notes, is that it locks the gold up behind the notes and makes it unavailable for use for the purpose for which it is mainly required. There were times in the nineteenth century when there might be an encashment of notes for gold owing to a severe lack of confidence. But by far the most important occasions when people wished to convert currency into gold was when there was an adverse external balance of payments ('foreign drain'). For such a purpose, of which more will be said later, notes would not usually be presented. If the operator was a bank with a deposit at the Bank of England, it would obtain gold by drawing down its balance there; or if the operator had no account at the Bank of England, he would draw a cheque upon his own bank and present it, which again would lead to a drawing down of that bank's deposit at the Bank of England. Thus the gold would be required by depositors at the Bank without there being any reduction of the number of notes in circulation. But the gold was locked up behind the notes, and by Peel's Act this could not be used unless the note issue was reduced. In practice the Banking Department normally itself held a certain quantity of notes. The ratio of the notes that it held to its deposit liabilities was known as the 'proportion'. If a client demanded gold for his deposit, the Banking Department could take any notes that it had around to the Issue Department and thus get a release of gold for the purpose required. Thus under the law the only free gold available to meet a foreign drain was an amount of gold equal to the quantity of notes in the Banking Department. This would be much smaller than the total amount of gold in the Bank of England, which continued to be locked up behind the notes which were in outside circulation or were in the tills of the commercial banks. It has often been pointed out that it is perfectly useless to have a reserve unless it can be drawn upon in a time of need.

Other central banks in due course imitated the Bank of England in making special provisions for the gold cover of a note issue, as a supplement to the more general obligation of the central bank that its notes must be convertible. But the other banks did not imitate the particular system adopted by Peel, and the British always contended that other systems were inferior. The system most commonly adopted was that of 'fixed minimum proportion'. By it the law laid down that the central bank must hold 30% or 35%, or whatever it might be, of gold against the note issue. This shared the disadvantage of the British system in having the gold locked up behind the notes and unavailable for the encashment of deposit liabilities, but it had a further disadvantage. It involves what is known as the 'cab rank fallacy'. Not only is the gold locked up in the wrong place, viz. behind the notes, but it is not even available if notes are presented. If there is a note issue of 100 million units and 30 million units of gold are held, in accordance with a law requiring 30% cover, not one unit of gold is available for converting the notes. For if one note was converted into gold, the note issue would fall to 99,999,999 units while the gold reserve would fall to 29,999,999, but the latter sum is less than 30% of the former, and thus the law would be contravened. Thus the only free gold available for the conversion even of the notes themselves would be gold held in excess of 30% of the note issue. The rest of the reserve would lie idle and be perfectly functionless. The cab-rank analogy is as follows. The kind authorities might think it desirable that citizens should always be able to find a cab on a recognised cab rank when they wish for one, and accordingly make a regulation that there shall never be less than two cabs on the rank at any one time. But if the citizen finds two cabs there, he cannot take one, because that would be in contravention of the regulation. Accordingly, in practice, if the citizen is to be convenienced, there will have always to be at least three cabs on the rank. All systems requiring a percentage ratio are of this character. It is to be feared that even so learned and astute a writer as Professor Robert Triffin has embodied the cab-rank fallacy in his proposal that national central banks should hold at least 20% of their reserves as a deposit in a world central bank.

A better system was that adopted by the Bank of France before the First World War. The object of these controls over the note issue is to restrain the central bank from making excessive issues. The French law laid down a maximum note issue and said nothing about gold. While perhaps exaggerating the importance of the size of the note issue, this system is at least fully rational. Strangely enough, the French went over to the fashionable system (fixed minimum proportion) when they restored the convertibility of the franc after the First World War. They also laid down at that time that a proportion of the reserve could be held in foreign currency, thus contributing to the build-up of a 'gold exchange standard' system, which they have criticised so strongly in recent years.

In 1939 the gold holding of the Bank of England was transferred to the Exchange Equalisation Account and the provision for a gold backing has been dropped. The British have a (flexible) maximum limit to the amount of notes that may be issued. Thus the British have gone over to the pre-1914 rational French system.

By the time that the Federal Reserve System came to be set up in the United States (1914), the idea that bank deposits were just as much money as notes was fairly firmly established. And so it was proposed that there should be a gold backing requirement for the deposit liabilities of the Federal Reserve System as well as for its note issue. But the old feeling of the priority of notes caused the authors of the Federal Reserve Act to fix the ratio for the gold backing for the notes at 40%, while the gold backing for the deposit liabilities was 35% only. Owing to the great enlargement of the money supply in the United States during the Second World War, and the possibility that the gold holding might be inadequate, both these ratios were reduced to a uniform 25%. Things can be done in war-time that would create a great rumpus in peace-time. Unfortunately the provision for the notes and for the deposit liabilities both involve the cab-rank fallacy, as the Americans have been finding to their embarrassment in recent years. When their external balance of payments began to come under heavy pressure (1958), it became obvious that the advantage of having a large reserve was its usefulness in financing a deficit on the external balance of payments, and that the law tying up the gold behind the notes and deposits was a piece of obsolete ritual. After deficits in the balance of payments had proceeded for about seven years, that part of the law which required gold behind deposits was repealed (3 March 1965). But the requirement for the note issue remained. Thus the ancient prejudice that a backing for the notes is more important than a backing for deposits has survived into the sophisticated America of today. It took a world crisis of unprecedented magnitude (16 March 1968) to get the note issue requirement also repealed.

During the nineteenth-century British crises, Peel's Bank Act was suspended on three occasions, in order to allow some of the gold locked up behind the notes to be released. On each occasion this suspension had a strongly curative effect on the crisis. On one occasion the facility did not even have to be used; the mere announcement of the suspension proved sufficient to unfreeze the money market. When the Reichsbank was founded in 1871, a formal provision was made for the temporary release of gold from behind the notes on payment of a tax to the Government. A similar provision was inserted in the Federal Reserve Act.

It has been noted that the British commercial banks work fairly precisely to an 8% ratio of cash to deposit liabilities. The need for a ratio of this order of magnitude was doubtless based on long experience. Before the Second World War the British banks are thought to have worked to a slightly higher ratio; it is not known exactly what this was, owing to the habit of window-dressing. Banks found means for adding something to their cash on the days of the monthly publication of their accounts. They published on different days, so that there might be a certain amount of inter-bank swapping. The ratio, as window-dressed, was about 11%, but the day-to-day ratio was probably 1% or 2% below that. After the war it was agreed that this rather futile habit of window-dressing should be dropped and that an 8% ratio would be sufficient. This ratio is purely conventional, i.e. without legal basis, but there could be trouble if one or other of the banks abandoned it. Under the Bank of England Nationalisation Act of 1946 the Bank of England has power to issue directives about such matters.

In the Federal Reserve Act the ratio of cash to deposits to be observed by banks that were members of the system was laid down by law. There were a number of different ratios: against demand deposits central reserve city banks were to hold 13%, reserve city banks 10% and other banks 7%, and against time deposits all banks were to hold 3%. For the purpose of these ratios only deposits with the Federal Reserve banks counted. Vault cash (till money) was excluded. In 1960 this was altered, the banks thereafter being allowed to count vault cash as part of their reserve. Thus is this respect the American system was assimilated to the British. The official reason given for the change was that it was more equitable as between different kinds of banks. The authorities may have had another motive also, namely, that the change would allow a certain amount of increase in the money supply without entailing an increased locking up of gold; the gold problem was taken to have become rather acute.

In 1935 the Federal Reserve Board was given power to vary these ratios between two limits, viz. the ratios as originally laid down and ratios double those amounts. By raising the required reserve ratios, the Federal Reserve could make it necessary for the member banks to reduce their lending, in fact could impose a 'credit squeeze'. Such a squeeze could also be imposed by a reduction of lending by the Federal Reserve banks which would take the form of sales from its holdings of government securities ('open market operations'). Thus two weapons seemed to have been established for doing the same thing, viz. open market sales and raising reserve requirements. The main reason for this duplication was probably as follows. The United States Government was at that time running deficits in connection with President Roosevelt's attempts to reflate the economy by public works, etc. It was envisaged that a time might come when the Federal Reserve would want to impose a credit squeeze, while the Government was still a net borrower. If the Federal Reserve began selling bonds or bills, in order to impose the squeeze, this might jeopardise the operations of the Government, which would also be wanting to sell bonds or bills to finance its deficit. Therefore it was thought expedient to introduce an alternative method for enforcing a squeeze, by which the Federal Reserve did not have to come into the market, selling bonds or bills; instead it would simply raise reserve requirements. The right to vary reserve requirements has been copied in other countries, such as Germany and Japan.

Finally, it has recently been copied by the British also, but with a different nomenclature. This consists in the requirement by the Bank of England from time to time that the commercial banks should hold 'special deposits' with it, the amount

required from each bank being designated as a percentage of
its deposit liabilities. The plan for requiring special deposits
was proposed shortly before the Radcliffe Committee reported,
and was stated to be a temporary expedient, pending the recommendations of the Radcliffe Committee bearing on this
subject. In fact, the Radcliffe Committee made no such recommendations, and the plan for special deposits has since
been put into operation from time to time. On the first occasion
special deposits successively of 1%, 2% and 3% were required;
later the requirement was rescinded. More recently there has
again been a requirement for 1% (May 1965), and then for
2% (August 1966). If 2% special deposits are required, this
means that the banks are in effect working to a cash basis of
10%, instead of the usual 8%. The peculiar nomenclature is
probably not due to the British just wanting to be different.
Other central banks talk of raising (or lowering) legal reserve
requirements. But the British 8% is not a legal reserve requirement, but a conventional rule. One cannot 'raise the legal
reserve requirement' if there is no legal reserve requirement.
So instead the British call it 'requiring special deposits'.
Although the 8% part of the reserve is conventional, not legal,
yet if, on the occasion of the Bank of England requiring 2%
special deposits, the banks decided to reduce the merely conventional part of their reserve ratio from 8 to 6%, there would
doubtless be trouble!

The reason for the British adopting this system of special
deposits was not dissimilar from that which activated the
Americans. As in the American case, a credit squeeze can be
effectuated by open market sales of securities by the Bank of
England. But there have been times, notably, for instance, in
1955, when it has been difficult to effectuate these sales without
undue disturbance to the capital markets. Again, as in the
American case, this difficulty arose from the British Government's having to borrow money for its own purposes.

One further point should be made in relation to reserve
ratios. By a long process of experience, the British banks found
that it was expedient to have a rule for maintaining a minimum
quantity of 'liquid' assets in relation to their deposit liabilities.
These liquid assets comprise the cash already referred to and
also money lent at call or invested in bills. In due course it

transpired that the minimum 'liquidity ratio' to which they liked to work was about 30%, and this 30% eventually became – the precise date cannot be given – a recognised convention. More recently (September 1963) the Governor of the Bank of England suggested that the banks might find that 28% sufficed. Unlike the 8%, which is the minimum from which the banks do not usually deviate upwards by more than two or three decimal points, 28% is a minimum from which they do deviate quite considerably upwards for considerable periods; in fact, they seldom fall quite so low. Broadly it may be said that the 8% is a rule to which they work regularly, while the 28% is genuinely a minimum. Both ratios play their part in the working of the system. Recent writers have tended to lay special stress on the 28% ratio. I am not yet convinced that they do not somewhat exaggerate its importance by comparison with the 8% ratio.

8. Working of the British System – a Case Study

The Discount Market plays a central part in the working of the British monetary system. The institutions called Discount Houses, in earlier days more often simply bill-brokers, have their roots deep in the past. Their task was to collect up spare cash wherever they could find it, and use it to lend on 'bills of exchange' for financing trade, both domestic and international. They worked to narrow margins and usually charged low rates of interest. London gained the reputation of being the cheapest place to borrow in at short-term, and it financed trade all round the world, often trade unconnected with Britain.

In due course the work of the Discount Houses was much assisted by the development of merchant banks (acceptance houses) in London. These banks were not mainly concerned with providing finance. The bills of exchange used in London normally had two names, that of the payee and that of the payer. When such a bill was discounted, the payee got his money right away, while the payer did not have to pay for three months, or whatever the period might be. There was naturally a vast multitude of actual and potential drawers of bills. It was the special task of the merchant bankers to 'accept'

these bills, which meant that they accepted the responsibility
for payment. The name of a merchant bank on the bill naturally
added greatly to its standing and facilitated the task of the bill-
brokers in deciding what bills they could discount without risk.
It was the duty of the merchant banks to get to know the credit-
worthiness of traders at home and all round the world. Thus
there was a division of labour. The bill-brokers specialised in the
actual handling of short-term loans and they had the task of
keeping their books straight. The merchant banks specialised
in the question of credit-worthiness; it was they who had to
have world-wide knowledge of the reputations of the particular
traders.

Before 1914 Treasury Bills played little part in the market.
They became much more important after the First World War
and more important again after the Second World War.
There was a period in which commercial bills seemed to be
fading out of existence altogether. But in the most recent
period their importance has greatly revived. Meanwhile the
Discount Houses have also branched out into dealing in short-
term government bonds. There was a long period, from 1932
to 1951, of ultra-easy money, with the bank rate at 2% and the
open market bill rate often at less than 1%. On the basis of
such narrow yields it became difficult for the Discount Houses
to pay their way; hence their branching out into the somewhat more remunerative asset of medium-term bonds.

Apart from their cash (till money and deposit at the Bank of
England) already mentioned, the most liquid form of asset that
the commercial banks hold is the money lent at call or very
short notice to the Discount Market. This is in line with the
historic tradition of the bill-brokers mopping up cash wherever
they can find it, and using it to discount bills.

The main categories of lending by the commercial banks are
money lent at call or short notice, the discount of bills, investment in securities of longer date, mainly government, and
advances to customers. These are listed in descending order of
liquidity and, usually, rising order of remunerativeness.

Most of the bills held by the commercial banks are not discounted on the day that the bills are drawn, but at a somewhat
later date. This gives them higher liquidity. As regards their
investments in Government Securities, the banks normally

arrange to hold a substantial proportion of short date so that, at a pinch, they can be sold without great loss of capital value. In the credit squeeze of 1955, when the banks felt it expedient to reduce their holdings of investments, as one way of curtailing total lending, they did experience substantial capital losses. Finally, loans to customers are the least liquid. They may be nominally for a defined period only, but are usually extendable in practice. If a customer explains his circumstances, the bank is unwilling to press him too hard, insisting perhaps on a repayment by instalments over a longer period. The bank will normally hold securities as collateral against its advances, but, if a customer was laggard in repayment, would only sell out the securities as a measure of last resort. In a certain sense it may be held that the primary purpose of a bank is to make advances to customers, the rest of its assets being needed to put it in a sound position to do so. A bank gathers together all the little rivulets of savings that people want to hold on deposit and canalises them into larger amounts available for industry and trade.

The discount market uses its call money, as already explained, to discount bills, Treasury and commercial. Call money must be taken in a literal sense. The banks and Discount Houses are normally in telephonic communication with each other every morning, to discuss how much call money needs to be called in. The banks have constantly to review their position in relation to the 8% ratio. If they are squeezed, their first immediate reaction will be to call in some call money. Every Friday the Discount Houses tender for Treasury Bills and have to take up their allotment day by day during the following week. They will be selling Treasury Bills to the banks from time to time. They will be offered a stream of commercial bills and constitute the money market engaged in very short-term lending. They are in constant telephonic communication with would-be borrowers or lenders all over the world. Thus the Discount Houses have a hectic life in seeing to it that their books are balanced each day, normally by three o'clock in the afternoon.

If, as a result of these operations, including a calling in of call money, they find themselves unable to balance their books, they can have resort to the Bank of England, and rediscount bills with it. Here the Bank of England operates in its role as lender of last resort. In normal conditions the discount market has to borrow from the Bank of England at Bank Rate. This is above the market rate on bills, and thus during the period of such borrowing the Discount Houses find themselves making a loss. They will have lent money on bills at one rate and have had to borrow from the Bank of England at a higher rate, commonly called a penal rate. It is accordingly highly expedient for them to get out of debt to the Bank of England as quickly as possible. They must therefore firm up their own rates, so as to discourage borrowers and attract lenders. The Bank Rate thus has a powerful effect on open market interest rates. When the market borrows from the Bank, this has the effect of increasing the money supply (deposits and notes) in the country, so long as this borrowing is outstanding. If the Bank had previously imposed a squeeze (by open market sales), the borrowing by the discount market *pro tanto* offsets the effect of this. But once the discount market gets out of debt to the Bank, the squeeze is 100% effective. The strength of the British system is that it makes the effect of the squeeze operative very quickly, since the discount market will feel an impelling necessity to get out of debt at the earliest possible date.

This may be contrasted with the operation of the Federal Reserve System in the United States. If the Federal Reserve Banks reduce the cash basis of the member banks by open market operations, the member banks may replenish their cash by borrowing directly from their Reserve Banks. For them the discount rate of the Federal Reserve Banks is not a penal rate. It will be below the average rate earned by the member banks on the whole spectrum of their assets. It may even at times be below the rate that they get on their more liquid assets, such as Treasury Bills. Accordingly, there is not the same imperative necessity for the member banks to get out of debt with the Federal Reserve Banks as there is for the discount market to get out of debt with the Bank of England. It is true that a member bank will not like to be in debt for too long, and may even be under moral pressure from its Federal Reserve Bank to reduce its borrowing. None the less the member banks may remain indebted to Federal Reserve banks for a substantial period of time. To that extent the action of the Federal Reserve system in reducing the money supply by open market sales may be in part frustrated, for the time being, by the member banks coming back on it and asking for direct accommodation, as they are entitled to do under Clause 13 of the Federal Reserve Act.

It may be said in passing that this difference has something to do with the different structures of the two countries. Traditionally the Bank of England has given most attention to the state of the external balance, although also having its eye on the state of the domestic economy in accordance with the prescription of Walter Bagehot. In Britain the external dealings represent a much larger fraction of total economic activity than they do in the United States. In relation to the external balance, notably the movement of short-term funds, the Bank of England requires to get a very quick adjustment. By contrast, until quite recently, the Federal Reserve has had to give little attention to the external balance of the United States. The sole objective of its policy was for long to maintain steady domestic credit conditions and iron out the business cycle. In this activity it would not expect that its operations should have their full effect within a matter of days. Thus it is not seriously hampered by the effectiveness of its methods being somewhat more slow working than are those of the Bank of England.

The normal functioning of the Bank of England control has been described; but sometimes the discount houses can borrow from it at what is called the 'back door'. This means that the Bank is willing to lend at the current open market rate of interest, so that the Discount Houses can borrow without being afflicted by the penal rate. The back door was very much used during the easy money period (1932–51), when the Bank seldom wanted to impose a squeeze, and the discount houses were finding difficulty in paying their way, as already explained. But it is also sometimes used currently. If the Bank of England judges that the discount market has been too easy in its policy, it will force it to borrow at the official Bank Rate. But the discount market may run short of funds owing to a number of fortuitous circumstances, and if the Bank judges that this is not due to laxity on its part, it may provide it with funds through the 'back door'.

Reference may be made here to another gadget. On an occasion when the Bank was anxious to firm up interest rates

c

for balance of payments reasons, but did not at the time wish this firming up to have a generally deflationary effect on the domestic economy as a whole, such as might be the consequence of a rise in Bank Rate and of the other rates conventionally aligned with it, it informed the Discount Houses that, if they came to borrow, it might charge them $\frac{1}{2}\%$ above Bank Rate. This had the effect of causing the open market short-term rates to rise to a position nearer Bank Rate than usual. There is some analogy between this and a policy of the Federal Reserve system, commonly known as 'Twist', when, for precisely the same reason, namely to improve the balance of payments on short-term capital account without having a deflationary effect on the domestic economy, they caused the rate on bills to rise relatively to the rate on bonds by dealing in both markets in an appropriate way.

The Bank of England, like the Federal Reserve System, has two principal weapons for controlling the money supply, namely, changes in the Bank Rate and open market operations. It is to be stressed that these are not alternative policy weapons but are interlocked with one another. There may be open market operations without any change of Bank Rate, when the change in the credit situation required is small only. It may happen that the open market short-term rate is falling below its normal level relatively to the Bank Rate, and the Bank may undertake open market operations to tighten things up; and conversely. Or the situation may be the other way round; the Bank may think that the open market rate is tending in the right direction, say downwards, away from Bank Rate, and adjust the position by lowering the Bank Rate; and again conversely. There may sometimes be a statement that the Bank Rate has been changed merely to get in line with market conditions. The authorities rather like to make a statement of that sort – anodyne words, which have played through history so important a part in monetary policy. The statement may sometimes be a little disingenuous, since the previous position of excessive tightness or ease in the open market may have been due to deliberate Open Market policy by the Bank of England in the preceding period. The point of doing things in this order would be to minimise the psychological effect of a change in Bank Rate, if it was thought desirable to do so.

There is no doubt that normally a change in Bank Rate does have a psychological effect, and this is operative in influencing conditions. If people expect that a period of easier or tighter money is in prospect, they may at once take appropriate action having regard to that.

The Bank Rate and Open Market Operations work together. When the Bank Rate is changed, there are certain rates that by convention are changed at the same time, notably the standard rate charged for bank advances to customers and the rate allowed on deposit accounts (time deposits). On the other hand, the all-important open market rates, which fluctuate from day to day, are governed by the forces of supply and demand. In consequence of a rise (or fall) in the Bank Rate, operators in the market will normally adjust their own rates by a similar amount very quickly. But if the Bank does not readjust its open market policy in accordance with, say, a rise in Bank Rate, the Discount Houses will find themselves with a surplus of funds, and rates in the market will tend to drop down again. Therefore it is imperative in such circumstances for the Bank to mop up surplus funds by open market sales; otherwise the rise in Bank Rate will be ineffective. Similarly with the case of a reduction of Bank Rate. The Open Market policy always has to be consistent with the Bank Rate policy. There is a given Open Market policy for the Bank that will make the supply and demand for credit in the open market establish a rate there that has a normal relation to the Bank Rate.

We next come to a very important point regarding what may be called the elasticity of the discount market. That market applies for Treasury Bills when they are put out to tender each Friday. By an agreement the main Discount Houses act as a group and quote the same rate, and they tender for the whole issue. All outside bidders who offer better prices (i.e. lower rates of interest) than the syndicated bid of the Discount Houses get their application met in full, and those who offer lower prices get nothing at all. The Discount Houses get what remains. Now let us suppose that the Bank of England wishes to impose a squeeze and conducts its open market operations accordingly. The Discount Houses will be short of cash and the open market rates will rise. This may attract outside funds into the market or deter borrowers. But in certain conditions it may

not have that effect. The discount market may be quite inelastic. None the less the Discount Houses are under an implicit obligation to take up the Treasury bills at issue each
Friday. If the rise in interest rates has not achieved an attraction of outside funds into the market, nor deterred borrowing,
the Discount Houses may be in a difficulty. The Government
cannot trim down at short notice the amount of Treasury Bills
it asks the market to take up. In such circumstances the Discount Houses will be unable to balance their books without
resort to the Bank of England. If they go to the front door, they
will lose money. They may have to put up with that for a week
or two. But if the market remains inelastic and the Discount
Houses have to go and borrow at the Bank week after week,
the situation becomes intolerable. The Bank may seek to ease
it by allowing borrowing at the 'back door'. To the extent that
it does this, or indeed to the extent that there is a borrowing
from the Bank of England at all, the purpose of the original
squeeze will be frustrated. The Bank will have reduced the
money supply by Open Market operations and have had to
replenish it again by 'back door' lending.

This kind of situation would not have arisen in the old days,
when the main mass of paper in the discount market consisted
of commercial bills. There was bound to be sufficient elasticity
for the supply and demand for these to be equated by a rise or
fall in the open market rate. This is also normally the position
at present. But there have been times when a change in rates
had little effect on attracting funds or repelling borrowers, and
meanwhile the inexorable demand of the Government through
its issue of Treasury Bills remained. Unless the Bank showed
some leniency, the Discount Houses might be driven to the
position in which they could no longer bid for the whole tender.
And that would be most embarrassing for the Government. At
such times the Bank was bound to show some leniency to the
discount market, thereby frustrating its own original intention
to make money tighter. In such conditions it would seem that
the system was not operating very smoothly.

It is necessary to look more closely at the supply of Treasury
Bills. What the Government will have to borrow week by week
is determined once a year by the Budget. Certain expenditures
are authorised and certain taxes are imposed, and the conse-

quences of this will be felt throughout the ensuing year. (This is subject to the use of what is known as the Regulator, whereby the Government can alter certain taxes between Budgets without Parliamentary authorisation.) The week-by-week borrowing of the Government will not be uniform since tax receipts vary seasonally. In particular receipts fall short of expenditure until the end of the year and then rise above it from the beginning of the year until Budget Day – the period of big tax payments. But the supply of Treasury Bills is not determined solely by this pattern. The Government may do some of its needed borrowing at longer term. It may 'fund' some of the Treasury Bills, if this is expedient from the point of view of monetary policy, e.g. for enforcing a credit squeeze. In such a case, when the Discount Houses are rendered short of cash, they do not have to go and reborrow from the Bank of England, because the supply of Treasury Bills will have been tailored accordingly.

It is necessary to distinguish between nominal funding and true funding. Either can occur without the other. Nominal funding is when the Government issues some long-dated stock and cuts down its issue of Treasury Bills by the same amount. The governmental departments, such as National Insurance, the Post Office, etc., have capital funds, which may consist of a mixed bag of long-dated stock, shorter-dated bonds and Treasury Bills. The most important of these and the one whose funds are said to be used most actively for the purpose that we are about to describe is the Issue Department of the Bank of England which has a capital fund of government securities amounting to some £3000 million (1968). That is a fairly ample fund. If the Government makes an issue and it is not taken up by the public (or only partly so), the Departments come to the rescue and take up the remainder. They can do that by running down their holding of Treasury Bills. To the extent that they run down their holding of Treasury Bills, these have to be issued into the market. They cease to be what are known as 'tap' bills and become what are known as 'tender' bills. Let us take an extreme case and suppose that none of the new long-dated issue is taken up by the public. In such a case there would be a nominal funding, i.e. a reduction of the *total* issue of Treasury Bills by the amount of the issue of long-dated bonds, but no 'true' funding at all. The quantity of *tender* bills would be exactly the same as before, the reduction in the total issue being fully offset by the reduction in the tap issue, the reduction in the tap issue being necessitated to make room in the departmental funds for the acquisition of the long-dated issue which was unwanted by the public. There can also be true funding without any nominal funding, as when the Departments unload some long-dated stock on to the public and at the same time absorb a larger quantity of tap Treasury Bills.

It has already been explained that a difficulty can arise when the Bank wants to impose a squeeze, if conditions in the discount market are inelastic and if the Government does not abate its offer of Treasury Bills, for the whole amount of which the Discount Houses are expected to bid. In such circumstances the latter may be put into an impossible position, unless they are able to balance their books by borrowing from the Bank of England at the back door. But if the Bank allows this to happen, week after week, it will simply be putting back into circulation the money supply that it took out by its initial squeeze, and thus its policy will be frustrated. It is at this point that the question of funding comes in. Academic economists and others criticised the Bank for not having in 1955 funded a greater amount of the National Debt and thus reduced the number of tender Treasury Bills. The trouble here is that in certain circumstances true funding, as distinct from nominal funding, may be easier said than done. To secure true funding the non-bank public, including the great institutional buyers like the insurance companies, have to be persuaded to make net purchases of long-dated government stock. Difficulties have arisen here. In the old days it would have seemed unthinkable that the government broker would not be able to sell, on behalf of the authorities, such amounts of government stock as were needed to effect a given open market policy, as desired by the Bank – except on occasions of very severe crisis.

In recent years the position in this regard has altered. The authorities have been subject to a pincer movement. On the one hand there has been a growing disinclination on many sides to invest in gilt-edged (government) stock, equities (the common stock of corporations) being preferred. The institutional investors have come to have a much larger proportion of equities in their portfolios. The Trustee Acts have been amended so as to allow trustees to hold a proportion of equities. Such humble bodies as colleges and schools have had their statutes altered to allow them to invest in equities. Coming down to the private individual, in the old days his banker or lawyer would not suggest flirtation with equities, except on the basis of a substantial capital already firmly invested in gilt-edged stock. Now all is changed.

The reason usually given for this, and it is probably valid, is that people have come to regard inflation as likely to be a long-run phenomenon, and seek equities as a hedge against inflation. Before the First World War there were periods of rising prices, but it was usually thought that these were likely to be followed by periods of falling prices; and that in fact happened. The inter-war period was prevailingly one of falling prices and depression. Inflation was naturally expected during and for a period after the Second World War, but since then it has appeared to have become a built-in phenomenon. Incidentally, it is to be noted that, when it began to appear in the later part of 1966 that the Government really meant business about an incomes policy and imposed a temporary freeze with legal sanctions, this led to a strengthening of the gilt-edged market.

Fear of inflation is probably not the sole cause of the movement out of 'gilts' into equities, a movement which had already begun before the war during the depression period. The basis of the preference for gilts in the old days was that no risk was attached to them. As time has gone on, the number of companies offering shares (common stock), the risk of serious loss on which is very low indeed, have grown. This has naturally made them more attractive. That is one arm of the pincer movement.

On the other side is the fact that year by year the British Government has to borrow large sums to find capital for the nationalised industries and also to find capital for the local authorities. Before nationalisation these industries found the capital they needed by borrowing in the market, as the private sector still does. In this respect a change was made in 1955, which was one rather of technique than of substance. Hitherto (1946–55) the nationalised industries, other than coal-mining, had raised their capital by specific issues, denominated by reference to the industry Board in question. These issues were not like those of private enterprise since: (1) they had a Treasury guarantee, and (2) they were not underwritten, any residue not taken up by the public being taken up by Governmental Departments. This really made them 'gilt-edged' issues under another name. When the Government changed the system and requested the nationalised industries to come direct to itself, when they needed capital, the object was a consolidation of all the gilt-edged borrowing operations, allowing the Government freedom to raise all the money it required, by whatever timing of issues and division between long and short borrowing might seem most advantageous from time to time.

Before the Second World War the Government did not borrow in peace-time. On the contrary, it had sinking funds for the repayment of debt. It is true that these sinking funds were often 'raided', but in the great majority of years there was some small net repayment of the National Debt.

And so we have the double pressure. The public has lost its taste for gilt-edged stock and the Government has to borrow far more than it has ever had to do before 1945, except in war-time. The situation is really deeply paradoxical. With one part of its thinking the public has, by due democratic process, decided to transfer a substantial part of industry, and especially of industry with high capital requirements, to government ownership. And with another part of its thinking it has decided that it vastly prefers to hold its capital in the form of investment in private enterprise rather than in government stock. Even strong socialists will talk glibly about the superiority of 'equities', without seeming to notice the contradiction inherent in their position.

We now revert to the question of funding. Having looked at the position of the discount market, we have found that in certain circumstances it is only possible to effect a credit squeeze by monetary policy in the ordinary sense, if it is possible to conduct a certain amount of 'true' funding, so as to reduce the 'tender' issue of Treasury Bills. But there have been phases when it has been found impossible to effect true funding on the required scale. Some have said that it must always be possible to fund any given amount, if the authorities are prepared to offer the stock at the right price. But it seems that this point of view is too academic. Of course the authorities will be willing to allow some increase in the long-run interest rate, and may even desire that as part of a squeeze policy. But at times there may be a danger of a downslide of stock prices getting out of hand. They do not want to create what is known as a 'disorderly market'. Even the Americans had some experience of this in the summer of 1953. And so it may happen that the government broker is just not able to execute the amount of true funding that is required from the squeeze point of view.

A situation of this perplexing kind arose in the summer of 1955, when inflationary pressures were rather strong and the authorities rightly wished to damp down the economy. It was the difficulties just described that led to the action of the Chancellor of the Exchequer, which surprised people at the time, in writing to the Governor of the Bank of England proposing direct requests to banks to limit their advances to customers. People wondered why the ordinary machinery of monetary policy was not used to impose a squeeze upon the banks and thus force them to reduce loans, without the need for a personal appeal to them. We may be sure that, if a squeeze on the economy has to be imposed, the banks would prefer to be free to play their part in the process in their own way and at their own discretion, rather than to have directives about curtailing loans to customers by a certain amount. We may believe that the authorities would also have preferred to conduct their squeeze in the orthodox manner, and that they were just unable to do so at that time for the reasons given. The nationalised industries happened to be borrowing at the same time on rather a big scale.

So much for direct interference. Another method for dealing with these difficulties has been the device of the requirement for 'special deposits' (see above, p. 47). By this method the authorities can effect a squeeze without having to conduct true funding. The Bank of England can withdraw tender Treasury Bills from the market and take them into the Banking Department while at the same time requiring special deposits, so that the absorption of the Treasury Bills by the Bank of England purchase does not give the banks any more cash to lend than they had before.

Putting together the possible inelasticities of the discount market and the possible difficulty of true funding, we may say that, in order to effect a squeeze, by regular methods, it is necessary to get Government Securities, whether short-term or long-term, taken up by the non-bank world.

Finally, a word may be said about the 'liquidity ratio' (see p. 49 above). If it is desired to effect a squeeze – and the argument applies in reverse for an expansion – it may be inexpedient that the commercial banks should make the whole of the adjustment, as required to maintain their cash ratio, at the liquid end of their assets. No doubt their immediate adjustment will be at that end. But it may be desirable that in due course they should make adjustments in their less liquid assets also, and notably in their lending to customers. A valid reason for this is that, if the whole adjustment is at the liquid end, this may create too violent and disproportionate a disturbance in the short-term markets. Another reason is that the authorities may regard a reduction (or increase) of customer loans as a primary objective. This may be well considered, but the matter is not certain. It can be held that the major effect of a squeeze or relaxation operates through changes in the total money supply and that it does not much matter through which channel of bank lending this change comes about. Without reverting to old-fashioned ideas of the quantity theory of money, one may yet hold that it is through alterations in the money supply as a whole that monetary policy primarily works. In the reaction from the crude quantity theory, there may have been a tendency to go too far the other way and lay too much stress on paternalism, as distinct from automaticity.

With a view to getting a contraction (or expansion) through all channels of bank lending, and not at the liquid end only, the rule for a minimum liquidity ratio comes in useful.

This is not the place to discuss the effect of monetary policy on the general state of the economy in purely theoretical terms. That will be done later. Some general remarks may be in place here.

There has been discussion about whether variations in the interest rates have a marked effect on investment and activity. Sir Ralph Hawtrey has, during his long period of active writing on monetary questions, continued to maintain that changes in interest rates have a strong effect on economic activity by inducing changes in the holding of stocks of goods. There has been widespread doubt about this. The Radcliffe Committee inclined to the view that these changes are not important. Sir Ralph has challenged its findings in relation to the evidence received. It is true that only a minority of witnesses admitted that interest rates were significant in this connection, but Sir Ralph has contended that, even if only a minority act in the sense required, that will suffice.

There are some general grounds on which it may be doubted if interest rates can have much effect in this area. First, we may go to the raw-material end of the spectrum of stocks of different kinds. Producers and traders will probably have some normal level for stock holding, above or below which, however, they may allow their stocks to go from time to time. Such variations, to the extent that they are deliberate, are primarily induced by the expectation of price changes; one holds more stocks if one expects the prices to rise in the near future, and conversely. At this end of the spectrum, changes in prices can be quite large within, say, a three months period. A man would not take up a position on the view that the price of the commodity in which he was interested would rise by, say, 1%. The uncertainties are too great to make it sensible to hold such a view with sufficient firmness to lead to action. But if he thought that the price might well go up by, say, 5% or 10%, within the relevant horizon, then he might act. But if he did hold such a view, then interest changes within the normal range would not deter him. Even a 2% change would mean only $\frac{1}{2}\%$ for three months.

At the other end of the spectrum stocks are held to meet the prospective needs of customers. It is not good business to be unable to provide what the customer wants. No one would run the risk of being in such a position because the current rate of interest was high. On the other hand a dealer does not want to hold excessive stocks of finished goods, if only because fashions can change quickly and the design, etc., of the goods in his stocks may become obsolete before he can unload them. Are there intermediate goods not covered by these two broad arguments? It does not seem likely.

Others have stressed the importance of the long-term rate of interest on long-term investment. About this too there has been some scepticism, although not nearly so great as that bearing on stocks and the short-term rate. It is contended that in the long term there is too broad a band of uncertainty for fine differences in interest rates to make much difference. Furthermore, the minimum acceptable rate of return on capital may be somewhat insensitive to changes in long-term interest rates as established in stock markets. It has not been fully made clear why the rates of return on capital that, by general agreement, are acknowledged to be accepted as minimum, such as 15% or 20%, are so much above the opportunity cost of raising capital. There is, of course, the risk element. But there may be other elements, which would make the opportunity cost irrelevant. For instance, an entrepreneur may believe that he can expand at the maximum feasible rate, consistent with management availabilities and constraints on growth, and earn 15% (or 20%) on all the capital deployed, at present or in the future. In that case a fall in the market rate of interest from, say, 7% to 5% will not cause him to do anything that he would not otherwise have done.

The publication of the results of findings based on detailed personal cross examinations of businessmen by a research group in Oxford shortly before the Second World War made some impression. The results in regard to the effectiveness of interest rate changes were largely negative. It is possible that this may have been influenced by the fact that interest rates had then been very low for a considerable time and that business memories are short. It seems to be conceded that in the case of very long-term investment, such as housing, where the interest charge is large relatively to the amortisation charge, the interest rate may have influence. It is believed, although this point is not absolutely certain, that low interest rates were in part responsible for the very great housing boom in Britain before the war.

In my own person I take the view that monetary policy has a very powerful effect on economic activity, even though the effects of interest rates, considered as arithmetical quantities, may not be very great. It must always be remembered that the capital market is for most people an imperfect one. There are bits of the capital market which function in the way of perfect markets, where at any one moment there is a going price at which the individual (other than some giant, like the government broker) can satisfy his needs. Such are the gilt-edged end of the stock exchange and the discount market. But most borrowing for capital outlay is not done in these markets. There are all the various channels for borrowing, the commercial banks themselves, the market for new issues, financial syndicates, insurance companies and, above all, trade credit, which plays a vital role. In these various markets it is not a question of just taking out as much money as one wants at a given going price. It is a question of negotiation. When the aggregate money supply is reduced, a would-be borrower may find it much more difficult, and even impossible, to raise money through his accustomed channels; and conversely. It is essentially the imperfection of the capital market that makes monetary policy a powerful weapon. This has surely been strongly evidenced by British experience in recent years.

3

FOREIGN EXCHANGE

---

1. The Gold Standard

As between two countries on the gold standard, the 'parity' of exchange is fixed by the statutory gold content of each of the two currencies. Being on the gold standard was always taken to imply convertibility. The holder of a note could present it for conversion into gold in accordance with the official gold valuation of the note. There was also, as already described, reverse convertibility, by which anyone could tender gold bars and obtain notes in exchange for them. Anyone who so wished could pay a debt to another country on the gold standard by presenting the notes of his own country for conversion by his own central bank, obtaining gold, remitting it to the other country, and there getting the notes of that country in exchange for gold at the official valuation. Most international payments were not made by this method, but through foreign exchange markets. In these markets the great mass of people who wanted to convert, say, sterling into dollars would meet those who had payments to make in the opposite direction, and the dealers in the market could marry the demand for a foreign currency to the supply of it.

Supply would not necessarily be equal to demand. If the demand for, say, dollars was greater than the demand for sterling, the sterling quotation would tend to fall. This would encourage those who foresaw the need for sterling in the not too distant future to buy it at once, while it was cheap. And conversely those wanting dollars might postpone their purchases, in order to obtain them later at a more favourable rate. To the extent that mutual needs were not rigidly fixed for a particular day, a helpful flexibility was introduced. Banks or other corporations having balances in both countries (or several countries) might have some latitude in regard to the particular day on which they replenished one or other balance. This adaptation to the existing rate of exchange caused what might be called 'helpful' movements of short-term funds. The currency for which the demand was weak on a given day would be helped to the extent that its cheapness would provoke purchases of it; and conversely. The rates quoted in different countries, and also the mutual rates of quotations of all the currencies of countries on the gold standard, would be kept consistent by arbitrage dealers.

Arbitrage, to which there will be subsequent references, may be defined as bilateral, or multilateral, deals, in which there is no risk of loss. Thus an arbitrageur may buy dollars for sterling in London and simultaneously sell an equal amount of dollars for sterling in New York. His assets will be the same as they were before these two deals. He would not make these deals if the dollar/sterling rate was not more favourable to sterling in London than in New York. But, since there is no risk involved in the operation, a very fine (negligible) superiority in the quotation of sterling in London compared with its quotation in New York will induce the arbitrage transaction. A multilateral arbitrage transaction might consist in a simultaneous sale of sterling for French francs, sale of French francs for dollars and sale of dollars for sterling, etc. 'Arbitrage' is, of course, to be sharply distinguished from 'speculation'. And both are to be distinguished from 'precautionary' movements of funds (see pp. 79–84).

The exchange rates, however, were flexible only between fixed points, known as the 'gold points'. For instance, if the dollar, having a parity of approximately $4·866 to the £, rose to about $4·85, this might constitute the 'gold export point' for Britain. The distance of the 'gold export point' from the parity was determined by the cost of remitting gold from London to New York, this cost including freight, insurance and interest during the period of transit. If it was possible, by converting notes into gold in London and presenting that gold in New York, to get $4·866 for £1, and if the cost of remitting this gold was not more than 1·6 cents, then it would obviously be disadvantageous to accept anything less than $4·85 for £1 in the foreign exchange market. This gave a bottom limit to the possible downward movement of sterling in the market. Similar considerations would apply to the gold import point. These points were not absolutely fixed for all time, since the freight and insurance charges might vary.

It is to be noted that it was the existence of these points that caused the 'helpful' movement of funds. If there were no such limits to possible fluctuation, then it would no longer be meaningful to say that the £ was cheap in any absolute sense at $4·85.

The actual movements of gold were normally carried out by arbitrageurs, who would execute the gold movement as soon as they saw that there was the finest possible margin of profit in doing so. The arbitrageur would sell sterling for gold in London, buy dollars for gold in New York and sell those dollars in London. As the three transactions constituted a closed circuit, no risk was attached to them. By the principle that no profit can be made where there is no risk, arbitrageurs did not make a profit in the ordinary sense. Their 'very fine' profit may be regarded as a service charge.

2. Modified Gold Standard (I.M.F.)[1]

Some countries which were on the gold standard in the old days are now members of the International Monetary Fund. The question may be asked whether these countries should be regarded, prior to 16 March 1968, as being 'on the gold standard'. The situation since 16 March 1968 will be discussed later. I believe that most uninformed people would hold that they were not on the gold standard. One sometimes heard people say, 'We do not want to return to the gold standard.' I would hold that, on the balance of considerations, it is more sensible to say that they were on the gold standard, rather than the other way round.

One may take the formal point that the various currencies have had in fact a statutory gold value and that the parities of exchange between them are determined by these values. This leads on to a point of great substance, namely that, as was the case under the regular gold standard, the currencies have fixed rates of exchange between them. The *machinery* for maintaining the gold value of currencies and the fixed rate of

[1] Prior to changes made on 16 March 1968 (see pp. 304–11).

exchange between them is (was before 16 March 1968) different
from that described for the gold standard proper. But this was
surely a minor point. In what follows the present tense will
continue to be used in describing the mechanism, since it is
not yet clear whether the 'two-tier' system of 16 March 1968
is more than a bird of passage.

It is sometimes urged that, whereas under the gold standard
proper the quantity of money inside the country was regulated
by the inflow or outflow of gold, that is no longer so. It is true
that there is this difference between the present system and
some very rigid forms of the gold standard, like that intended
by Peel's Bank Act. But it would be an entire misuse of language,
the sense of which should be determined by its actual meaning
as intended by a mass of literature extending over many
decades, to say that a country which did not regulate its
quantity of domestic money supply precisely by the inflow and
outflow of gold was not 'on the gold standard'. For instance,
by no usage of speech could it be denied that the United States
was on the gold standard between 1922 and 1933. Yet during
that period the amount of money supply in the United States
bore no relation whatever to the inflow of gold experienced by
that country. The same is true of Britain in the period from
1925 to 1931. Conversely, under the present system it cannot be
said categorically that the inflow or outflow of gold has *no*
influence on the domestic money supply. It is arguable that the
tightness of money obtaining in the United States in 1966 was
due, in part at least, to the United States authorities having
anxieties about the large outflow of gold. In the United Kingdom the tightness of money in the recent period (1964–68) has
been unquestionably caused by the adverse balance of payments.

There is really only one important difference between the
present system and a gold standard proper – and this is probably not one which would be normally cited by the man in the
street – namely, the existence of what is known as the 'adjustable
peg' in the Articles of Agreement of the International Monetary
Fund. Under those articles a member is allowed to alter the
gold content of its currency, to correct a 'fundamental disequilibrium' in its balance of payments. Under the old gold
standard it was understood that a nation, which had the gold

content of its currency fixed by law, implicitly committed itself
to maintaining that content unchanged *for ever*. It would be
recognised that this commitment might not be honoured in the
event of some catastrophe, such as a major war or revolution.
'For ever' seems a strong expression. But it is not altogether
inappropriate. It must be remembered that Britain did maintain the metallic valuation of its currency unchanged, subject
to some trivial adjustments, and subject to suspension during
two major wars, from 1561 until 1931. The gold value of the
dollar was kept unchanged from 1834 until 1933. There is a
very great difference between a system, the background implication of which is that it will be maintained for all time, and
one the background implication of which is that it may be
altered in certain circumstances (viz. in the event of a 'fundamental disequilibrium'). This is the main difference between
the I.M.F. system and the gold standard in the old sense. It is
one of rather profound importance.

It may be noted here that the trend of official opinion in
recent years has been that the 'adjustable peg' should be used
as seldom as possible. To the extent that this opinion has
authority and has influenced conduct, it might be said that we
were moving towards a gold standard of the more old-fashioned
type. But official views about the working of the monetary
system were shaken by the devaluation of sterling (18 November
1967) and the suspension of the working of the 'gold pool'
countries to maintain a fixed price for gold in the gold bullion
market of London (15 March 1968), and it will be some time
before new coherent views are formed.

In regard to the *machinery* for keeping foreign exchange rates
fixed between narrow limits, many countries do not allow
individuals to hold gold and the balancing payments in gold
are no longer made by arbitrageurs. Therefore the gold points
no longer operate. 'But the rates of foreign exchange can still
fluctuate within fixed limits in the foreign exchange market.
The limits instead of being, so to say, natural ones, governed
by the cost of transporting gold, are artificial ones fixed by
agreement with the International Monetary Fund.

Article IV, Section 4, of the Articles of Agreement of the
I.M.F. lays down that 'each member undertakes, through
appropriate measures consistent with this agreement, to permit

within its territories exchange transactions between its currency and the currencies of other members only within the limits prescribed under Section 3' (i.e. the agreed upon limits). This is the central undertaking .What are the 'appropriate measures'? The Government cannot have a policeman in every house in the country to ensure that people are not exchanging currencies outside the limits behind closed doors. The authorities have a very simple method of preventing such transactions. They must be prepared themselves to support their own currency in some market located in their territory when it reaches the bottom limit and to support the foreign currency of a member of the I.M.F. when the domestic currency reaches the top limit. This automatically prevents any exchange transaction within their territory outside the limits. No one is going to pay more than $2.42 for £1 sterling, if he is absolutely sure of being able to get sterling at the top rate of $2.42 in the market; and no one is going to accept less than $2.38 for £1 sterling, if he can always get at least that amount of dollars in the market. The authorities do not confine their interventions in the market to occasions when the currency is at one or other of the limits. They often support the domestic currency when it is above the bottom limit, and buy foreign currency when the domestic currency is below the top limit. Some might argue, however, that the interventions except at the limits are not desirable.

In any foreign exchange market there will be a number of foreign currencies being exchanged. The authorities might operate in all of them. In most countries the currency especially favoured for these operations is the dollar. If each authority keeps the exchange rate for the dollar in terms of its own currency within the limits, then arbitrageurs can be relied on to ensure that the cross rates between non-dollar currencies are mutually consistent. The widespread use of the dollar by the authorities puts it in rather a special position and causes the authorities to hold more dollars than other currencies in their reserves. Owing to this use the dollar has been called a 'currency of intermediation'.

The dollar is in a special position in another way also. Article IV, Section 4, of the I.M.F. already cited, has a further sentence: 'A member whose monetary authorities, for the settlement of international transactions, in fact freely buy and sell gold within the limits prescribed by the Fund under Section 2 of this Article, shall be deemed to be fulfilling this undertaking.' The American authorities do freely buy gold from and sell it to other central banks at the official parity, and this is deemed to fulfil the requirement of this section. Their willingness to buy and sell in this way is required by an act of Congress. Until quite recently, the American authorities did not intervene at all in the foreign exchange market in New York; accordingly, in the discussions prior to the establishment of the International Monetary Fund, they represented that the method laid down for maintaining currency parity did not suit them. It was for this reason that the alternative method for fulfilling Fund requirements was inserted in the Articles of Agreement. The thought behind this alternative is obviously that, if a country undertakes to buy gold from and sell gold to other central banks freely, this will serve in substitution for intervention in its own foreign exchange market. It is by no means certain that this thought is correct.

The real reason why the dollar remained within the prescribed limits in the foreign exchange market of New York *before* the Federal Reserve System began to operate in it, was not this at all. It was that, if the foreign exchange rate of the dollar is kept within the limits by the authorities in all other countries, it will be kept within the limits in New York by arbitrage. It is not clear whether if all countries, or even a number of countries, took advantage of the *second* sentence in Section 4 and *refrained* from intervening in their own foreign exchange markets, the various foreign exchange rates would in fact be kept within the limits laid down. This is one among a number of instances in which the drafters of the Articles of Agreement of the International Monetary Fund lacked a grip on reality.

It is argued that the Act of Congress referred to puts the United States on a gold standard in a sense in which other countries are not on it. Some have even gone so far as to say that the other countries have adopted what they call a 'gold exchange standard'. I believe that this terminology confuses certain issues, as will appear later. And I would suggest that the statement that the United States is the only country on a full gold standard is a point of form only and not of substance.

In all monetary matters it is what actually happens that counts, and not the form. The fact that Bank of England notes were legal tender after 1833, but not before 1833, and the fact that Federal Reserve notes were not legal tender in the United States for many years after they had come into circulation, are of no significance whatever in monetary history or theory.

The statement that the United States is (was before March 1968) the only gold standard country is sometimes made a prestige point. No one would grudge the Americans prestige. But if the other principal countries are just as much in effect on the gold standard as the United States, this prestige point may confuse thought. It is arguable that the British should have an Act of Parliament similar to the Act of Congress. It would make no difference to the position. It is to be noted that in Britain also (and in other countries) there is a Parliamentary sanction, since its adhesion to the I.M.F. required an Act of Parliament. Its obligation to give gold to another central bank holding its currency, is laid down in Article VIII, Section 4 – provided that it does not hold an equivalent value of the other member's currency whereby it could make a direct swap.

Article IV, Section 4 takes the place of the old gold convertibility in maintaining fixed exchange rates between the member countries in the I.M.F., subject to the margins allowed. The link of the various currencies with gold was, until March 1968, maintained in gold bullion markets, of which the most important was in London. In order to maintain the gold value of each currency the authorities may have to intervene in this market also. The price of gold is almost the same in the various free gold bullion markets, but may be at a premium in some countries where there is restriction on the import of gold. Gold was at a premium in all markets between the Second World War and the reopening of the gold bullion market in London in 1954. The International Monetary Fund objected to this, but there was nothing that they could do about it.

It was not at first clear to everyone, although doubtless it was always so to the British, that intervention by the authorities in the gold bullion market would be necessary if the *de facto* currency value of gold was to be kept at its official level. The matter was brought to a head in 1960 when there was a crisis of confidence in the dollar and there were heavy purchases of gold in the London market. The proper procedure was for the Bank of England to sell gold for sterling in the bullion market while sustaining the dollar in the London foreign exchange market and to tender the surplus dollars thus acquired to the United States under Article VIII, in exchange for gold. There was for a few days some doubt as to whether the United States would honour the dollars, so acquired, in gold, on the ground that the Article did not require this when the acquisition of dollars was the result of speculation, as it could be represented to be in this instance. Some trans-Atlantic telephoning was required. Meanwhile, pending British intervention, gold stood at a heavy premium in the market. In due course the Americans recognised the necessity for preventing this, and there was no trouble subsequently until 1968. Shortly after the crisis of 1960 a 'gold pool' was formed whereby on occasions when there had to be heavy selling of gold by the authorities in the London market to prevent its rising to a premium, the participating countries agreed to provide a proportionate share of the gold required for this purpose, swapping it against currencies. The United States contributed 59%.

If the gold bullion market had not been reconstituted in London in 1954, gold premia in markets in the Middle East and elsewhere would doubtless have continued. It seems likely that, as the years wore on, there would have been a tendency to equality among these markets, so that a uniform and recognised world-wide dollar price of gold would have been established at a level above the official one. It would have appeared more and more that the official gold parities of currencies in the International Monetary Fund were unrealistic and meaningless. This is liable to happen again after 16 March 1968 in relation to the so-called 'two-tier' system. It might even have happened that central banks, including the American authorities, would have been reluctant to continue disbursing gold against their own currencies at a valuation of gold that was *de facto* substantially below the world valuation. I recall that at some date before 1954 I was asked to write a statement to be produced in evidence on behalf of the Iraq Petroleum Company at a trial in which the Iraq Government claimed that the sterling value of contracts expressed in golden shillings should be assessed, not by the official I.M.F. valuation of sterling, but by the then current sterling price of gold, as established in such places as Beirut, Baghdad and Macao. The case was settled out of court on the morning when the trial was due to begin. I confess that I was facing the ordeal of submitting myself to cross-examination with some trepidation, since the Iraq Government seemed to have rather a good case.

3. Short-term Capital Movements
(Full Confidence in Parity)

Foreign exchange rates fluctuate, under the influence of supply and demand, between the outside limits, whether, as in the old system, those of the gold import and export points, or, under the I.M.F. system, the limits officially prescribed. So long as there is absolute confidence that existing parities will continue to be maintained, the fluctuations induce helpful movements of short-term capital. Commercial banks and business corporations which have balances in more than one currency have a latitude as regards when they will replenish or draw down one or other of these balances. If they have need to replenish, say, their dollar balances, they will naturally be on the look-out for an occasion when dollars are relatively cheap, i.e. nearer the bottom than the top limit. If they buy dollars on such an occasion, this means helping the dollar when it is weak, i.e. when the supply is tending to be in excess of demand. Their purchase of dollars constitutes a flow of short-term capital into the United States, and thus serves to bridge a temporary gap when the United States balance of payments is in deficit. And conversely. It is to be noted that the expression 'relatively cheap' has a definite meaning only when there is a fixed rate of exchange and complete confidence that it will not be altered. If there were any belief that the dollar parity might be revised downwards within the relevant time horizon, there would then be no definite meaning in saying that it was cheap now, since it would be expensive now relatively to what it was destined to be after the downward revision, if such occurred.

There is a further 'helpful' movement of short-term capital which can occur only when rates are fixed and there is absolute confidence that they will not be changed. Interest rates may rise in the centre of the currency that is under temporary pressure. This rise in interest rates can provide a further inducement for the purchase of that currency if it is near the bottom limit. The maximum possible loss by a fall in the rate to the bottom limit will be more than offset by the higher interest rate. If the interest rates do not rise under the influence of market forces, they can be given a push by the central bank. Raising the Bank Rate was over many decades the regular way by which the Bank of England tided over temporary deficits due to seasonal or random causes. It was a very effective method indeed. It was always available, since there was absolute confidence that Britain would continue to maintain the existing parity of sterling, as it had done, subject to minor adjustments and to suspension during the Napoleonic Wars, for several centuries. The ability of the Bank of England to induce substantial movements of short-term capital by this method gave great confidence in the future of sterling, and, since sterling was the predominant currency in the world, may be regarded as having been the centre-piece of the world monetary system at that time.

Note may be made of the difference between the effect of a rise in Bank Rate in attracting short-term funds and its effect in deterring short-term borrowers. Before 1914 it was the latter effect that was more important in the British case. A rise in Bank Rate would cause foreign traders to reconsider whether it was profitable to discount bills of exchange in London, or whether they might get cheaper finance at some other financial centre, or even secure the necessary trade credit by raising money locally. One is naturally in a much stronger position if one can rely mainly on the effect of a rise in Bank Rate in deterring borrowers than if one has to rely on the attraction of temporary funds. That added to the strength of the British position at that time.

These aids to maintaining an even balance in the face of adverse short period fluctuations are not available if there is no fixed rate of exchange; and, if there is a fixed rate, but a belief that it may be altered within the relevant time horizon, many perverse movements of short-term capital are likely to occur, i.e. movements that increase, instead of offsetting, a temporary imbalance.

4. *Forward Foreign Exchange Market*

Before explaining this, it is necessary to refer to the forward foreign exchange market. A forward purchase of, say, dollars, in exchange for sterling by A at time X consists in a contract that A will furnish sterling to a dealer at some specified future date in exchange for dollars, which the dealer agrees to furnish, the rate of exchange being agreed upon at time X. The rate at which dollars can be bought forward is not normally identical with the rate at which they can be bought 'spot', i.e. for immediate delivery. The rate at which forward dollars can be acquired will normally be below the rate at which spot dollars can be acquired, if short-term interest rates are higher in New York than in London, by an amount equal to the excess of the total interest accruing in New York during the period of contract over the interest that would accrue in London. Conversely, if short-term interest rates were lower in New York, the forward dollar would normally stand at a premium. When the forward exchange rate bears the relation defined above to the spot rate, the forward rate is said to be at 'interest parity'.

The reason for this may be seen by examining the position of a dealer. Dealers exist, as such, to satisfy clients. It would not do if a regular dealer had to inform a client that he was unable to oblige by furnishing forward currency. Accordingly, from this point of view, the dealer must be regarded as passive. (Of course he may have other business in which he is taking the initiative.) The dealer will endeavour to 'marry' his various contracts for furnishing forward dollars and for furnishing forward sterling, so that they cancel out against each other, and, if he can marry them all, nothing further has to be done by him for the time being. But there may not be an equal balance of contracts; for instance, there may be a greater demand for forward dollars than for forward sterling. On the occasion of each particular contract, the dealer, on stating his terms, must assume that this contract is a marginal contract, i.e. that it will not be balanced by a contract in the opposite direction. In the event of there being a marginal contract, not married, the dealer will have to cover himself by buying the

requisite quantity of dollars spot. If he did not take this precautionary action, then he would be leaving himself in an
exposed position. Of course, if he or his firm chooses to speculate
on the basis of the dollar becoming cheaper later, he can do
that, but this must be considered quite separately from his
daily duty in passively meeting the needs of his clients. If he
has to cover his forward deal by buying spot dollars, then, so
far as he can see at present, he has got to accept the rate of
interest prevailing in New York on short-term money, until the
contract matures, instead of the rate of interest prevailing in
London. If the forward dollar rate were identical with the
spot rate, and if the rate of interest were higher in New York,
then the dealer would be making a riskless profit on the two
transactions (buying spot and selling forward dollars). As these
operations are subject to active competition, market forces will
not allow the dealer to make such a riskless profit. Hence
dealers will be willing to supply forward dollars at a discount
compared with spot dollars, the discount exactly offsetting what
would be a riskless profit, if the forward rate were equal to the
spot rate.

The question may be raised as to what particular interest
rates in the two centres are chosen to determine the value of the
forward discount or premium. At one time it was said that the
rates on Treasury Bills would usually be chosen for this purpose.
At the time of writing (1968) it is understood that the 'interest
parity' is governed by the interest rates on Euro-dollars and
Euro-sterling, entities the nature of which I leave for explanation
to a later stage.

If there is a one-way movement in the market, e.g. a much
greater demand for forward dollars than for forward sterling,
the balance of supply and demand may tend to raise the
premium (or reduce the discount) on the forward dollars,
taking it away from the interest parity. In such conditions
arbitrageurs may enter the market by buying spot dollars and
simultaneously selling them forward, since if the forward dollar
is tending to be above its interest parity, there is a clear riskless
profit in doing so. This action by the arbitrageurs should
normally avail to keep the forward rate very near indeed to its
interest parity. There is, however, a difference between this
type of arbitrage, known as interest arbitrage, and some other

types of arbitrage. In this case the arbitrageurs have to lock up funds, whereas they do not do so if, for example, they simultaneously buy and sell spot exchange in different markets. There may be a limit to the amount of funds available for this purpose, the consequence of which is that, if there is a big one-way movement, arbitrage may not suffice to prevent the forward dollar from standing for a time above (or below) its interest parity. It is to be noted that, when there is an excess of demand for forward dollars over the demand for forward sterling, the difference is always covered by the sale of spot sterling, whether by dealers or arbitrageurs. This means that the excess in question imposes an immediate drain on the reserve of the central bank of the currency under pressure. This can be obviated only if the authorities themselves operate in the forward market.

5. Short-term Capital Movements (Lack of Confidence)

We may now revert to the question of short-term capital movements, when there is a lack of confidence in the maintenance of a given parity within the relevant time horizon. Britain has had much experience of this in recent years. The movements may be considered under the heads of covering, hedging and speculation. At times when sterling has been under pressure there has been much reference in the Press and otherwise to 'speculation against sterling'. But it is most unlikely that speculation has constituted more than a very small part of the total movements of funds in question. Covering and hedging, which constitute the main part of the movements, should properly be called precautionary.

I. *Covering.* In relation to a particular country we have to consider: (*a*) payments due out, and (*b*) payments due in within the relevant time horizon. These dues out and dues in relate not only to merchandise trade and services but also to capital movements. In perfectly normal times, i.e. when there is no thought that the exchange rate may be altered, many great corporations 'cover' all future commitments, as a matter of ordinary office routine, as soon as they are entered into. But not all firms do this. When there is a doubt as to the possible movement of a given exchange rate, upwards or downwards, the position is altered, both in respect of covering and uncovering. The change is due to advice given by the foreign exchange departments of great corporations and by bankers responsible for the affairs of more humble businesses. Both sets of advisers have to keep a weather eye open for possible change, and they would be rightly held culpable if they did not advise their employers or clients to take precautionary actions at appropriate times.

The appropriate occasion for giving such advice is not only when there is a 'probability', viz. more than half a chance, of a currency being revalued, but also when there is a possibility of more than a small degree of importance that this may happen. The theoretical principle is that the likely loss due to devaluation, if it occurs, multiplied by the fraction representing the probability of its occurring, must be greater than the cost of taking covering action.

For the analysis of what occurs when a doubt arises about the continued maintenance of a given parity within the relevant time horizon, we may take initially the two extreme cases: (i) when no one normally covers, and (ii) when everyone does so. We may combine this with another extreme hypothesis, namely that, when a doubt arises, *everyone* is advised to take appropriate precautionary action and does so. We may take sterling by way of illustration:

a. Dues out denominated in non-sterling currencies. Advice will be given to buy the foreign currencies in question at once in the spot or forward market. Which market is chosen will depend on the liquidity position of the firm in question and also on the fine margins when the forward rate is not at interest parity; but this decision on the choice between spot and forward, on the occasion of distrust in the parity of a currency, makes little difference, since the preponderance of forward purchases in one direction will necessitate dealers in forward exchange making equivalent spot purchases; the drain on the reserve of a suspect currency (or the inflow of funds into a country thought to be likely to value upwards within the relevant time horizon) will be the same, whether the particular firms buy spot or forward. This drain on the reserve can, however, in the case of forward purchases, be obviated, if the central bank of the country of the suspect currency itself operates in the forward market, as the Bank of England did on a considerable scale in periods before the devaluation of sterling in November 1967. Similarly in the case of a currency believed to be likely to be valued upwards the central bank can reduce the inflow of funds by operating in the forward market as the Bundesbank did before February 1961.

b. Dues out denominated in sterling. Under the suspicion of a possible devaluation of sterling, foreigners due to receive sterling will be advised to sell it at once on the forward market. This imposes an immediate drain on present reserves, for the reasons already given.

c. Dues in denominated in foreign currency. No action should be taken.

d. Dues in denominated in sterling. No action should be taken.

The summary is that, on the hypothesis that no positions were previously covered, and, on the advent of suspicion, *all* positions are covered, when that is appropriate, the drain on sterling will be equal to the sum-total of dues out within the relevant time horizon.

Now let us take the extreme opposite case when *all* positions are normally covered:

a. Dues out denominated in foreign currencies. No fresh action need be taken. These positions should continue to be covered, as before.

b. Dues out denominated in sterling. No fresh action required. These positions also should continue to be covered by the sale of sterling forward by the foreigners due to receive it.

c. Dues in denominated in foreign currency. Here fresh action is required. Firms should *cease* to cover these positions (and uncover positions previously covered). There is no point in selling foreign currency forward if there is a chance of getting more sterling for it later within the relevant time horizon. The *cessation* of covering in this class of cases has the same adverse effect on the reserve that fresh covering has in cases (i) (*a*) and (*b*).

d. Dues in denominated in sterling. Foreigners who have to make payment should *cease* buying sterling in advance either in the spot or forward markets, since they may be able to get it cheaper before the due date of payment.

On the hypothesis that all positions were previously covered and that, on the occasion of loss of confidence, all positions under (c) and (d) cease to be covered or are uncovered, the loss to the reserves is equal to the sum-total of expected dues in within the relevant time horizon.

The sum-total of changes of direction classified under (i) (a) and (b) and (ii) (c) and (d) are known as the 'leads and lags' in trade payments. These can add up to very large amounts indeed. In the case of the United Kingdom, supposing the relevant time horizon to be three months, taking current account payments only and ignoring long-term capital flows the total movement of funds involved would be about £2000 million.

This may give a somewhat exaggerated picture, since not all people take appropriate action when there is a loss of confidence. Some may go forward in a carefree manner and allow themselves to be caught unawares if devaluation actually occurs. But there may be occasions when the loss of confidence is very severe indeed, as, for instance, a few days before the devaluation of sterling on 18 November 1967, when the great majority do take appropriate action.

In another respect the estimate may understate the position, as the relevant time horizon may be more than three months. When there was a persistent expectation before 1961 that the Deutschemark would be valued upwards, as eventually it was, but by a smaller amount than expected, it was reported that some foreign firms who had contracted to buy German equipment were buying Deutschemarks to cover payments due as far as two years ahead.

It is an interesting, and perhaps surprising, result of the foregoing analysis, that it makes no substantial difference to the size of the leads and lags movement whether no positions are covered normally i.e. in the absence of a break in confidence, or all positions are covered normally. In the one case the maximum size of the movement will be equal to the value of payments due out within the relevant time horizon and in the other case it will be equal to the value of payments due in. Dues out may not be exactly equal to dues in – indeed, they are presumably somewhat greater if a currency becomes suspect – but this difference will be small in relation to the magnitudes we are considering.

If some firms normally cover and some do not – the actual case – the same result follows, provided that the proportion of out-payments that is normally covered is equal to the proportion of in-payments normally covered. If the proportion of out-payments normally covered is greater than the proportion of in-payments normally covered, the leads and lags movement consequent on loss of confidence will be *pro tanto* less; and conversely.

For a time I supposed that leads and lags movements in relation to a suspect currency would be greater if a high proportion of the country's trade, imports and exports together, was invoiced in this currency. The analysis shows that this is not the case. The total amount of precautionary action required will be the same in whichever currency the trade is denominated. The only difference is that, if a higher proportion of the trade (both ways) is denominated in the home (suspect) currency, a larger proportion of the covering (or uncovering) actions will have to be undertaken by foreigners, while, if a lower proportion of the trade is invoiced in the home currency, a higher proportion of the covering actions will have to be undertaken by residents.

2. *Hedging*. Foreign firms may hold sterling assets in the ordinary course of their business. These may consist of currency balances, of securities denominated in sterling or of 'real' assets like factories, stock in trade or real estate. If the plight of the United Kingdom was considered to be very desperate, with a communist revolution threatening round the corner, they might decide that the United Kingdom was no place to do business in and sell the lot outright. The mere possibility, or even probability, of sterling being devalued within a relevant time horizon would not be likely to cause them to take such drastic action. But they may feel that they ought to take *some* action to protect the value of their sterling assets in terms of the dollar or in terms of whatever their own currency may be.

In the case of real assets they might indeed argue that the effect of a devaluation would be to raise the sterling value of their assets, owing to the inflationary process consequent on the devaluation, and thus to conserve their dollar value. But this would be a somewhat precarious argument. The inflationary process might take a long time to work through. Meanwhile the United Kingdom Government would presumably do its best, by all policy measures available, to prevent the sterling price level of goods and services rising in full proportion to the devaluation.

So the foreign owner may decide to protect himself by the forward sale of sterling in amount equal to the whole or to a part of the capital value of his sterling assets. If sterling is devalued before his contract matures, he will be able to buy spot sterling, with a view to discharging his forward contract, at a lower price. By the profit he makes on this transaction he will recoup himself in large part for the loss in the dollar value of his sterling assets due to the devaluation. If sterling has not been devalued but is still under suspicion, he can renew his forward contract. If the suspicion has blown over, he can just wind up his position.

This protective action may cost something, as in the case of covering. There will be the commission; the price of spot sterling may have risen by the time that he has to buy it in; forward sterling may have been – probably will have been – below its interest parity at the time when he sold it. Thus the risk of devaluation must be sufficient to justify his incurring these costs.

Both the covering and hedgings operations should be regarded as precautionary in the strict sense. They are operations under-taken to avoid the risk of loss.

3. Speculation. The word speculation has been used much too freely in relation to the great 'runs' on sterling and on the dollar that have occurred in recent years. This has been unfortunate, because it has created a wrong impression. The word should not be applied to precautionary actions taken to protect existing positions. It should be confined to the actions of those who take a view about a currency and sell it (or buy it) with the object of making a profit, should their view prove correct. A man may say: 'I believe that sterling will be de-valued. I shall have a flutter, and there will be a handsome profit for me if I am right.'

Those close to foreign exchange operations do not report that speculation in this sense played a large part in the 'runs'. And it is inherently unlikely that it should have done so.

Speculation doubtless plays a great part in commodity

markets and still more in security markets. But this type of speculation is a continuing process. The relevant factors are carefully studied over a period of time. An *expertise* is gradually built up. There can also be specialisation, by which a speculator concentrates on a particular sector of the market. It is not likely that vast sums are ventured even in this type of speculation without the existence of a considerable body of knowledge about relevant factors.

The occasions on which an important currency may be devalued do not occur frequently. There cannot be a continuing study of how the relevant factors work in practice. The economic issues involved are usually complex. Political factors also often play an important part. Doubtless some speculation occurs. But there cannot be such a large background of understanding as would justify venturing really massive sums. Speculation, like covering and hedging, costs money.

It may be asked why the coverers and hedgers are justified in incurring such costs and not would-be speculators. The answer is simple. If the coverers and hedgers do not incur these costs, and if the currency in question is then devalued, they will make substantial losses. If the would-be speculator refrains from incurring these costs and does not speculate, and if the currency is then devalued, *he loses nothing*. Thus his position is entirely different from that of those who cover or hedge.

From all of the above it is clear that, in relation to short-term capital movements, the central bank will require larger reserves to meet occasions when a lack of confidence may develop than it would need to have if there was no provision in the Articles of Agreement of the I.M.F. allowing devaluation in certain circumstances. It would be assumed that the country would make greater efforts to avoid devaluation, if this were downright illegal. The I.M.F. clause, by making devaluation 'respectable', makes it seem more likely, from time to time, that a country will have resort to it than it would be if there was no such provision.

The consequence of all this is that, given the existence of the devaluation clause, the central bank ought to keep larger reserves to cope with short-term capital movements than it would need to have if the devaluation clause did not exist.

D

6. Short-term Capital Movements (Flexible Exchange Rates)

Some words should be said about short-term capital movements when a currency has no fixed rate of exchange. The most important example of this – apart from disorderly episodes – was sterling between 1931 and 1939. The main features of that episode are described in Chapter 4, Section 2.

When there is no fixed rate, all future commitments will normally be covered. There may be some carefree people. If the sum involved is not large, an individual may feel that he does not mind taking a risk of loss, which will be offset by a possibility of gain. But most people will usually cover.

First it must be noted that the 'helpful' movements of short capital that occur under fixed rates when there is absolute confidence in them (pp. 75–6 above) will not occur with flexible rates. This is because a flexible currency cannot become 'cheap' in any absolute sense, as a currency is when it is near its bottom limit under the fixed rate system. Of course an individual may take the view that at a certain rate a currency is cheap, because he thinks that it will rise later. But being cheap in the mind of a particular individual is quite different from being cheap as a hard fact, as is the case, from time to time, with fixed-rate currencies. Moreover, it is of the essence of the flexible system, in which the rate is fixed from day to day mainly through the influence of market forces, that it will move to a level at which there are as many who think the rate too high as think it too low.

Secondly, there will not be helpful movements of short-term funds to take advantage of interest rate differentials, since the exchange risk is too great. Under fixed exchange rates the maximum exchange risk in moving short-term funds to take advantage of a higher interest rate is less than the gain of interest, when the exchange rate is near its bottom limit.

It is true that there may be *covered* movements of short-term funds under the flexible rate system (viz. spot purchases combined with sales forward). But covered movements are not 'helpful'. If the inward movement of covered funds towards the high interest centre exceeds the outward movement of covered funds from it, the dealers will not be able to marry all their forward contracts and will have to sell the currency in question spot, in amount equal to the excess inflow of covered funds.

Some advocates of flexible exchange rates have held that the rates should be allowed to 'float freely' without any official intervention. The idea is that the correct rate will be established by the market forces of supply and demand.

In order to assess the value of this contention, an analysis is necessary. The balance of market supply and demand depends, in one part, on what may be called the fundamental position. This position depends primarily on the competitiveness of the country in question in establishing an appropriate flow of exports and imports of goods and services in relation to what is happening (rightly or wrongly) on its long-term capital account, and on its short-term capital account also, to the extent that this is of long-term significance.[1] If, at a given point of time, there is, looking at the matter from the point of view of what will happen in a two- to three-year period, an equal balance, the country in question may be said to be in 'fundamental equilibrium'. But at the same point of time there may not be an equal balance of supply and demand at the ruling rate of exchange owing to seasonal, cyclical or random causes. Owing to these causes, the balance of supply and demand on a given day may serve to alter the rate of exchange, in an upward or downward direction, away from the rate which, by the aforementioned definition, is consistent with fundamental equilibrium. Under the system of fixed exchange rates, there would be in such circumstances a 'helpful' short-term capital flow of sufficient amount to fill the gap between supply and demand due to these seasonal, cyclical and random factors. But under the system of a freely floating rate there can be no such helpful movements for the reasons already given. How then will the gap be filled? Let us take the situation in which, owing to these short-term causes, the supply of a currency exceeds the demand for it. The gap will have to be filled, in the absence of official intervention, by a special inflow of private short-term capital.

If this flow is to occur, it is needful for the foreign exchange rate to move to a point at which more people think that it is

[1] See pp. 91 and 219.

likely subsequently to move upwards than think it likely to move downwards. And conversely. If we suppose that people have a true idea about what the exchange rate consistent with fundamental equilibrium is, it will have to move to a level substantially *below* that rate (or substantially above it in opposite circumstances), in order to induce speculators, having regard to the costs of speculation, to operate in such a way as to get an equal balance of supply and demand in the market. This means that, in order to get an equality of supply and demand from day to day, there will have to be departures from the true equilibrium rate, upwards or downwards.

The authorities, watching events, and knowing that aberrant oscillations in the foreign exchange rate are detrimental to the optimum flow of foreign trade and investment, will be sorely, and, I would suggest, rightly, tempted to intervene, when they know that the imbalance of supply and demand, and the consequent movement of the market foreign exchange rate, is due to seasonal, cyclical or random causes. The doctrinaire view that they must *never* intervene will, again rightly, seem to them to make no sense. If the view of the authorities on this point is correct, and in fact they ought to intervene on such occasions, it follows that they will need to have larger reserves on this account than they would have to on a system of fixed rates, when gaps due to seasonal, cyclical or random causes would be filled by 'helpful' private movement of funds under the influence of the incentives described above.

The account just given was based on the hypothesis that private potential speculators continually have the right assessment of what the rate consistent with fundamental equilibrium is; even on that hypothesis there appeared to be need for official intervention. It is a dangerous hypothesis. Factors determining the rate consistent with fundamental equilibrium are frequently changing, and it is very difficult to assess the effect of these changes on what the equilibrium rate should be. Simultaneously there may be causes due to seasonal, cyclical or random factors operating on the balance of supply and demand in the market. How can the unfortunate operator (or his adviser) disentangle the one kind of cause of an excess supply of a currency from the other? At this point I should like to record with some emphasis that the ebbs and flows of confidence in sterling in the period before 18 November 1967 seemed to me to make little sense; in particular, lest, being a British man, I should be deemed to have some bias, I should like to record that the return flows of confidence in sterling seemed to me to make little sense, since to an economist making a careful and fundamental analysis, the United Kingdom position did not appear to have improved on those occasions. From this I infer that 'advisers' on foreign exchange operations, although thoroughly honest and well-intentioned, are not very competent in assessing what the fundamental equilibrium rate of exchange should be.

If this view about their competence to discern the difference between fundamental and merely transitional causes is correct – and it is really no discredit to them to assume that it is – how can they do better than they do in all the difficult circumstances of the case? – it follows that a still more substantial drop in the foreign exchange rate of a currency below its 'fundamental equilibrium' level, on the occasion of merely transitional weakness, will be needed before the advisers will begin to recommend their clients or employers to speculate in favour of a currency. If this is right – but it may not be – rather large oscillations in the foreign exchange rate will be needed, in the absence of official intervention, to secure a day-to-day balance between supply and demand. This, if true, would make the case all the stronger for intervention by the authorities to fill gaps due to seasonal, cyclical or random causes, about which they will have more detailed information than the would-be speculators could possibly have. The consequence of intervention would be a steadier rate than would otherwise obtain.

There is, however, a possible disadvantage of intervention. It was stated above: (i) that under the system of flexible rates the great majority of commitments will be covered, and (ii) that, at any given rate, there will be as many people, if any, who believe that the existing rate is above the equilibrium level as there are believing it to be below that level. That is the consequence of the rate being allowed to move under the influence of market forces. These two classes, if such exist and if their respective views are sufficiently firmly held, will cease covering – in opposite directions. The effects of these two 'cessations' on the rate of exchange will cancel out.

But if the authorities intervene to offset seasonal, cyclical or random imbalances, and, accordingly, the rate does not perfectly reflect the contemporary balance of private supply and demand, it is possible that the opinion that the rate is too high, in relation to long-run equilibrium, may overweigh the opinion that it is too low. In this case, an unfavourable cessation of covering will outweigh the favourable cessation of covering (or conversely). And in this case there will be a net short-term outflow (or inflow) of funds on precautionary account. When the movement is unfavourable, the authorities will need to use their reserves, not only to offset the seasonal, cyclical or random factors but also the net short-term capital outflow ('leads and lags' and hedging) due to the adverse opinion about what they are doing.

We may summarise the foregoing considerations in relation to the size of reserves that the authorities need to hold:

1. This is minimal with fixed exchange rates in which there is absolute confidence, since helpful movements of private short-term capital will normally fill the gaps due to seasonal, cyclical and random causes.

2. It is maximal under the system of fixed exchange rates combined with an 'adjustable peg' (as under the I.M.F. system) owing to the large perverse movements that are liable to arise when a country is seen to have an adverse balance of payments.

3. It is nil, when there are absolutely freely floating exchange rates; but this system would lead to intolerable oscillations.

4. It is betwixt and between under the system of floating rates with official intervention.

Finally, it could be argued that, although the authorities would need more reserves under system (4) to deal with short-term capital movements than they would under system (1), they would need less reserves under system (4) to deal with imbalances on current and long-term capital account than they would under system (1), since, under system (4), such imbalances would be corrected more quickly. They might well be corrected somewhat more quickly under system (4); but experience suggests that system (4), or indeed system (3), is not at all a *quick* remedy for curing an imbalance.

My own, very provisional, opinion is that the extra reserves that the authorities would need to have in hand for dealing with perverse short-term capital movements under system (4), as contrasted with the helpful movements under system (1), would exceed the saving in reserve requirements owing to system (4)'s securing a somewhat more rapid cure of a fundamental imbalance on current and long-term capital account.

In this section and the foregoing three sections short-term capital movements have been discussed only as regards their helpful or perverse action in relation to imbalances of payments on all other accounts. But some short-term capital movements should not be regarded in this light at all. If country A has rising direct long-term capital investments in country B, it may need also to place some short-term capital there. Such short-term capital outflow from A to B would have nothing whatever to do with short-term capital outflows, whether helpful or perverse, that are geared to fundamental imbalances of payments or interest rate differentials connected therewith. Short-term capital outflows of the former character should be included in the assessment of a country's fundamental equilibrium in its balance of payments. It is obviously of the greatest statistical difficulty to distinguish between these two types of short-term capital flow. This is connected with the notorious difficulties in reaching a correct estimate of the United States balance of payments.

7. The 'Crawling Peg'

Before concluding this broad topic, I should say a word about a proposal that is designed to secure a long-run flexibility in exchange rates, as a method of curing fundamental disequilibrium, like the 'adjustable peg' of the I.M.F., without provoking perverse movements of short-term funds. It is also designed to reintroduce the automaticity that prevailed under the gold standard, thereby immunising the system from erroneous judgements by the 'authorities'. I am not seeking to expound any particular one of the various forms that this general type of proposal has taken, so that I cannot be charged with misrepresentation! It seems better to attempt, in my own version, to incorporate what strike me as the valuable features. I believe that the name of this kind of scheme 'crawling peg' is due to Professor John H. Williamson.[1] The contrast between 'crawling' and 'adjustable' is apposite.

It is proposed to broaden 'the band' that has previously existed on either side of an official parity, whether that bounded by the 'gold points' of the full gold standard system or that bounded by the support limits agreed upon with the I.M.F. In the former case the band, although narrow, gave a motive for *helpful* movements of short-term capital; the I.M.F. bands do the same, provided that there is no fear that the 'adjustable peg' is likely to be used, in respect of one of the currencies involved.

The 'crawling peg' system would allow the *parity itself* to move more or less continuously. The best chosen intervals between each movement are subject to consideration; I should favour a *daily* movement. The amount of this movement would not be determined by the judgement of administrators, but automatically by reference to the *actual* average market valuation (the relevant market for any currency would presumably be the home market) in the preceding period. One might take the preceding two years, or even the preceding five years. If a lengthy back period were laid down, the maximum possible change of parity on any one day would be miniscule. A two-year backward calculation would be quite enough to ensure this.

There should be some maximum for the downward adjustment of the parity, such as 2% a year. The requirement for a broader band on either side of par may be needful to ensure that the average of actual quotations over the back period moves down (or up) sufficiently to ensure that the whole amount of the maximum revaluation, as allowed by the 2% per annum restriction, could in fact be secured by the formula.

There is a two-fold objective, namely: (i) to ensure that, as under strictly fixed exchange rates, the maximum possible change in an exchange rate, whether upward or downward, for so long as the system is faithfully maintained, is not sufficient to be a legitimate motive for substantial precautionary movements of funds, and (ii) to ensure that the parity of exchange

---

[1] I elaborated such a scheme in detail in *1933*. See *International Economics*, Ch. 8. This chapter disappeared in later editions.

will in due course be moved so as to adjust for a 'fundamental disequilibrium'.

It is needful to express reservations.

1. The allowable change in the exchange rate in, say, one year must be sufficiently small for the likelihood of its actually occurring to make it not worth while for cautious people to make big movements of funds. It has been stated by some proponents of the scheme that a country on the downward path would have to maintain its interest rates at a higher level than that of the interest rates in relevant foreign countries, and, thereby, possibly at a higher level than suited its own domestic economy. If that were indeed true, I would reject the proposal outright. But I do not believe that it is true. The maximum (and problematic) decline of a currency by 2% in a year would not be sufficient to motivate precautionary people to take covering action, who would not otherwise have done so, owing to the service charges and other inconveniences of taking such action in relation to a maximum movement of the exchange rate of $\frac{1}{2}$% only in a quarter.

There is a different point, which would not, however, arise if an unfortunate currency was continually bumping along at the bottom of the band. If we suppose that, at some blithe moment, it rose up just for a time, then, with a wider band the precautionary movements would be greater than they would be with a narrower band. I should therefore suppose that, with a wider band, precautionary movements would give more trouble than they would with a narrower band.

2. Secondly, the method of adjustment to a 'fundamental disequilibrium', as provided by the 'crawling peg', would be very slow-working. If the maximum allowable change in the rate of exchange is to be such as to avoid the large precautionary movements of funds that occur when there is a fear of a bigger devaluation, as under the 'adjustable peg', the maximum allowable change in any one year must be *small*. I have given the figure of 2% per annum. This provides for a possible 10% over a five-year period and 20% over a ten-year period. This should be quite sufficient for a mature country that is not the victim of uncontrolled inflation.

But it does mean that, within the five- (or ten-) year period, during which the 'crawling peg' is supposed to put matters to rights, reserves will be required to finance a basic deficit due to a structural change, like that which the Americans experienced in 1956, over a five- (or ten)-year period.

The 'crawling peg' might or might not – but I believe that it would – reduce the need for having reserves to cope with precautionary movements. But, owing to the very slow working of a 2% per annum devaluation, there would be long time intervals after a structural change before the basic balance came to rights.

I would think that the 'crawling peg' would reduce the need for reserves a little, as compared with the 'adjustable peg', but not nearly to the extent that a rigid exchange rate, in which there was complete confidence, would reduce it.

In this modern world, in which we aim at having greater 'flexibility' than before, this 'crawling peg' – not, unfortunately, likely to be adopted in the near future – is appropriate. But it does imply a need for *large* reserves, and this need is not much recognised by the various authorities at present.

8. Fundamental Disequilibrium

The foregoing sections have been concerned with the technical methods, under various systems, of coping on a short-term basis with inequalities in the balance of payments, when such inequalities occur. The underlying assumption has been that these are for a finite period only; the remedies considered do not cater for deficits of indefinite duration. We have also to consider how a fundamental long-term imbalance may be cured. This can be done effectively only after we have considered the theory of the working of a monetary system more deeply than we have done so far.[1]

[1] See Part Two, Ch. 9.

4

EROSION OF THE GOLD STANDARD
(OLD TYPE)

1. 1914–32

IT is expedient once again to make a retrospect. The gold standard was maintained in Britain during the First World War. The gold points widened very considerably, owing to the rise of insurance charges in consequence of the submarine menace. Sterling was pegged at $4·75, which was above the then gold export point. This was effected with the assistance of loans from the United States negotiated by J. P. Morgan. In 1922/23 Baldwin, the British Prime Minister, got a settlement on the terms for the repayment of these loans, and instalments were paid for a number of years. On one of the occasions of renewed negotiations about the division of German reparations, the British waived their claim to a proportionate assignment of them, viz. in accordance with damage suffered, and said that they would take no more than was required to meet their annual payments to the United States for interest on and amortisation of the war loans previously received. Thus, in a sense, they stood aside from the whole post-war settlement, their share of the German reparations simply by-passing them and going direct to the United States. During the great world slump President Hoover negotiated a moratorium in regard to German reparation payments, and in that year the British praetermitted their American debt payment. When in due course it appeared that no more reparations would be forthcoming from Germany, the British announced that it would be impossible for them, for balance of payments reasons, to pay any further instalments on the American debt. This caused great annoyance in the United States, and may have been one reason for fierce legislation by Congress to the effect that the United States Government must never in future allow any credit to be extended to a belligerent. Britain suffered much from this legislation in the early years of the Second World War.

The gold standard was suspended by the U.K. in April 1919 and restored six years later. In the interval the pound 'floated'.

Prior to the restoration there was some controversy about whether Britain should go back to the pre-war parity. It will be recalled that there was a similar discussion after the Napoleonic Wars. A number of experts, including Keynes, argued that she should accept the *de facto* depreciation, as established in foreign exchange markets, which was something less than 10%.[1] During the course of 1924 the United States was in mild recession, and the Federal Reserve System took reflationary measures which tended to make the dollar 'soft' for the time being. Prices in the United States rose somewhat. By one of those pieces of wishful thinking, which have occasionally recurred in Britain from that time to the present day, the word went around that the Americans were all set for a new bout of inflation, so that the British could safely restore the old quotation for sterling against the dollar. Of those who agreed with Keynes that, if there was to be a return to the gold standard a new and somewhat lower parity should be established, all except one person fell away from him, so that he was almost alone in his advocacy towards the end of the period of inconvertibility. The one person was Lord Beaverbrook. Churchill was Chancellor of the Exchequer at the time of the restoration. This was the only major policy measure in his life which he subsequently acknowledged to have been mistaken. The episode caused him to attach weight to the economic opinions of Lord Beaverbrook in subsequent years, including those of the Second World War.

During the course of 1924 sterling rose in the foreign exchange market, in the first instance because of the American reflationary policy. This gave much satisfaction to the British authorities, since there is nothing that authorities like more than saying, when they adopt a course that they wish anyhow to adopt, that they are merely doing it to comply with market forces. As sterling rose, there was a growing opinion that Britain would

[1] Six per cent in 1923 as a whole and 12·5% in the first half of 1924, after which the pound began climbing.

in fact restore the previous parity, and this opinion caused sterling to move up further; and by April 1925 all that had to be done by the authorities to return to the pre-war parity was to clock in at the existing rate. But the predicted American inflation never eventuated, as the Federal Reserve System was firmly in the saddle and reversed course during 1925, so that the return to the old parity by Britain involved an over-valuation of sterling.

Keynes was against a return to the old parity, but also, unlike his associates in this opinion in the early days, he did not think that there should be a return to any parity at all. He wanted to keep the sterling/dollar rate flexible and argued in favour of this in his *Tract on Monetary Reform*. He thought that sterling should be 'managed' so as to maintain a stable price level in Britain. He recognised that the Americans had a similar aim, but argued that stability of prices in both countries would not necessarily entail a constant exchange rate, since events might occur that would alter the equilibrium exchange rate, even though prices were held stable in both countries.

The most important monetary event in this period, and perhaps the most important monetary event in this century, occurred in the United States in 1922. During and after the Second World War the United States had had a favourable balance of payments and been the recipient of large quantities of gold, which went into the coffers of the Federal Reserve System. Both in Britain and in the United States there had been great inflations during the First World War, which were followed by intense deflations, causing much unemployment in both countries. The American economy revived much more quickly than the British, and there were signs of renewed inflation setting in during 1922. The American gold reserve was very large for the reasons aforementioned, rising at one time to over 80% of the note issue and deposit liabilities combined of the Federal Reserve System. By the regular maxims of the gold standard the System should have accordingly expanded credit on rather a large scale. But in the autumn of 1922 it seemed that this would have increased the inflationary tendency then prevailing. It was therefore decided to pursue a somewhat tight monetary policy, despite the very large size of the gold reserve.

This was explained in the tenth annual report of the Federal Reserve Board (1923). This report, although rather sketchier than that of the Bullion Committee (1810), may be regarded as having an almost equal rank with it, as one of the few great classical documents in monetary history. Just as the Bullion Report set out the principles on which Britain was to conduct its monetary policy for the following century, the tenth annual report of the Federal Reserve System set out the main ideas, much modified in detail later, by which the Americans were destined to conduct their monetary policy during the twentieth century – at least until 1958.

The publication of this report marked the demise, anyhow in the United States, of the old semi-automatic gold standard, as it was previously understood. The quantity of the money supply was no longer to be fixed by reference to inflows and outflows of gold, but was to be regulated in such a way as to iron out the business cycle. While this may be deemed to have been an excellent reform in relation to domestic monetary policy, its implications on the external side were not clearly thought out. There was no reason for them to be so thought out in the United States, since its very large gold reserve was to exempt it from all worries about its external balance of payments for nearly forty years. Other countries also have been influenced by the American policy, namely by the idea of regulating credit conditions more by reference to the domestic business cycle rather than by the external balance of payments, but they have not been equally lucky in regard to the size of their reserves.

It is not implied that the Americans acted in an unneighbourly manner. It would have been injurious not only to themselves but also to the whole world had there been a large-scale inflation in the United States in 1922, or indeed in any of the following years, when their gold reserve remained grossly excessive in relation to the domestic circulation.

The American policy of aiming at a stable price level was undoubtedly a step forward. The fact remains that the relation of this type of policy to the working of a gold standard on the external side, or to any fixed exchange rate system, has never been properly thought out by the authorities, and we have continued to live in a schizophrenic world until the present day.

It is true that some thought was given to the subject in the discussions prior to the conference at Bretton Woods (1944). Matters had to be decided somewhat hurriedly at that time. The proposal for an 'adjustable peg' was an attempt to deal with this problem, but this technique has not subsequently been applied in any systematic way, and the Bretton Woods plan must be regarded as having been a failure. This is discussed in a later chapter. It is certainly a most striking case of what the Marxists like to call a 'contradiction'. And it is a very big one. The matter is made worse by some tendency to wishful thinking inclining to the pretence that the contradiction does not exist. Such a tendency was especially prevalent in Britain between 1955 and 1967.

The problem has been looked at in a report by Working Party No. 3 of the Economic Policy Committee of O.E.C.D. (the Balance of Payments Adjustment Process, August 1966). Although this is a thoughtful document and shows some appreciation of the problems involved, it cannot be said to go to the root of the matter or provide for a resolution of the contradiction.

Another event of some importance in monetary history also occurred in 1922, namely, the meeting of an International Conference at Genoa. During the 1920s there were recurrent anxieties about the shortfall of gold production relatively to the work that gold had to do in the international monetary system. Despite the post-war deflation, the prices of goods remained well above the pre-war level, but the price of gold had not been altered. A similar situation has occurred in the period after the Second World War. But the problem has not been so fairly and squarely faced as it was at the Genoa Conference. Does this betoken a decline of intellectual grasp at the top level? Or may it be that, while the individuals concerned are just as intellectual as they were before, decision-making has become more diffused, so that reason has less chance of influencing the outcome?

The Conference at Genoa recommended two things to meet the prospective shortage of gold: (1) Nations were requested not to re-issue gold coins on the occasion of a return to the gold standard. This was on the lines of Ricardo's recommendation for Britain after the Napoleonic Wars, already mentioned,

which was not adopted then. (2) It was recommended that central banks should hold some part of their reserves in the form, not of gold, but of foreign currencies. Although this had been done to some extent at an earlier date by certain countries, it had not before been elevated into a principle of policy. Both recommendations were acted upon, and in certain cases the provision for holding part of the reserve in foreign currencies was embodied in central bank statutes. The system has continued.

By a gross exaggeration, this Genoa system has been referred to in some recent controversial writing as a 'gold exchange standard'. This expression should be applied only to countries which hold all, or the main part of, their reserves in the form, not of gold but of a foreign gold standard currency.

The over-valuation of sterling led to troubles for Britain at a fairly early date. Exports came under pressure. At that time coal exports made a major contribution to British foreign exchange receipts. These exports could not be maintained unless the supply price of coal in terms of sterling was reduced in proportion to the upward valuation of sterling in the foreign exchange. At that time wages constituted about 85% of the cost of production of coal. Putting these two points together, it became apparent that wage rates in coal-mining must be reduced. In 1926 the mine workers struck against this proposal, and there was a General Strike in sympathy, which, however, lasted for less than a fortnight. The strike of the mine workers lasted for more than six months, and some export markets for coal were permanently lost. This was the occasion of Keynes's classic little pamphlet *The Economic Consequences of Mr Churchill*. Unemployment continued to be at an uncomfortably high level (an average of 11·6% of those engaged in industrial production in 1926–28).

The next episode to be noted is the great world slump, which was triggered off by the Wall Street crash of October 1929. This was the largest slump that has been recorded in human history. Although many years have passed since then and much research work has been done, no one knows why it occurred.[1] There was some tendency at the time to believe that it was due to the strains connected with the German Reparations pay-

[1] I gave my own account of its causes not long afterwards in *The Trade Cycle* (1936), pp. 207–13.

ments, but this does not seem plausible when we look at the matter in quantitative terms. The fact that the proximate cause was the Wall Street crash, that the American economy weighs so heavily in the whole world scene, and that the slump hit the United States with exceptional severity, has inclined many to believe that the root cause of the slump was some feature in the American economy. But this is by no means certain. It is possible that the United States was afflicted by the effects of causes lying outside her domain. After 1922 the Federal Reserve System had a considerable measure of success in maintaining the American economy on an even keel, adopting expansive measures in some years and restraining measures in others. Prior to the crash there were no *general* signs of overheating in the American economy. Unemployment was rather high and prices not rising. Almost the only abnormal feature was the great boom in Wall Street, supplemented by ancillary phenomena like real estate speculation. There was controversy about whether the Federal Reserve should act so severely, in order to check the speculation, as to induce a general recession in the economy, or should adopt a middle of the way policy, which was in fact done. It may be that the basic cause had something to do with a lack of balance between saving and investment in the world as a whole, or, alternatively, with a lack of balance between world agricultural and industrial production.

Britain was less severely hit by the slump than the United States and Germany, although unemployment rose towards the 3 million mark. In monetary history, however, the incidence on Britain was very important, since it toppled her off the gold standard, which had been restored six years earlier. As sterling had been by far the most important currency in relation to international trade and settlement before 1914 and continued to be very important after the First World War, the departure of Britain from the gold standard had great international significance.

Four reasons for the departure may be set out in ascending order of importance:

1. The resolution of the Genoa Conference concerning the holding of foreign currencies in reserve was adopted by a number

of countries, and the currency thus held was usually sterling, as being still the foremost in the world. This altered the balance of Britain's position as borrower and lender on short-term capital account. Although claims still exceeded liabilities, the margin was not as great as it had been before 1914. This was pointed out in the report of the Macmillan Committee,[1] another classic document, which appeared shortly before Britain's departure from the gold standard in September 1931. The report recommended that Britain should aim at holding a somewhat higher reserve, her ancient tradition having been to manage sterling on the basis of a very narrow reserve. It has sometimes been said in criticism of the British authorities of the time that they 'borrowed short and lent long'. This is not quite a fair statement, since the 'borrowing short' was not a deliberate act of policy, but rather the consequence of the initiative of other countries (in deciding to hold sterling reserves) in pursuit of the Genoa Conference recommendation. It is true that, if these other countries had not let their sterling holdings run up, Britain's overall balance of payments would have been less favourable in this period, and she might have been compelled to take drastic measures to rectify it. There was in fact some restraint on British long-term lending in this period operated informally by the Bank of England.

2. Churchill was not alone in thinking that he had made a mistake in restoring the old sterling parity in 1925. There was a rather widespread belief to this effect, confirmed by the trouble in the coal industry and the continuing high level of unemployment in Britain. Thus confidence in the parity was undermined. When Britain, like other countries, became involved in the turmoils of the great slump, her balance of payments deteriorating a little, the sterling parity seemed to be a weak spot.

3. The collapse of the important Austrian Bank, the Credit-Anstalt, led to widespread banking troubles in Germany, which culminated in the declaration by that country of a general moratorium there. This immediately involved Britain in difficulties, since a large amount of her acceptance credits were due to be paid by German firms. Thus an important section of her short-term foreign exchange assets was suddenly frozen.

---

[1] Committee on Finance and Industry, Cmd 3897, June 1931.

The London merchant banks succeeded in negotiating a gradual repayment of these credits by what was known as the 'standstill agreement', but the liquid position of London was obviously gravely impaired. This was widely known.

4. The domestic slump caused large and rising deficits in the British Budget and in the Unemployment Insurance Fund. The general opinion was that effective measures should be taken to terminate these deficits. This is not in line with modern thinking, which regards such deficits, when arising during a recession, as 'built-in stabilisers'. It may well be that it was precisely because of these deficits in 1929–31 that the slump was less severe in Britain than it was in the United States. There was at that time no equivalent in the United States of the important British Unemployment Insurance Fund.

In April 1931 Philip Snowden, the Chancellor of the Exchequer – a Labour Government was then in office – introduced what was generally regarded as a 'phoney' budget, it being optimistic in its forecasts of revenues and expenditures. He may well have felt this himself, since he did not resist a proposal by the Liberal Party, which, although not in the Government, held the balance of power in the House of Commons at that time, to have an independent committee (the 'May Committee') look into the state of the national finances. No Chancellor of the Exchequer ought ever to allow such a thing to happen, and Snowden ought certainly to have resigned, had the Liberals pressed their point. The May Committee produced an exaggerated picture of the parlous state of the nation – Keynes said that the report was one of the silliest documents that he had ever had the misfortune to read. It was widely read around the world and made a deep impression. It stressed the points that the Budget and Unemployment Insurance Fund deficits must be immediately remedied.

This view was almost universally held in Britain, and it was understood that most members of the Labour Cabinet agreed with it. Keynes was almost the only opponent of importance in the country. He adopted the modern view, which has since gained ascendency, doubtless partly through his influence, that terminating the deficits would make matters worse.

It is not clear whether the Labour Government could have maintained a sufficient amount of foreign confidence, had they adopted Keynesian doctrine and rejected the May report. In 1964–68 the only thing that has seemed to give confidence to foreign central bankers has been deflation, and it was presumably so in 1931 also. But the British position was stronger at that time.

Certainly the adoption of a Keynesian line would have been better for confidence than what the Government actually did. It was known to favour the May report but was publicly obstructed by the Trades Union Congress, which refused to allow a 10% reduction in unemployment benefits, which was needed as a measure to terminate the deficit in the Unemployment Insurance Fund. Thus the British Government was shown to the world as being unable to do what it thought it was right to do, owing to the opposition of the Trades Union Congress. This was a really disastrous blow to confidence. A political crisis boiled up and a National Government was formed, but that was already too late. Foreign balances were withdrawn from London on a large scale. The British borrowed an amount equal to the total of their gold reserve (£130 million) from the Federal Reserve System and the Bank of France, but this was not enough to offset the withdrawals. And so convertibility of the pound had to be suspended.

Then two things happened: (1) Some of the export industries, notably textiles, began to feel benefit from the depreciation of sterling. Almost everybody, including Keynes himself, had been opposed to any voluntary departure from the gold standard once it had been re-established; but, after the departure had happened, many people thought that it might be a good thing, owing to a slight consequent improvement in export prospects, in those ghastly days of world-wide unemployment and depression. (2) There was a return flow of confidence in sterling. The newly formed ('National') Government was prepared to buttress the balance of payments by abandoning Britain's ancient policy of Free Trade. The deficits in the Budget and the Unemployment Insurance Fund were in due course terminated, and this, although it may have been bad for employment in Britain, was good for confidence abroad. (How like the situation in 1968!) Meanwhile things were getting worse in the United States, and the German moratorium continued and was followed by a complex system of exchange controls, which put the mark out of action as a respectable currency. And then thoughts turned to the other European countries, which had so far not fared so badly in the slump. Incidentally the Scandinavian countries stayed with sterling when it left the gold standard and became, for the time being, part of the 'sterling area'. Might not those other European countries in due course have to follow in the wake of sterling and abandon their old parities? In consequence of this there was a return flow of capital into sterling as being by this time the safest currency. Sterling rose.

And so there came about a certain conflict. People did not want sterling to go back to the old gold parity, and yet market forces seemed to be pushing it back there, or nearly there. The Bank of England came into the market and bought foreign currencies, in order to hold sterling down. This was an unusual action for the Bank of England to take. The consequence was the setting up of the Exchange Equalisation Account in April 1932.

2. British Experiment with a Floating Rate (1931–39)

The Exchange Equalisation Account was set up as an office of the Treasury. From a practical point of view it can best be regarded as a ledger in the Bank of England, which operated the Account. The Bank had to obtain concurrence by the Treasury for its general lines of policy, but the day-to-day dealings were doubtless left to its discretion. These operations were not substantially different in quality, although they were in quantity, from those to which the Bank was accustomed. I give three reasons, again in ascending order of importance, why this Account was placed under the ultimate authority of the Treasury:

1. We have seen that in the winter of 1931/32 the Bank of England began buying foreign currencies to prevent sterling rising too high in the foreign exchange markets, and that this was anomalous. A more natural, and traditional, procedure would have been for it to buy gold.

The purchase of gold by the Bank was, however, allowed only at the official price. If the object was to hold sterling down at a level below its old parity, gold would have had to be bought at a premium and this was not allowed. The suspension of the gold standard in 1931 had consisted merely, as in 1797, in a relief for the Bank from its duty of converting bank-notes into gold at par. Nothing had been said about the official valuation of the pound sterling or about the Bank of England's statutory buying price of gold. The Treasury, on the other hand, was perfectly free to buy gold at whatever price it liked. The objector might wonder whether it would not have been simpler to pass an Act through Parliament enabling the Bank also to buy gold at whatever price it thought fit. The matter was not quite so simple. There may be a lesson here for 1968.

Any such Act would have caused a serious break in confidence. The measures adopted at this time were regarded as provisional and designed to meet a crisis of unprecedented magnitude. The whole world was being rocked by a slump, such as had never occurred before. The causes were not known, nor was it understood what should be done to remedy this state of affairs. Some economists seriously thought that the capitalist system was on the verge of breaking down completely. Although there were slight signs of recovery in England at this time, in most of the world the slump was continuing on its downward course.

In these circumstances what was done was regarded as provisional and contingent. No one knew what the shape of things would be, when the slump was terminated, if ever. A proposal to alter the official valuation of the pound sterling, although in the changed climate of today it might seem natural enough, would then have seemed a major break-down. To suspend was one thing; that had been done already in connection with two major wars, and the slump seemed, from an economic point of view, to be as serious as either. This was not mere jitters. It has been computed that more wealth was lost to the world through this slump than had been lost through the First World War. The official valuation of the pound dated back, as we have seen, to Sir Isaac Newton, and, to all intents and purposes, to Queen Elizabeth I. The official valuation had not been changed in the two major wars. Accordingly, to have changed it at this time would have given a major shock to confidence, and British troubles were enough already, without needlessly bringing about such a shock. So the official valuation of gold was retained, so far as the Bank of England was concerned, while the task of buying gold at a premium, as was needed in order to hold sterling down, was made, from a formal point of view, the responsibility of the Treasury.

2. It was desired to keep the operations in gold secret for the time being. Ever since Peel's Bank Act the Account of the Bank of England, including its gold holdings, had been published once a week. To have suspended publication, which had not been suspended during the First World War, would also have given a major shock to confidence. One way of describing the setting up of the Exchange Equalisation Account is to say that it constituted a division of the account of the Bank of England into that part published each week and that part not published. The part published had exactly the same form as it had always had, including the gold holding. But the additional gold acquired by the Exchange Equalisation Account was not shown, so that the public was kept ignorant of the fluctuations of the gold stock. The foreign currencies that had been acquired by the Bank of England were transferred to the Exchange Equalisation Account.

Whether this secrecy was really desirable is uncertain. This was, after all, a new experiment. The public was told about the holdings of the Exchange Equalisation Account only about two years after the event. What is curious is there was no sense of the need for secrecy after the Second World War, when the reserve position of Britain was much more critical. Soon after the end of that war the gold holdings of the Account were published each month. It seems clear that this publication has done harm. Downward fluctuations in the gold holding, which might be due to some fortuitous or quite harmless event, have on a number of occasions produced a bogus crisis, or anyhow a needless lack of confidence. So perhaps the originators of the Exchange Equalisation Account were wiser in their generation.

3. The most important point was that in the new situation the responsibility for exchange rate policy had to be placed fairly and squarely on the shoulders of the Government. It must be remembered that at that time the Bank of England was still in

essence a private enterprise institution, subject only to the regulations laid down in successive re-enactments of its Charter, and that it had its own depositors and shareholders. The over-riding constraint had been that the Bank was obliged to maintain the convertibility of its notes into gold. It was free to use its discretion as regards the manner in which it discharged this obligation, by changing Bank Rate, by open market operations, etc. There was also the over-riding responsibility, never formulated but long since accepted by the Bank, of maintaining the economy on an even keel and doing its best to iron out the business cycle. In the discharge of this duty it was responsible neither to the Government nor to Parliament.

In the previous periods in which the gold standard had been suspended the duty of the Bank remained clear. It was to do all in its power to limit the depreciation of the pound to the smallest possible amount, to prepare for the return to the gold standard at the earliest possible date, and to use all its influence upon the Government, an influence which it held owing to its duty of managing the National Debt, to keep inflationary spending by the Government down to the lowest feasible level. But now the scene was entirely changed. It seemed that people no longer wanted to return to the old parity at the earliest possible date; on the contrary, they wanted, for the time being, to avoid doing so. What then was the duty of this private enterprise institution in such circumstances? Its duty was no longer definite, but blurred. It was to manage the foreign exchange rate in the way that best suited the interests of the country. But what was the criterion?

Foreign relations were also involved. A movement of the sterling/dollar rate could have world-wide repercussions. Indeed, towards the end of 1932 the Americans were annoyed with the British for having let sterling slip; they held that the consequent drag on world prices, as expressed in dollars, had frustrated the vigorous attempts made by the Federal Reserve System in the summer of 1932 to reflate the American economy. It would have been an impossible position for the Chancellor of the Exchequer, when subject to such representations, to have had to say, 'that is none of my business; I cannot possibly interfere with the Bank of England, which is an independent institution'. It was, therefore, necessary that the official responsibility for exchange rate movements should be transferred to the Government.

The problem of those days has relevance to the proposals made by some at the present time (1968) that the dollar should be allowed to 'float'. The Federal Reserve System is responsible for foreign exchange operations, as conducted by the Federal Reserve Bank of New York. Those operations are subject to the Act of Congress that dollars coming into the possession of other central banks must be redeemed at a fixed gold value. Would it really be feasible to give the Federal Reserve System, with its present independent constitution – although one not quite so independent as that of the Bank of England in 1931 – the right to manage the foreign exchange value of the dollar according to its own discretion? The idea of having a floating dollar would surely require a radical reconstruction of the law of the United States, whereby the Federal Reserve System would have to be made subject to the United States Executive powers. I believe that this point has not yet been fully appreciated by advocates of a floating dollar.

It is time to turn to the objectives of the Exchange Equalisation Account, as they developed after its inception.

The proximate objective was to prevent sterling rising in the foreign exchange markets to an extent that might be deemed deleterious to British export prospects and to the recovery of the British economy. A further point very soon appeared. There had been the experience of the flight of money out of sterling in the summer of 1931, which was due, in substantial part, to political motivation (distrust of the Labour Government). Subsequently there was a strong return flow, due largely to a feeling of insecurity about the future of other currencies. It seemed that, in this world of great depression, there were likely to be movements of funds from country to country on a large scale, owing to uncertainties about the future. These movements came to be known as 'hot money' movements. They were destined to continue until the outbreak of the Second World War – and after it. They might be caused specifically by fears of an impending devaluation of some other currency. Or they might be caused by wider political uncertainties, as, for instance, on the part of those who were not sure of the wisdom of President Roosevelt's New Deal, or, at a later date, by those who were frightened by the advent to power of a Socialist government under M. Blum in France, or again when there were fears that war might break out in Europe.

It was accordingly felt that special provision should be made for this movement of hot money. Its advent should not be allowed to influence the foreign exchange rate or the domestic circulation, as would an inflow due to a regular surplus in the balance of payments. It was obvious enough also that, if hot money flowed in, it might also flow out again, e.g. owing to the removal of the political uncertainty that had caused it to take flight to England. Accordingly, it was expedient to build up a reserve against a potential outflow. The British authorities did not wish to be taken by surprise again, as they had been by the outflow in 1931, and they, therefore, decided that they would allow the British reserve to rise above the amount traditionally supposed to be required, in order to have funds to meet such a reflux.

Then another point came up for consideration. The heavy level of unemployment, which was continuing in 1932, in due course built up an opinion that the British authorities should take more positive steps to reflate the economy. A distinction must be drawn between monetary policy on the one hand and fiscal policy on the other. Currently it is widely accepted, and even by countries most adverse to all forms of state control or planning, that monetary and fiscal policies are appropriate for ironing out the business cycle and maintaining growth, since these can be executed by impersonal leverages, without interfering with free competition and private enterprise.

But at that time in Britain only monetary policy was accepted. The same may probably be said of the United States also, since, although President Roosevelt incurred deficits in order to boost the economy out of its slump by Public Works and other spending measures, the best opinion appears to be that President Roosevelt did not himself recognise a deficit as such as an instrument of recovery (although there may have been some economists at a lower level in his government machine who did so). Rather, it is believed that the President regarded public expenditure as itself the prime agent and held that it would have been better, had this been balanced by extra taxation, if only that were politically possible. In the world Economic Conference held in London, in 1933, the British spokesman said that the British had some experience of Public Works and decided that they could have no good effect on the level of employment. The doctrine still persisted at that time that so much more public demand, e.g. on account of Public Works, meant that much less private demand, *even if* the authorities borrowed the money for the extra government spending. Work on a ring-road round Oxford was suspended in 1931, after only one-quarter had been completed, despite the fact that unemployment at that time was near the 3 million mark; that work was only resumed a quarter of a century later, much to the embarrassment of the traffic problem in that university city meanwhile. The suspension of this road plan was designed to reduce the budget deficit and thereby to strengthen the economy. The inclusion of 'fiscal' in the now widely accepted 'monetary and fiscal policies' should be attributed almost entirely to the subsequent influence of the thinking of Keynes.

But the desirability of monetary policy was recognised. The first big success in Britain was the Conversion Loan put through in 1932 by Neville Chamberlain, who was more expert in domestic finance than he was in foreign affairs. The traditional British interest rate on long-term Government Bonds before 1914 had been 3%, but, after the First World War was over, this interest rate had stuck at around 5%. In 1932 £2000 million worth of Government 5% Bonds, a large sum in those days, and constituting about a quarter of the whole British National Debt, was due for redemption. A Conversion Loan of $3\frac{1}{2}\%$ was offered in its place and about £1850 million of this was subscribed to by the holders of the previous 5% Bonds, despite the consequent loss of three-tenths of their income. The commercial banks took up the remainder. This success was partly due to the idea that it no longer made sense for government stock to yield 5% when the great mass of business had become totally unprofitable owing to the slump. The conversion issue was accompanied by easy money. The long-term rate fell to 3% soon after that; meanwhile the Bank Rate was reduced to 2% and continued to be held there until 1951. It was generally believed that this lowering of the rates of interest should stimulate investment, including house building, and thereby lead to a recovery of the economy. It was therefore thought to be expedient that the Bank Rate should be held down to 2% continuously, so long as there was heavy unemployment.

But traditionally Bank Rate had been moved up and down in accordance with the state of the foreign exchanges and the inflow and outflow of gold. Although in the early part of 1932 gold had been coming in, there was an obvious danger that it would go out again, and it was thought most undesirable that such an efflux should entail a rise in domestic interest rates, thereby impairing the domestic reflationary policy. It was, therefore, thought desirable that, so long as the unemployment condition obtained, the domestic economy should be screened from the influence of gold inflows and outflows.

A similar decision had been reached by the Federal Reserve System in 1922, as we have seen. But that decision was reached on the basis of a gold reserve of vast magnitude, so that the authorities did not have to worry about their domestic policy leading to an outflow of gold or, conversely, about an outflow of gold imposing a constraint on their domestic policy. The British position in the 1930s was different. Although the gold reserve was much larger during this period than it had ever been before, much of it was potentially ear-marked against an outflow of hot money, and what remained was by no means sufficient to enable the British to be oblivious of their external balance in the conduct of domestic policy.

What then was to be done? Britain lacked the cushion of a big reserve that had enabled the Federal Reserve to conduct its bold new experiment of using its monetary weapons solely to iron out the domestic business cycle. If the balance of payments became adverse, what were the British authorities to do?

This required something wholly new. In the event of an adverse movement in the balance of payments, they should let the foreign exchange rate move downwards. The idea was that there *must* be an equilibrium foreign exchange rate at which foreign payments would balance.

And so there emerged the rough principles of a system, not spelt out in detail, but generally understood. Bank Rate policy was to be governed by the needs of the domestic economy while external payments were to be kept in balance by movements in the foreign exchange rate. Many hoped at the time that this might become a permanent system. But it was terminated at the outbreak of the Second World War and not revived. There are many economists who now believe that the system, as worked by the Exchange Equalisation Account, was a sensible one and should be adopted generally. Some difficulties have already been discussed and I shall return to them later. Unfortunately the British experience of this system was not long enough to afford decisive evidence of its viability; and there were many cross-currents.

The principles, thus, were that reserves should be used by official intervention to hold the foreign exchange rate steady in the face of hot money movements and also in the face of seasonal, cyclical or random fluctuations in the balance of payments. It was recognised that a larger reserve than was ever held before was required for this purpose, *not only* because of the hot money movements, *but also* because it was recognised that, with the fine movements in foreign exchange rates and the Bank Rate weapon no longer available for influencing the flow of short-term funds, the authorities would have to provide out of their own reserve funds enough to offset temporary deficits due to seasonal, cyclical and random causes. (See above, pp. 75–6 and 87.)

Subject to the ironing out of short-term oscillations, the authorities were to allow the foreign exchange rate to *move* gradually towards its equilibrium level, whatever that might be. The duty to hold the rate fixed had gone.

Then, as regards domestic policy, the line was to have, for the time being, conditions of the utmost monetary ease, as were needed to cure the heavy unemployment still prevailing. That was likely to be a lengthy task.

In regard to the actual mechanism of insulation, a sharp distinction must be drawn between hot money movements and movements arising from surpluses or deficits in the balance of payments, exclusive of hot money.

1. There should be no difficulty in principle, although there may be in practice, in insulating hot money movements, whether inward or outward. A certain amount of controversy arose at the time, and Keynes at one point held that the

process of insulation was having a deflationary effect. Contemporary writers on the subject made rather heavy weather and presented a needlessly complicated picture.

In order to elucidate this matter, let us suppose, for example, that members of the French public become fearful of a devaluation of the French franc or distrustful of the Government, as happened on the accession of M. Blum. Accordingly, many decide to transfer some of their money into sterling. For simplicity we may name this group 'a Frenchman'. We may suppose him to bring over £100 million worth of French francs, convert them into sterling and hold sterling on deposit account for that amount at a British bank.

If the Exchange Equalisation Account knows about this and does not wish the movement to have any effect on the exchange rate, which, we must remember, is a floating one, it will buy that amount of French francs in the market (or, perhaps, directly from the British bank at which the Frenchman has made his deposit). Unless it has some special reason for wishing to hold French francs, it will swap this amount for gold at the Bank of France.

The Exchange Equalisation Account was given a fixed amount of capital at the outset, which was enlarged from time to time, as its operations grew. Initially this capital was in the form of Treasury Bills. As these were issued to it directly, they constituted part of the 'tap' issue. As and when the E.E. Account acquired gold or foreign exchange, the Account reduced its 'tap' holding of Treasury Bills by an equal amount. One will not go seriously wrong if one thinks of the Exchange Account as part and parcel of the Bank of England. But in the technique of operations, there was this difference from the previous system.

In the old days, when gold came into the Bank of England through its normal operations, this, in the first instance, increased the 'cash basis' of the commercial banks at the Bank of England (cf. pp. 34–5). It was then up to the Bank to decide whether it wished to allow this to have its consequent effect on the volume of credit in the country, or wished to offset the increase of liquidity by selling securities and thus cancelling the extra cash that had come into the hands of the commercial banks, or, alternatively, to re-enforce the effect of the inflow. The last-mentioned alternative might be especially important in the case of the opposite kind of movement, namely an outflow of funds. The Bank of England might then think it needful to re-enforce the effect of the outflow of gold on the cash of the commercial banks, so as to produce a greater tightness in the monetary system than would be caused by the outflow of gold alone, with a view to rectifying the adverse balance of payments and thus protecting its reserve.

When the Exchange Equalisation Account was set up, the *second* of these three alternatives was adopted as a matter of automatic routine, in the first instance. Treasury Bills of value equal to the gold inflow were disposed of, and, therefore, the tender issue would be increased by £100 million. The effect, thus far, would be the same as if, in the previous days, the Bank had decided to offset an inflow of £100 million in gold by selling Treasury Bills of equal amount. But in the old days such large sums never came into play.

We are considering, so far, the case of an inflow of hot money, and supposing that the Frenchman wishes to hold his sterling in the form of a deposit account at his bank. Two facts may be noted: (*a*) the increase of the tender issue of Treasury Bills will, if nothing further is done, tend to raise the interest rate on Treasury Bills above its previous level; (*b*) supposing that the total money supply has not been changed, the holding by the Frenchman of £100 million on inactive deposit at an English bank, pending his decision to withdraw it at a later date, will temporarily take £100 million out of active circulation. Thus, so far we have noted a deflationary effect on the domestic monetary system, having two aspects, namely: (*a*) a rise in short-term interest rates, and (*b*) a withdrawal of £100 million worth of bank deposits out of active circulation. It may have been something of this sort that Keynes complained of. Be it noted that this £100 million finds its way into the Frenchman's account ultimately, although perhaps circuitously, by being transferred from the accounts of those who take up the extra Treasury Bills coming on to the market. If the commercial banks, directly or via the discount market, take up some or all of the Treasury Bills, then, their cash basis being unchanged, they will have to reduce loans in other directions, and the deposits of those repaying the loans will be (indirectly) transferred to the Frenchman.

In order to prevent this deflationary effect happening, it will be needful for the Bank of England to take up £10 million worth of the Treasury Bills released from the Exchange Equalisation Account. We suppose that the commercial banks are working, as they were, roughly, at that time, to a 10% cash ratio. Thus of the £100 million of Treasury Bills, £10 million will stay within the 'tap' issue (Bank of England) and only £90 million will be added to the tender. Since the purchase by the Bank of England of £10 million Treasury Bills adds £10 million to the cash basis of the commercial banks, they will be able to purchase the other £90 million of Treasury Bills, either directly or through the discount market, without their cash ratio being affected.

Sometimes the Exchange Equalisation Account transferred gold to the Bank of England. This would be when the Bank of England needed more gold in the Issue Department, in order to provide more notes in accordance with the growing requirements of the economy. The gold had to be transferred, in compliance with the law, at the old valuation. This involved a loss to the Exchange Account. But, since the profit of the Issue Department had been transferred to the Government by the Act of 1926, the Government made a countervailing gain through the Issue Department having bought gold below its market value. If such a transfer happened to coincide with the inflow of the French money, the net effect would be that the Exchange Account would hold only, say, £95 million of extra gold, the other £5 million going to the Bank of England, and would release only £95 million of Treasury Bills. Of these the Bank would purchase £5 million. The cash basis of the commercial banks would be raised by £10 million, £5 million in respect of the gold purchased by the Bank of England and £5 million in respect of the Treasury Bills taken up by it. They would thus be in a position to purchase the remainder of the Treasury Bills released by the Exchange Account, viz. £90 million. Their cash basis would thus be up by £10 million, which would cause them to increase loans by £90 million and cause their total deposits to increase by £100 million, but this increase would be exactly offset by the fact that the Frenchman was holding his £100 million deposit inactive. Since the commercial banks would have had their cash basis increased by

£10 million they would be able to take up the extra £90 million worth of Treasury Bills and there would be no tendency for open market interest rates to rise. Thus the two deflationary effects of the inflow of French funds noted above would be obviated. The domestic monetary system would be completely insulated.

Alternatively, the Frenchman might prefer to hold his capital in the form of Treasury Bills. That would make possible the simplest kind of insulation of all. The Exchange Account would take the £100 million worth of French francs brought over by the Frenchman, encashing them for gold at the Bank of France, while the Frenchman would take up the £100 million worth of Treasury Bills previously held by the Exchange Equalisation Account. The banking system would be entirely unaffected by the operation. The insulation would be perfect.

But the Frenchman might decide to go further and enter the gilt-edged market. In practice, of course, he might well confine this venture to a part of his capital, keeping the rest more liquid. Let us suppose he embarks the whole of his £100 million into the gilt-edged market. What is required for insulation is then as follows. The Government Departments should take up the Treasury Bills and release longer-dated Government Securities (see above, p. 57). If the Frenchman desires to hold his capital in gilt-edged stock, what is needful, in order to get complete insulation, is for these Departments to release £100 million from their holdings of gilt-edged stock, and to absorb in their place, the £100 million of Treasury Bills released by the Exchange Equalisation Account. Once again the domestic monetary system will be completely insulated. The money supply and interest rates will be unaffected.

But the Frenchman may go further still and decide to venture into British equities. This would make matters a little more difficult, since the Government Departments do not hold equities and, therefore, cannot release them to meet the Frenchman's demand. Perfect insulation is in this case not possible. What the Departments can do is to release £100 million worth of gilt-edged stock, as on the last alternative, and hope that the Stock Exchange will be able to sort the matter out by a change in the differentials between the yield on gilt-edged and the yield on equities. The market will have £100 million of

E

extra gilt-edged stock to digest, while the demand for equities will be increased by £100 million, namely by the Frenchman. Subject to this disturbance in the Stock Exchange, the monetary system will be insulated.

The whole of the above is basically quite simple. But the narrative implies that the authorities know exactly how much hot money is coming over, and what the Frenchman is doing with it. In practice this information is not available, or anyhow, not in detail. What is happening may have to be inferred. The authorities may be aware that there is strong pressure for the purchase of sterling by the sale of francs in the foreign exchange market, and the commercial banks may inform them that large monies are coming in from France. It will not always be easy to put a precise figure on the amount of hot money coming in. In practice, of course, there is not one Frenchman, but many Frenchmen. The flight of hot money may become entangled with normal day-to-day commercial operations. A Frenchman may bring money in simply in order to conduct perfectly ordinary trading operations in England. Naturally a bank cannot ask every French customer why precisely he is depositing money in London. The Treasury Bills may be purchased directly on behalf of French clients by foreign banks operating in London. The money may come in by all sorts of methods and be disposed of in various ways, the holding of Treasury Bills, gilt-edged stock, etc., without the authorities at once knowing how much hot money there is coming in or how it is being disposed of. In these circumstances one cannot assume that perfect insulation can be carried out in the manner described in the foregoing paragraphs. All this applies in reverse, when hot money is withdrawn.

2. It is not only from the effects of an inflow or outflow of hot money that the authorities may desire to insulate the domestic economy. An inflow may be due to a genuinely favourable balance of payments, omitting hot money, or an outflow may be due to a deficit. In these cases the process of insulation may be more difficult. It is to be remembered that it is still required to insulate the domestic economy, the necessary adjustment in the balance of payments being effected by allowing an appropriate movement in the foreign exchange rate.

There should not be any difficulty about insulation in the

case of a deficit, if this is desired. But difficulties may arise in the case of a surplus. It seems likely that no serious difficulties arose in the period under review, first, because there were not many surpluses of substantial amount, and secondly, because, with the continuing objective of ultra-cheap money and the desire to raise the level of employment, the authorities may not have minded if a trading surplus had some reflationary effect, i.e. was not completely insulated. But difficulties have arisen on occasions in the post-war period, when, from time to time, it was needful for the authorities to contain inflationary tendencies.

If money flows in because there is a surplus, it is not likely to be held idle, as in the foregoing account of the Frenchman. On the contrary, British producers or traders or investors, having foreign exchange proceeds coming in to them, will normally, having, when necessary, converted them into sterling, push them on into further transactions in the ordinary way. There is no presumption that any of this money will stay idle.

In this case, therefore, it is not expedient that the Bank of England should increase the cash basis of the joint stock banks by £10 million, thereby causing the total of the money supply to rise by £100 million. That would be definitely inflationary. How then are the £100 million worth of Treasury Bills released by the Exchange Equalisation Account to be disposed of?

In the former case, (1), if the Frenchman held his money on idle deposit, the Treasury Bills could be disposed of by the Bank of England allowing an enlargement of the cash basis and enabling the banks to take up £90 million of Treasury Bills without causing any inflation. Or (2) the Frenchman might be at hand to take up the Treasury Bills. Or (3) if he wanted other securities these could be released for him by the Government Departments which would swap them for Treasury Bills. The Frenchman was always standing by, so to speak, to take up the redundant securities due to the purchase of gold by the Exchange Equalisation Account.

But where there is a genuine surplus and the authorities have to dispose of the Treasury Bills, released by the Exchange Account, who will take them up? By hypothesis the commercial banks are not going to be given any extra cash, since in these circumstances such action would be inflationary. If the Treasury

Bills are to be sold, whether themselves or having been swapped for other kinds of securities in the Government Departments, it is the non-bank public that will have to take them up. For this purpose the Discount Houses should be considered as part of the banking system. It may well be that the non-banking fraternity will not want £100 million worth of extra Treasury Bills. In that case they can be swapped in the Government Departments. Then we come to the question whether the non-bank fraternity will want to take up £100 million worth of other Government Securities. This brings us right up against the question, which has already been discussed, of the limitations of the gilt-edged market. There may be genuine difficulty in getting the whole of the £100 million disposed of with the non-bank public, and this may mean a genuine difficulty in preventing the trade surplus from having a domestic inflationary effect.

One must point out the contrast with the old régime. Under that it was understood that a trade surplus would tend to have some inflationary domestic effect. That was part of the ordinary working of the gold standard, as it was understood before 1922. The gold would come into the Bank of England and not normally be offset or not fully offset. This would enlarge the cash basis of the commercial banks and cause immediately a fall in short-term interest rates. In the British case the domestic inflation might be mild only, or even nominal, owing to the international operations of the Discount Market. As soon as the commercial banks had some extra cash owing to the gold inflow, they would pump it into the Discount Market, where interest rates would fall in consequence. This would at once attract foreign borrowers, entailing a short-term capital outflow. This outflow would largely offset the favourable balance of payments on other accounts. The British system was essentially one that repelled gold as soon as it came in, so that a surplus would normally have only a small domestic inflationary effect, the surplus being quickly offset by large lending abroad on short-term capital account.

In conditions in which the London Discount Market is not sufficiently attractive to foreign borrowers, and in which the gilt-edged market is relatively narrow, so that it is not always easy to dispose of Government Securities of the required amount, there could be genuine difficulties in preventing a surplus on the overall balance of payments having a substantial domestic inflationary effect.

There is no corresponding difficulty in insulating the economy from the effect of an external deficit, if it is desired to do so, for the simple reason that it is always easy for the authorities to buy Government Securities! This might seem to be a rake's progress. But the philosophy of this system is that an external deficit should be cured, not by allowing it to cause domestic deflation and unemployment, but by a movement in the foreign exchange rate. The theory was that the authorities would always allow a downward movement, when they were satisfied that the outflow of funds was due not to a withdrawal of hot money or to merely seasonal, cyclical or random factors, but to a fundamental disequilibrium.

This British experience of floating rates cannot be regarded as decisive. After the first impact, the movements in the exchange rates were not large. During this period the British had a substantial recovery, and it is often said that this was because she enjoyed the benefit of a devalued currency. This was not in fact the case for the greater part of the period. In 1933, about a year and a half after Britain's departure from the gold standard, President Roosevelt embarked on a course of devaluing the dollar. This was done by successive stages during that year. During the course of them the pound rose against the dollar and from the end of 1933 until the Treaty of Munich it stood at a higher value in terms of the dollar (on average, $4.98 = £1$) than it had done for a century. Thus, for most of the time, sterling was not devalued against the dollar but, on the contrary, had been valued slightly upwards. It may, however, have had an advantage for another couple of years against the 'gold bloc' currencies, before they in turn were devalued.

In 1936 the Tripartite Agreement was formed between the United States, Britain and France to help France out of her difficulties. This laid down that the three countries were to give each other's currencies mutual support. Other countries subsequently associated themselves. This really meant that Britain had lost much of her freedom to operate a floating rate system. If she let sterling fall too much, that would have been violating the spirit of the Agreement by stealing a competitive march, and, if she let sterling rise too much, that too would have violated the spirit, since it would have meant allowing a fall in the French franc, which the Agreement was designed to obviate.

Some have suggested that in this period the British should have used the floating system to push sterling down farther, in order to cure domestic unemployment more rapidly. But actually the British record of improvement was superior to that of most other countries, except for Germany, which was a special case, as she lived in a closed system and embarked, first, on large-scale public works under the Nazis and later on large-scale rearmament. It cannot be said with certainty that Britain could have had a more rapid expansion had she pushed sterling down, since there is the question whether, in this time of great world depression, the demand for her exports was sufficiently elastic to make this manoeuvre profitable.

3. Sterling Holdings Outside the United Kingdom

There has been much talk in recent times of 'reserve currencies'. Once again it is impossible to understand the true nature of this phenomenon without an historical retrospect. It is expedient to deal, first, with sterling, and, secondly, with the dollar, following the temporal order.

The reference to sterling as a reserve currency proper should be confined to its use by the central banks of the Commonwealth, other than Canada, as their main medium of reserve is a use which dates back to their foundation.

The system of a floating exchange rate was abandoned by Britain, when the war broke out, and the pound was pegged at $4·03. A very strict system of exchange control was put into force, although, until the fall of France, foreigners were allowed to withdraw their balances. It was thought that it would have been bad for the reputation of sterling, had these been blocked; but it is questionable whether people would have taken a blocking so much amiss in the special circumstances of Britain in the period 1939/40. One might think that the authorities in question were rather slow in appreciating what would be required for the war effort.

It was impossible for Britain to borrow from the United States, owing to the Congressional legislation that has already been referred to (p. 95). American assets held in Britain were mobilised by the authorities and sold in the open market in the United States. Heavy losses in capital value were incurred in these sales. Somewhat later it proved possible to make an arrangement with the Reconstruction Finance Corporation (United States) within the framework of the United States legislation, by which money was advanced to the British against the deposit of what remained of their American securities. It was only in the spring of 1941 that the 'lend–lease' system, the idea of President Roosevelt, was made available for the British, and real resources began to arrive in quantity only towards the *end* of that year. For the first two years of war there was a terrible dilemma about the use of shipping, which was in short supply; from the shipping point of view it was desirable to bring as much as possible over the short-haul from North America, but from the foreign exchange point of view it was desirable to ship from more distant parts, like Australasia and South America, where the facility for payment was easier. In the first two years of war the foreign exchange consideration was, on the whole, dominant. After 'lend–lease', purchases were concentrated to the greatest possible extent on North America owing to the short-haul. Canada meanwhile made large gifts to the British to finance their purchases from that country.

Between 1931 and 1939 what came to be known as the 'Sterling Area' consisted of the British Commonwealth and Empire, except Canada, and a number of other countries, notably the Scandinavian countries, which preferred to keep their currencies pegged at a fixed rate against sterling, rather than against gold. The membership of this loosely conceived sterling area fluctuated from time to time. For (different) periods it included Japan, the Argentine, Portugal and Turkey. It did not rest on a legal basis, but depended on whether the monetary authorities of the countries in question chose to keep their currencies pegged to sterling or to gold. After the outbreak of war the British authorities had, much to their regret, to give a legal status to the sterling area, its members, other than Britain, being known as the 'scheduled territories'. The need to do this arose out of the British exchange control and the measures of enforcement involved. Members outside the Commonwealth had to be shed for this legal purpose, with one or two exceptions, like Egypt and Iceland, which were involved in belligerent activities. A free movement of funds was allowed inside the newly defined 'sterling area', but this area was walled around with exchange controls, operated voluntarily by the independent members of the Commonwealth and by London for the dependent members. Imports were subject to licence and the proceeds of exports had to be surrendered to the authorities. These proceeds were in turn surrendered to the Bank of England and constituted what at that time was known as 'the dollar pool'. This was by no means a new system; it merely gave formal expression to what had been done as a matter of routine by the Commonwealth members of the sterling area before the war. Throughout the war and after it, sterling remained 'convertible' for sterling area members, but each separate member voluntarily agreed to limit its need to draw on this convertible sterling to the greatest possible extent.

In 1940 'payments agreements' were reached with most countries outside the sterling area, whereby they agreed to pay sterling accruing to them into 'special accounts'. Sterling held in these accounts could be used to make remittances only to the sterling area, and not elsewhere. It may be asked why countries outside the sterling area were willing to accept such an arrangement. The answer is that these countries thought it worth while to continue to trade with Britain for payment in sterling, the use of which was temporarily limited, since trade around the world was greatly restricted, and they knew that, if they did not consent to these terms, they would have to forgo their trade with the sterling area, as Britain lacked the means to pay in any other way. Goods consigned to Britain enjoyed the advantage of British convoys. Meanwhile, as the pressures of war got ever more severe, the British authorities limited exports to the minimum needed to sustain the economies of the countries, co-belligerent or neutral, which, on their side, were providing Britain with much-needed goods. In this phase Britain was deliberately *not* trying to pay its way on foreign trade account, thinking it necessary to divert all her productive resources, subject to the exception mentioned above, to the war effort. At the worst point British exports sank to about one-third of their pre-war level.

The consequence of the sterling area arrangements and of these payments agreements was a large pile-up of sterling balances held outside Britain up to 1945. These, including the balances held in the ordinary way by central banks of the Commonwealth, amounted to the large figure of about £3500 million. It was obvious that so large an amount could not be paid off at once, either in gold, which Britain did not possess, or in goods, since this would have taken up about three years worth of exports without Britain being able to import anything at all!

Under the Anglo-American Loan Agreement, negotiated in November 1945, whereby the United States made Britain a large loan for post-war reconstruction on generous terms, these balances were to be dealt with in three ways: (1) Some moderate amount was to be made available at once, out of the proceeds of the United States loan, to liquidate a fairly small proportion of the sterling held in special accounts right away. (2) It was hoped that some part of the externally held sterling balances would be scaled down as a post-war contribution to Britain's war effort by the countries concerned. (3) The remainder of the balances was to be funded, viz. 'released by instalments over a period of years beginning in 1951'. Britain was to enter into negotiations under the second and third heads.

It was probably a great mistake to mix these two questions (2) and (3). There was found to be no willingness to scale down the balances, although Australia and New Zealand in due course made certain contributions. Nor was there any willingness to accept a funding operation. This is where a sharp distinction should have been drawn. Britain was obviously not in a position to insist on a scaling down, if creditors did not wish it. It is arguable that she could have insisted on a funding, despite the unwillingness of creditors. It would obviously have been a perfectly reasonable thing to do, since outright repayment was physically impossible, and it was unsound to maintain sight liabilities of so large an amount in existence. Furthermore, the British had agreed to the principle with the Americans, as a condition of the American loan obtained on generous terms. However, the creditors were unwilling, and the funding was not done. Britain could claim that she had fulfilled her agreement with the United States by trying her best to get a funding, which was all that the Agreement laid down that she should do. These outstanding liabilities proved a great embarrassment for a number of years. Funding would have put Britain into a much sounder position.

Under the Anglo-United States Loan Agreement, Britain undertook to make sterling 'convertible' a year after the Loan Agreement came into effect (summer of 1946), which meant in the summer of 1947. There remained in the minds of even the most notable Americans a considerable amount of misunderstanding about the working of the sterling system and about the nature of 'inconvertibility'. They had the feeling that what we may call the 'sterling system' militated against their interests by diverting demand away from the purchase of American goods. They also held, justifiably, that the system, as it was working immediately after the war, was inconsistent with the development of a world-wide open non-discriminatory multilateral trading system. But there seems no doubt that there was confusion in their minds between the effects of the sterling area itself and the wider holding of 'inconvertible' sterling in other countries. The latter was a greater block to the realisation of their aims than the former.

This is not to imply that the sterling area countries did not discriminate against dollar goods. They certainly did so. But this was not because their sterling reserves were inconvertible – they were *always* convertible – but because there was voluntary co-operation throughout the sterling area in husbanding resources and adopting commercial policies limiting the purchase of American goods. In the dependent countries this was doubtless looked after by the British themselves.

Sterling at this time had three main categories:

1. What was called American account sterling, which meant sterling held by residents of the United States and of other countries in America, whose currencies were convertible into the United States dollar, had been freely convertible into sterling throughout the war and remained so. The reason for this was that those countries would have refused to have any debts denominated in sterling, had sterling not been convertible for them. They were in a power position.

2. All sterling area sterling was throughout convertible, in the event of sterling area countries having settlements to make outside the sterling area. There was voluntary co-operation in limiting the amount of liabilities incurred there. The foregoing was subject to the exception that certain sterling area balances, notably parts of the large balances held at the end of the war by India and Egypt, where British war-time expenditures had been heavy, were temporarily blocked after the war, or, to use the word more favoured by the authorities, 'restricted'. This blocking meant that the balances were temporarily unusable even to make payments inside the sterling area, so that there was a distinct difference between blocking and 'inconvertibility'. These blocked balances were in due course unblocked by stages.

3. It was in the rest of the world (viz. *outside* the sterling area and the American account area), which was largely covered by payments 'agreements', that sterling was inconvertible in a meaningful sense.

The term 'inconvertible', itself ambiguous, should therefore be confined to sterling held abroad outside the American Account area, and outside the sterling area. In earlier times a currency had been said to be 'convertible' if it could be exchanged for gold or some gold standard currency at a fixed rate of exchange. An 'inconvertible' currency was one having *no* such fixed rate, the holder having to take his chance as regards the question at what rate he might be able to convert it. Sterling was inconvertible in this sense between 1797 and 1821, between 1919 and 1925, and between 1931 and 1939. In the period with which we are now concerned (1945–55) sterling was convertible into other currencies at a *fixed* rate, to the extent that it was convertible at all. But there were restrictions on the rights of holders to convert at *any* rate. This kind of restriction was made possible by the development of administrative arrangements, unknown in the earlier periods, except perhaps during the later part of the First World War. It might have kept our language clearer and prevented misconceptions, if the new status had been described by the term, 'non-negotiable'. Thus instead of a return to 'convertibility', one would have had to return to 'negotiability'. In that period there was some discussion of return to 'convertibility at a floating rate'. That usage did violence to the historic meaning of 'convertible'. If such a usage became, as it may still become, general, many economic history books will have to be reworded. A currency negotiable only at a floating rate was always described as 'inconvertible'. Indeed, during the classic periods of inconvertibility referred to above, sterling was in fact freely negotiable, but, at an undetermined rate.

In the summer of 1947 this third class of sterling was made convertible, i.e. freely usable for remittance to countries outside the sterling area, in accordance with the Loan Agreement into the United States. This was despite the fact that arrangements for funding had not been made, as envisaged in the Loan Agreement. That Agreement contained a waiver clause by which the British could represent to the Americans that they were not ready for convertibility. It is understood that no such representations were in fact made, and some have wondered why this was. It appears to have been an example of blithe optimism. The British authorities had conversations with important creditors and received assurances that they would not dream of drawing down their sterling balances just because sterling was made convertible. But in the event many did so. This type of optimism seems to have been recurrent with the British authorities in relation to external questions since the war, and has often, although not always, proved unjustified. This is in striking contrast with the morbid pessimism which seems to have prevailed for most of the time about the potentialities of the domestic British economy. Owing to the drawing down of the external balances, the convertibility experiment had to be terminated after a few weeks. It is difficult to infer from the figures exactly what happened, but it is certain that the funds provided by the United States Loan, which were supposed to last for four or five years, were sorely depleted.

Two years later (1949) sterling was devalued by a big amount, namely, from $4·03 to $2·8. This devaluation was probably premature and certainly unnecessarily large. By the criterion of price and wage indices, sterling had not in 1949 lost value relatively to the dollar, by comparison with the pre-war period. Owing to a remarkable increase in exports, British trade had come into balance. There was some weakening in the summer of 1949, but this must be attributed to a holding back in the purchase of British exports in anticipation of a devaluation of sterling which, by that time, despite disclaimers by British Ministers, had come to be thought likely to occur. It is true that the British still had very severe import restrictions, and it may have been in the mind of the Americans, whose thinking had much influence in promoting the idea that sterling devaluation would be a good thing, and indeed in making it inevitable, that, in consequence of the devaluation, the British would be able to remove those restrictions. This, however, did not prove feasible. On the contrary, in the following period restrictions were tightened both in Britain and in the rest of the sterling area. This was in consequence of a Commonwealth meeting, which occurred two months before the devaluation, when it was agreed to have an all-round tightening of restrictions as a measure to 'save the pound'. After the pound could no longer be saved, i.e. after the devaluation had taken place, the plan was none the less adhered to. This was probably sensible. A further time was needed for the British to increase their exports yet further, before it would be safe to allow greater freedom of importation. Exports increased in volume after the devaluation, but at a somewhat slower rate than they had been increasing in the preceding years. But, owing to the worsening in the terms of trade due to the devaluation, the British merchandise balance did *not* improve in 1950; indeed, it got slightly worse. There is no reason to suppose that the volume of British exports would not have continued its upward course in 1950, had there been no devaluation. In that case the British balance would actually have been better in 1950 than it was. The balance of the rest of the sterling area improved somewhat in 1950, but this appears attributable, not to the devaluation of sterling itself, but to those very measures of increased import restriction that had been agreed upon in London before the devaluation.

It is not implied that there need not have been any devaluation at all. Before the final dismantlement of import controls, it might have been expedient for Britain to have had some devaluation, although by no means so large a one as actually occurred. The reason for the decision to have a big devaluation was the sense that this would make people convinced that there would be no further devaluation, and thus eliminate any lack of confidence in the sterling parity in the future. By contrast the more moderate devaluation of 1967 left an aftermath of lack of confidence about whether another devaluation would not be needed. This has caused a continuation of embarrassment on the part of those responsible for sterling. I am convinced that, in this *one* respect, heads have been wiser in 1967 than in 1949, the temporary embarrassments owing to a continuing lack of confidence in sterling being of much less detriment to the country than the over-devaluation of 1949 with its aftermath of price and wage inflation inside the country.

The policy of over-devaluation worked for a time in maintaining confidence; but unfortunately at a later date the lack of confidence in sterling recurred. In any measure for realigning an exchange rate, the utmost care should be taken to strike the right equilibrium rate; any over-devaluation for some such psychological reason as to secure confidence should be strictly avoided, since such an over-devaluation is bound to cause further troubles later. In retrospect it seems that the ideal time for a moderate devaluation of sterling would have been in 1952, when world prices were falling, so that the devaluation might have been effected without causing domestic price and wage inflation in Britain, and when the British economy had a certain amount of slack which could have been used to take advantage of extra export opportunities due to the devaluation.

In 1949, by contrast, the British economy was not slack and the devaluation, after a certain time lag, had a serious effect in raising the cost of living in Britain. This in turn caused a spiralling inflation, wages and prices chasing each other upwards for a number of years. In 1949 Stafford Cripps had succeeded in implementing what we now call an 'incomes policy'. For two years wages rose at only 2% a year, which was decidedly less than the simultaneous increase in labour productivity. This policy was destroyed by the devaluation. It is not contended that Stafford Cripps's rather austere incomes policy could have been maintained in perpetuity; but any relaxation would have been more moderate, had it not been for the rise in the cost of living caused by the devaluation. This spiralling inflation had deleterious effects, lasting to this day (1968). It was only in about 1954 that wages had risen enough merely to keep pace with the higher cost of living due to the devaluation although productivity had increased substantially during those five years; thus further wage increases were due in equity. It may well have been this further period of wage increases, following on the immediate post-war period of adjustment, that was responsible for what seems to have become a built-in habit on the part of wage earners in Britain to expect a round of increases every year.

After the war a system of 'transferability' was developed whereby 'inconvertible' sterling could be used for remittances, not only to the sterling area but also to certain other countries. This 'transferable account system' was developed by agreement with the countries thus grouped together; for the countries making payment in sterling under the system this arrangement meant a clear additional privilege; but it had to be agreeable to the countries in the transferable account area receiving the sterling. It would not be agreeable to strong currency countries; but for a weaker country it could have the advantage that, if it agreed to accept payment in sterling, it might be able to sell exports which it could not otherwise have done at all. Eventually – but this is to anticipate a little – in the spring of 1954 almost all countries outside the American Account area and the sterling area were brought into the transferable account area, so that thereafter there were only three main types of sterling, viz. American Account sterling, sterling area sterling and transferable account sterling. This development was facilitated by the existence at that time of the European Payments Union, which gave some protection to Britain in regard to sterling held within the Union. The E.P.U. which was set up by negotiation among recipients of Marshall Aid, and partly financed by that Aid, provided for multilateral settlement within the group – and this included the whole sterling area – and for mutual credits.

During the period between 1945 and 1955 'black markets' developed. Sterling was quoted below its official parity in these markets. There was one quotation for transferable account sterling and as many other quotations as there were countries not in the transferable account area. Thus there might be French sterling, Saudi Arabian sterling, etc. I recall during this period seeing quotations in a Japanese newspaper for no less than fifty-two different kinds of sterling.

The existence of black markets meant a loss of reserves to

Britain to the extent that these markets were used. Transactions of most complicated and varied kinds developed. It must suffice here to describe a very simple type of case by way of example. If an American wanted to make a remittance to Australia, for instance in payment for wool, he would ask his bank what was the 'cheapest' available kind of sterling in the market. A little 'avoidance' would be involved, which was not necessarily illegal from a non-British point of view. If the sterling chosen for the negotiation was, say, French, the wool in question could be invoiced to a buyer in France who would resell it to the American who really desired the wool. It would then seem to the Bank of England that some Australian wool had been bought by a French holder of sterling, a perfectly proper operation, since French sterling was available for remittance to the sterling area. But in fact the American would have bought the wool and paid for it by buying cheap sterling in the 'black' market, viz. French sterling. The consequence of this process would be a loss of dollars to the Bank of England, since, if this device had not been used, the American would have had to acquire sterling for the purchase of the wool by the sale of dollars in the official market. Those dollars (gold convertible) would have accrued to the Bank of England, as banker to the sterling area. But as a result of the black market operation all that the Bank of England gained (more than nothing) was a transfer of its liability from France to Australia.

It is needful to explain the motives actuating the operators in the black markets. It is obvious why the American desired to use such a market; he got the sterling required to pay for the wool by the surrender of a smaller number of dollars than he would have had to pay, had he operated through the official market. For the Frenchman the gain depended on the circumstances. He would have had to sell his sterling at a discount and thus make a paper loss. His willingness to do that depended entirely on how he regarded the prospect of sterling convertibility. If sterling eventually became convertible, he would be able to dispose of it at the official rate. Consequently what was all important was the question whether sterling would in fact become convertible in the near future. If there was a good chance of this, then it would be foolish of him to sell sterling at a discount rather than to await the time when he could dispose of it at par. It was therefore incumbent on the British authorities during this period to hold out lively hopes that sterling would shortly become convertible, so as to give an incentive to foreign holders to continue to hold sterling and not to inflict a loss upon the British reserves, which would follow from a black market operation. If there had been no prospect of convertibility, most of the sterling balances held outside the sterling area would gradually have seeped away, to the extent that they were not wanted for prospective payments into the sterling area, and this would have necessitated a corresponding loss to Britain of reserves. If the situation had become bad enough, the British authorities might have had to declare a moratorium, namely by blocking, in the fullest sense of that word, all external holdings of sterling.

There were some illusions prevalent at that time. Some thought that the inconvertibility of sterling, as described, was quite a good idea, on the ground that Britain could continue for an indefinite period to avoid its liabilities, as represented by the outstanding sterling balances, and in order to induce people to buy British exports as the only method of using their redundant sterling. But in fact, if there had been no prospect of an early return to convertibility, this would not have been the course of events. The black markets would have been actively used, and the outstanding sterling balances would gradually have been redeemed in this way at the cost of the British reserves. Further to this, in due course, customers would have refused altogether to have had their trade invoiced in sterling or to accept payment in sterling. They would have insisted on the British paying for all imports in dollars.

In relation to the hope that sterling would become convertible in the not too distant future, the Commonwealth meeting in the Autumn of 1952 was useful. Transferable sterling was quoted at as low a rate as \$3 to the £ in 1948, when the official rate was \$4·03 to the £, and in 1951 it was quoted at \$2·4 to the £ when the official rate was \$2·8 to the £. After the Commonwealth meeting the transferable rate rose above \$2·7 and remained within that range. In some periods in the winter of 1953/54 the transferable rate was above the bottom point for the official rate (\$2·78).

At the meeting of the International Monetary Fund in

September 1954, the British Chancellor of the Exchequer made an unfortunate remark. He suggested that the time would not be fully ripe for sterling convertibility until the Americans adopted a more liberal commercial policy. The world at that time did not believe that the Americans would alter their commercial policy, based doubtless on grave reasons of state, just to enable the British to restore convertibility. The transferable rate relapsed to $2·73, which made the use of the black markets once again worth while. It is to be observed that, when the black market rate was only slightly below the official rate, as in the preceding two years, this did not make it worth while for buyers of sterling to use black markets, since incidental expenses were necessarily involved, by payments to intermediaries, etc., in using this devious channel. British reserves suffered in the winter following the Chancellor's statement in Washington, through the more active use of black markets.

On 24 February 1955 the Bank of England took a bold step. It began intervening in the black markets, which it had previously ignored, in such a way as to prevent the discount on transferable account sterling getting big enough to make the use of the black markets worth while. The decision to intervene at this point should be recorded in history as the moment when there was a true *de facto* return to sterling convertibility. From that time onwards anyone could convert sterling into dollars at a rate below the official rate by a negligible amount only.

It is to be assumed that the Bank could not have taken this step without notifying the Cabinet. It was doubtless represented that the step would be technically advantageous. Had the Bank gone to the Cabinet with the proposal to 'restore convertibility', there might have been ideological resistance at that time, and the proposal might well not have gone through. Doubtless there was another motive in the minds of the Bank, namely that it would be expedient to try out the effects of intervention before making sterling *formally* convertible. If the operation had proved very costly, then the Bank could have withdrawn.

But in fact it did not prove costly. It is understood that the amount of reserves that had to be used to support prices in the black markets was very small indeed. This fact shows that by this time the amount of sterling held outside the sterling area was not considered redundant by its holders. Some of the balances had already been used for payments into the sterling area. The outside balances had gone down and the inside balances up. Further to this, the rise in prices and in the volume of foreign trade since 1946 had greatly reduced the size of the outstanding sterling balances in ratio to trade turnover. In February 1955 externally held sterling balances stood at 271 (1933 = 100) while United Kingdom exports stood at 298. What had clearly been redundant in 1946 was no longer so in 1955. And if some holders registered that they considered their holdings redundant by sales at a discount in the winter of 1954/55, this was doubtless because the British Chancellor's remark, already quoted, had suggested to their minds that, in the absence of any near prospect of convertibility, sterling might fall further in the black markets and had therefore better be disposed of at once. It may well be that the Bank of England made sterling *de facto* convertible in the nick of time.

There were, it is true, some troubles later in the year owing to another unfortunate statement, this time by the British delegate to the O.E.E.C. meeting in Paris in June. Incidentally this followed a General Election, always disturbing to foreign confidence, and a rather severe railway strike. People were then considering what would happen in the event of most European currencies becoming convertible once more and the European Payments Union being wound up, as being redundant in those circumstances. The British affirmed that, in the event of convertibility, they would like to have a 3% margin of fluctuation of sterling on either side of par. This was probably a hang-over from the Commonwealth Conference of 1952, when such a proposal had been made in somewhat different circumstances. The Continentals at once took this to mean that the British in effect wanted a devaluation of 3%, and this caused an adverse movement in the exchanges. The British Chancellor corrected this at the International Monetary Fund meeting in Istanbul in the following September, by saying that statements about wider margins of fluctuation were 'irrelevant and unrealistic'. (But why had they ever been made?) This did not quite end the trouble since the British economy was subject to some inflationary pressure in 1955 and a second Budget, imposing some mild extra taxes, was introduced later in that year.

Sterling was made more completely convertible in December

1958. This followed the breakdown of the British negotiations for the formation of a European Free Trade Area and was immediately succeeded by the return to convertibility of the principal European currencies. The final formal step was taken early in 1961, when Britain renounced the privileges allowed by Article XIV of the Articles of Agreement of the International Monetary Fund (transitional clause) and came under Article VIII. This may have been influenced by the British desiring to be in a fully privileged position on the occasion of a drawing on the I.M.F. later in the year, which was then considered probable (and happened).

Since *de facto* convertibility was restored in 1955, the British have had more frequent and more severe troubles in the management of sterling than they had between 1949 and 1955. But it would be quite fallacious to argue that these troubles were 'caused' by the return to convertibility. It is true that the British position was in a certain sense protected by the inconvertibility prior to 1955. But this protection was operative only to the extent that the world hoped that there would be an early return to convertibility. It was a temporary shield against some of the trying facts of life, the use of which Britain was able to enjoy owing to her great prestige at the end of the Second World War and owing to general confidence that she would eventually put her house in order. The return to convertibility brought her into more direct contact with the facts of life, which she would have had to face anyhow, sooner or later, if she was to avoid the total collapse of her position. The 'shield' was just not available for permanent use, and it is wrong to imply that her casting it aside at a particular date was responsible for the troubles that have occurred since.

Two facts appearing in the above narrative are to be noted:

1. There was a large pile up of sight (or short-term) debts, in the form of sterling balances held by non-residents, when the war was over, far exceeding what it was possible for Britain to redeem in the near future. So far as the *sterling area* was concerned, there was no question of the holders of the balances seeking to substitute gold or dollars for them; the trouble for Britain would arise only if they sought to use an excessive amount of them to buy *goods* from outside. There was, of course, a

pent-up demand for goods everywhere. Britain met this difficulty by securing voluntary restraints in the sterling area on
the purchase of goods from outside the sterling area. The more
serious difficulty, namely that of the balances *outside* the sterling
area, Britain met by making these 'inconvertible' for the time
being as described.

2. It has been seen that, when *de facto* convertibility was
restored in 1955, no serious trouble arose. The courageous
intervention by the Bank of England in the black markets
proved justified. It was able from then onwards to maintain
'transferable' sterling very near the official parity for sterling
by the use of a moderate quantity of funds only. Sterling holding
outside the sterling area and the dollar area stood at £682
million at the end of 1954 and at £639 million at the end of
1955. This total dropped by a larger amount in 1956, namely,
to £528 million, after which the amount remained roughly
steady and later began to climb.

What did the fact that the balances were not further drawn
down signify? Holders of sterling were now free to obtain
foreign currencies for it at quite a small discount. The fact that
they did not draw them down further signified that they were
no longer holding sterling under *force majeure*, but were holding
sterling for their own motives of convenience.

The current references to the use of sterling as a 'reserve
currency' suggest some confusion of thought. Holdings of
sterling by the central banks of the sterling area represent the
continuance of a practice, dating right back to the beginning
of those central banks, of holding the major part of their reserve,
available for external settlements, in the form of sterling. It is
really only by reference to those reserves that sterling should be
called a 'reserve currency'. But people often imply, when they
use this expression, that they refer to the much larger quantities
of sterling held outside Britain by commercial banks and trading
concerns as well as by central banks outside the sterling area.
This usage is really misleading.

Sterling is held by these bodies for convenience. They hold
it because, sooner or later, they expect to use it to make payment. Much international trade is invoiced (and settled) in
sterling. The ratio of trade so invoiced to total world trade is

larger than the ratio of British trade to world trade. The reason for this is that not all currencies are suitable for invoicing. Trading contracts and commitments often have to be made long before the time at which the transactions in question will actually occur. Some currencies, such as those subject to frequent devaluation or official restrictions, are not acceptable as a medium for invoicing trade, since one may need to feel secure about the trustworthiness and stability of the currency used in contracts for a number of years ahead. Much international investment and other forms of international finance are denominated in sterling. It is a matter of convenience and security. The holding of sterling by the various bodies outside Britain is a consequence of the denomination of trade and finance in sterling.

There has been loose talk in recent times about putting an end to the use of sterling as a reserve currency. Among the non-British this has come from distinguished experts as widely different in their fundamental views as Professor Triffin and M. Rueff. But there has also been a growing amount of talk inside Britain about the desirability of terminating the use of sterling as a 'reserve currency', on the ground that it is a mill-stone round the British neck, which is supposed to hamper British policy in various directions.

The traditional use of sterling by the central banks of the sterling area is not in fact a mill-stone and has had no connection with the 'runs' on sterling which have been embarrassments to Britain in recent years. There is no stroke of the pen by which the holding of sterling by others not resident in the United Kingdom could be terminated. To do this it would be needful to have a law prohibiting people from denominating trade and financial dealings in sterling. This would not be very convenient to the British; nor would it be so to non-British.

This matter will be further discussed in relation to the devaluation of sterling in 1967.

4. Dollar Holdings Outside the United States

External dollar holdings have in part a different origin, but there are similar misconceptions in relation to references to it as a 'reserve currency'. The external holdings of dollars appear to have been rather small before the war, but have been built up since on a scale that overtops the sterling holdings. By 1963[1] the external holdings of dollars were more than double the external holdings of sterling.

There is nothing exactly corresponding, in the case of dollars, to the use of sterling as a 'reserve' by the central banks of the sterling area. Dollars are indeed held in considerable quantities, both by central banks and by commercial banks and others. As regards the holdings by commercial banks and others, these are of much the same nature as the sterling holdings of commercial banks and others. In 1963 this constituted 39% of all external holdings of dollars. Such sterling holdings were 42·2%. Here too these dollars are held for convenience, because a large amount of international trade and finance is denominated in dollars. This is for a reason similar to that which applies to sterling. The dollar is used as an international medium for invoicing and settlement because some other currencies would not be so satisfactory.

The question remains how far it can be said that the dollar holdings by the central banks, which are undoubtedly large, constitute the dollar as a 'reserve currency' in the sense in which that part of sterling held by the central banks of the sterling area may be called a 'reserve currency'.

Developing countries tend to hold dollars (and/or sterling) in preference to gold as their reserve. The developing countries that hold sterling lie mainly, but not exclusively, in the sterling area and have already been dealt with. Developing countries prefer currencies to gold as a medium of reserve, since it is possible for them to obtain interest on the former. Central banks of such countries hold these currencies also as a matter of convenience, so as to be able to provide their own commercial banks from time to time with a medium that they require for international trade and finance for the reasons already stated, especially in countries lacking a well-developed foreign exchange market.

It may be argued that the dollars held in the central banks of

---

[1] The year 1963 is chosen here, and in subsequent passages, rather than a later year, because support operations in relation to crises may have introduced abnormalities since then.

the developing countries which do much trade with the United States, especially when the reserves of these banks consist in large part of dollars, have a status similar to that of the sterling held by the central banks of the sterling area. Once again, in monetary affairs it is the basic need and motive, rather than the legal forms, that count. The existence of the formal sterling area is due to the accidents of history as already described. The economic motive that induces the central banks of some developing countries to hold a preponderant proportion of their reserves in dollars is largely the same as that which induces central banks in the sterling area to hold sterling.

When we come to the holdings of *other* central banks, a difference may be discerned.

In the first place a considerable amount of dollars are held because it is a currency of 'intermediation' as described in the chapter on the 'modified gold standard'.[1] The primary obligation of member countries under the I.M.F., in relation to the maintenance of a fixed exchange rate, is no longer to tender bars of gold on demand but to intervene in their own foreign exchange markets, to prevent their own currencies going outside the agreed upon limits, *vis-à-vis* the currencies of the members, under the influence of supply and demand in those markets.

As it would be tiresome for the authorities to have to intervene continually by the purchase and sale of a large number of different currencies, they find it simpler to steady the rate of exchange of their own currencies with all others by the purchase and sale of one foreign currency only, and to leave the rest to arbitrageurs. For this purpose the dollar has generally been chosen, as being the most important world currency. It is convenient to have dollars on hand in reserve, wherewith to effect such interventions as may, from time to time, be needed. This motive is somewhat different from that which prompts central banks to hold the *major* part of their reserves in dollars.

This is not quite the end of the story. There seems no doubt that since the war dollar holdings have been built up above the level required for the intermediation function, not merely by the central banks of developing countries or of countries doing heavy trade with the United States, but also by those of other

---

[1] Ch. 3, Section 2.

countries. A tell-tale fact is that in 1963, whereas only 8·9% of all central bank holdings of sterling were in Europe, 58·8% of all central bank dollar holdings were there.

The factors responsible for this are subtle, and it is not possible to give a definitive account of them now; perhaps it never will be. But such an account, if only it could be given, would be of the utmost importance in elucidating differences of opinion that have arisen in recent years about how the monetary problems of the future should be tackled. There was a change in the operative factors in 1958, when the United States began to run a series of heavy deficits, or not long after that. We may take the two periods in turn:

1. It does look as though in the earlier period a number of advanced countries were beginning to think of using the dollar, not as their main medium but as an important supplementary medium of 'reserve', in the full and proper sense of that word. Why so? They were under no obligation to hold dollars. Were they tempted by the interest obtainable, which was, however, moderate by recent standards? Official European holdings rose from $2.38 billion in 1950 to $6.29 billion in 1957. It may be that Marshall Aid was a contributory factor towards inclining the authorities in the countries concerned to hold some of their reserves in the currency of the generous donor. It has been noted that a portion of Marshall Aid was specifically allocated towards enabling the European Payments Union to carry out its duties, while it lasted. This would further incline people to think of the dollar as a regular reserve medium. One may have to be content to say that it was 'just one of those things that happen'. I am not aware of a systematic investigation that has yielded a fully rational explanation of the phenomenon.

2. There is no doubt that some time after the heavy United States deficits began to occur (1958), additional dollar holdings were taken on with the express purpose of *helping* the Americans through their difficulties. American officials repudiate any reference to a 'Gentleman's agreement'. But it is difficult to define such an agreement; it does not imply a specific undertaking, even an oral one. Something uncommonly like a gentleman's agreement occurred in 1960. There were discussions. There is no doubt that a number of countries deliberately

added to their dollar holdings simply and solely to *oblige* the Americans. By 1963 the European holdings had risen to $9.71 billion. Unfortunately the foregoing figures, which are provided by the International Monetary Fund (International Financial Statistics) include non-official bank holdings. But the trend of the official holdings only would be the same. The I.M.F. also provides a European figure for 1963 (but not for earlier years) purged of non-official bank holdings. This stood at $7.87 billion in 1963, i.e. at more than three times as much as the European official and non-official bank holdings together in 1950.

But there is also a third phase:

3. Owing to the continuance of the rather large United States deficits, by about 1965, or perhaps earlier, there appeared over the horizon a question-mark as to whether the dollar might not have to be devalued. This had a double effect. The simple one (i) was doubt whether the countries concerned should go still further in accumulating more dollars to 'oblige' the Americans. Had the Americans not by then had sufficient time to take appropriate adjustment measures – whatever these might be – to terminate their deficits? The idea of 'obliging' them by an unwanted holding of dollars had not been entirely without limit of time in the minds of the holders, although, at the first onset of the problem, it is probable that no specific time-limit was consciously formulated. In such matters the thought may be a vague one only. But vagueness is not the same as non-existence and does not entail that the thought lacks operative force.

The more subtle effect (ii) was that this embarrassment – viz. 'the Americans must understand that our gentleman's agreement must not be taken to last for ever' – brought into the surface of the minds of those concerned the more general question of the *large* size of their dollar holdings. This size had become large already before 1957, viz. before there was any question of 'obliging' the Americans. Before that year there had been little explicit probing of the question of whether, in the abstract, it was a good thing to hold dollars as a medium of normal reserve. The long continuation of the United States deficits, which in themselves have probably done no harm to the world economy, has not only led to an aversion on the part of continental European countries to the idea of increasing their dollar balances still further, to 'oblige' the Americans, not only to a consideration of how long the excess holdings of dollars to 'oblige' the Americans since 1957 (or 1960) is to go on, but also, more important, it has led to the *general* question about the use of the dollar as a 'reserve currency', so-called. Such a question does not seem to have been raised before 1960, or, anyhow, not in an important way. What, before then, was just a habit that had grown up, without theoretical analysis, was afterwards elevated into a general question of principle. Some, but by no means all, of those expressing views about the proper working of the international monetary system, and a smaller, but not negligible, minority among those who actually have to work it, have raised the *general* question – is the use of 'reserve currencies', as an essential ingredient in the world monetary system, a good thing? Some have criticised this use as introducing an 'haphazard' element into the rate at which world monetary reserves increase, this depending on fortuitous variations in the balances of payments of the so-called reserve currency countries.

If the large United States deficits had not continued for more than two or three years after 1957, this wide general question would probably never have been raised. There is really a twofold moral. From a narrow standpoint the Americans, just because of their importance in the world economy, ought to have been on their toes to correct their deficits very promptly, knowing that Caesar's wife must be beyond reproach. From a wider point of view, which many Americans probably adopted, even if only implicitly, their sustained deficits were doing the world no material harm – rather good – because they contributed towards preventing the world from going into recession or stagnation, and – quite a different point – they were providing an increase, in the form of dollars, in total world reserves at a time when gold was making an inadequate contribution.

Unfortunately, the powers that be are inclined to take the narrower viewpoint. In consequence there is a question-mark, not only over further increases in official dollar holdings – the European official holdings have declined since 1963 – but also over the level of dollar holdings in 1957 and over the use of the currency of a particular country as a 'reserve currency'.

The appearance of these question-marks has also, naturally enough, raised questions about sterling, the other 'reserve currency'. It is desirable to revert to a comparison between the dollar and sterling.

5. Sterling and the Dollar – Comparison

The strong point of similarity is the widespread holding of dollars and sterling by foreign commercial banks and other business corporations. These holdings are related to the widespread use of these currencies for the invoicing of trade and other transactions, and for settlement. It cannot be too much emphasised that this use is only indirectly connected with the use of these currencies as central bank reserves. If those who object to the holding of 'reserve currencies' by central banks had their way, this would probably have little effect on invoicing and settlement or on the level of unofficial holdings. When it is desired to assess the magnitude and importance of the use of these currencies as 'reserve currencies', the figures of official foreign holdings only should be taken; non-official foreign holdings should always be omitted.

These unofficial holdings may rise or fall in future, that depending on business convenience. Their size has little connection with the problems confronting those who seek to restructure the world monetary system.

The main link between the problems connected with the official monetary system and the unofficial foreign holdings is that, if either currency became subject to repeated devaluations as against other currencies, this would weaken the tendency to invoice international transactions in it. A devaluation in terms of gold, as part of an all-round devaluation of currencies in terms of gold, would probably make no difference. It remains to be seen (1968) whether the devaluation of sterling on 18 November 1967 will reduce the long-run inclination to denominate international transactions in sterling. It is doubtful if it will do so. A second devaluation of sterling would, however, surely have that effect. I do not believe that a once-only devaluation of the dollar against other currencies, should that at any time seem desirable, would have any appreciable effect.

It is probably not a point of paramount interest to a country that much world trade should be denominated in its currency. But a reduction in the amount of trade so denominated and a consequent reduction in unofficial holdings of it would have an adverse effect, while it was proceeding, since it would constitute a negative item in the country's balance of payments and lead to a decline in its own official reserve. That would be a serious inconvenience to the United Kingdom or the United States at the present time (1968). It is a powerful and valid argument why the United Kingdom authorities should give top priority to the avoidance of a second devaluation.

When we come to the use of the currencies for official reserves the similarity is not so great. The use of sterling has deep roots in history; it has not increased in recent years and has fallen in ratio to trade. It is concentrated in areas which have past or present political connections with the United Kingdom, and which have many business relations with it. The United States holdings have, by contrast, grown strongly in recent years, i.e. since the war. A majority of them are located in Western European countries; although these have large business dealings with the United States, the amount of those dealings in ratio to all their foreign dealings is not notably great.

The British may, perhaps, be deemed unlucky in that the chain of events relating to reserve holdings of dollars, as described in the last section, has raised in the minds of some the *general* question of the use of foreign currencies for official reserves. It is unlikely that, if there had been no dollar problem, the question of *principle* in regard to the use of a foreign currency for reserve would ever have been raised in relation to sterling alone. It might, of course, have been raised as a *practical* question owing to the weak United Kingdom balance of payments position. To some extent fortuitously, sterling has become enmeshed in the dollar problem.

PART TWO

Monetary Theory

5

INTRODUCTORY

MONETARY theory is a department of general economic theory. The latter is usually divided, in these days, into micro-theory, macro-theory and growth theory. Since money is but one among many objects that have value in exchange, like cotton, one might at first suppose that the theory regarding it would fall into the micro category. The fact, however, that money enters into an exchange relation with most, or, indeed, all, other valuables, entails that macro-theory and growth theory also have a bearing on monetary theory.

Micro-theory considers, in relation to a particular object, how much of it is likely to be produced, if it can be produced, and what its exchange value is likely to be; these two quantities being jointly determined by supply and demand conditions.

We may begin with supply. When silver and/or gold were the principal, if not exclusive, constituents of money, their marginal cost of production was clearly of importance on the supply side in governing the value of monies embodying them. They differed, however, from most other commodities, as noted in Chapter 1, Section 2, in that current stocks of them have been large in ratio to current production. This meant that the ratio of demand to current stocks had a greater influence, in governing their value, than was the case with most commodities. While the amount of current production had some influence, and on occasions an important one, the marginal cost would be equated to the value established by the relation of demand to current stocks by appropriate adjustments in the amount produced. This applies, of course, to some extent to all commodities, but to a more marked extent to the precious metals. In the case of gold the decision has had to be made from time to time between mining high-grade ores only or also mining ores of lower grade, a matter currently (1968) of great importance.

A complexity, and, indeed, perplexity, is introduced into this

F

question by the fact that gold and silver have not been demanded for monetary purposes only. One might be tempted to make use of the concept of *net* supply, that consisting of existing monetary stock splus current production minus that part of it which is siphoned over into other uses. Monetary stocks might be defined as the sum total of coins in circulation plus the gold (and/or silver) in the vaults of banks, or, perhaps, only in the vaults of central banks. The trouble is that it is not clear that all the non-bank demand for gold is for non-monetary purposes. Some of the non-bank demand is undoubtedly for industrial use. But some gold may be desired for holding. And in this part a subtle distinction can be drawn between those who hold it simply because it is a valuable object, just as they might hold diamonds or rubies, and those who choose to hold it in store precisely because it is a monetary medium. The last-mentioned category should strictly be regarded as part of the monetary demand. Unfortunately it is not statistically possible to calculate how much is in this category. Currently (March 1968) certain actions have been taken, the intention of which is said by some to be to 'de-monetise' gold. Whether this is a right description cannot yet be known. It would be extremely relevant to those concerned with these measures to know how much of the private holdings of gold are truly of a monetary character.

For centuries token coins and paper documents have come into monetary circulation, as described in Chapter 2, alongside gold (and/or silver), as a supplementary monetary medium. Thus the total money supply has consisted of gold (and/or silver) plus the supplementary media. We have accordingly to consider the supply conditions of these supplements. It is unfortunately very difficult to do so. Consisting, as they do, mainly of paper, their marginal cost of production has been negligible. At least in the early days, their supply seems to have been governed in part by the convenience of individuals, who might prefer to carry paper about and to store it, rather than the precious metals, and in part by the number and diffusion of banks whose paper was credit-worthy. In this phase there was surely something haphazard in the supply conditions of the total quantity of circulating medium.

More recently the supplementary medium has been brought under control as described in Chapter 2. At first the 'control' tended to regulate the quantity of the supplementary medium simply by laying down that it must be convertible on demand into one of the precious metals. By this plan it would seem that the proportion of precious metal money to total money inside a country still depended on the convenience of citizens. Later attempts were made to regulate, or partly regulate, this proportion by establishing minimum reserve requirements.

Later still there has been a tendency for the amount of paper money to become quite detached from the amount of monetary precious metals inside the country. It does not follow that in this last phase the quantity of money became indeterminate. On the contrary its determination passed into the hands of the central banks.

Accordingly, if we approach the problem of the value of money by the supply and demand theory of micro-economics, we have to say that in these advanced cases the supply is determined by policy decisions of the authorities. They doubtless have some criteria, but these are usually not defined and may often be in fact quite vague.

In regard to the demand for money inside a country, an analysis of which is necessary to complete the supply and demand approach, Keynes made a study in depth of a magisterial quality not matched in the present century. This will have to be explained at length in due course.

There still remains the question of the use of money as a medium of exchange between nations. This is a much more perplexing topic. The trouble is that different nations have different monies. In the case of a commodity such as tin it is expected that, subject to transport costs, subject to tariffs, subject to any other obstacles to trade, it would tend to have the same value in terms of other commodities in different countries. The same was true of gold when that could be handled freely by individuals. And, when units of a country's currency were freely convertible into gold by individuals, it was expected that these units would tend to have roughly the same value in terms of other commodities in the different countries, just as gold did. But these conditions no longer obtain. It is not possible to push further with an elucidation until we have explored the equilibrium of foreign trade.

There is a still more difficult problem. Not all the units of money circulating inside a country can be used for making payments to foreign parts, but only the gold possessed by the central bank (or by others, where this is allowed), and the foreign currencies, notably the dollar and sterling, as described, and we, perhaps, ought to add here foreign currencies held in the country outside its central bank.

What governs the world supply of monetary media available for use in international settlement? That will have to be looked into. And what governs the demand for such media, mainly the demand by the world totality of central banks? Unfortunately there has been no one to give an analysis of the demand for money available for international settlement comparable in quality with Keynes's analysis of the domestic demand for money. This is really virgin territory.

Meanwhile we may return to the domestic scene and revert to the 'quantity theory of money'.

6

QUANTITY THEORY

---

1. Quantity Equation

THE operational heyday of the quantity theory was in Britain in the century that followed the report of the Bullion Committee. Not only economists but also top officials accepted it as the main guideline for policy purposes. Things were rather different on the continent of Europe, where members of the 'historical school' found it too rigid for their taste, and, in many cases, the official world was somewhat lacking in clearly defined notions.

In the last fifty years in classrooms Professor Irving Fisher's formulation of it has been much cited. He is by no means to be regarded as the inventor of the theory, but merely gave it a convenient pedagogical shape.

It may be written in the form:

$$MV = \Sigma pq$$

or

$$MV = PT$$

or again,

$$MV + M'V' = PT$$

M is the quantity of money, V the average number of times that each unit of money is used in circulation, p is the price of each (non-money) article entering into exchange and q is the quantity of each of the items so entering. It may be convenient to express the summation of prices and quantities in the form of index numbers, P for the price level and T for the level of transactions. In this case the quantities in the left-hand side of the equation will be expressed as some multiple of 100, representing the base year. The longer equation divides the stock of money into notes and coins (M) and bank deposits (M').

The first thing to be said about these equations is that they are necessary truths, provided that the coverage of the variables is complete, and that the index numbers on the right-hand side are properly weighted. The formulae do not require verification. If one gets out some figures to see how things have been proceeding, the equality of the figures on the two sides of the equation would not serve to verify what is stated in it; on the contrary, the equation would serve to show whether the data used were accurate or not. The equation verifies the data, and not the other way round. I recall Keynes in his lectures poking gentle fun at Irving Fisher for supposing that the statistics that he assembled in his book could possibly serve to verify his equations.

The necessary truth of the equation may be illustrated by the purchase of a packet of cigarettes. The act of a customer in handing money across the counter is one part of the totality of MV in a given period of time. It does not matter whether for the purpose of evaluating T we count a cigarette as a unit, or a packet of twenty as a unit. The tautological nature of the equation, if this is the right term to use, springs from the fact that the price of a packet is *defined* as being the amount of money that is given for it. What is handed out in payment for the packet is the same as what is received for the packet. The necessary truth of the equation is simply a generalisation of this for all transactions within given limits of time and space.

There may be certain difficulties in getting a full coverage. For instance, gifts figure in MV. Accordingly they must figure in PT also. This could be done in various ways. One might regard gifts as having a constant 'price', so that the rise and fall in amounts given would be reflected in a rise and fall in T; gifts must of course be given a correct weight, as governed by the fraction that they constitute of all transactions.

More important is the case of loans, where money is handed across the counter (part of MV) in exchange for a promise of repayment. The repayment will also enter into MV. Such transactions may presumably be treated in the same way as gifts. Sir Ralph Hawtrey made the subtle point in relation to the discount of trade bills that if an increase in the aggregate value of, say, cotton bills were due to an increase in the amount of cotton shipped, this should figure in the T index, but if it was due to an increase in the price of cotton, this should figure in P. Perhaps these subtleties are hardly operational.

From a practical point of view, Fisher's equation may be thought to suffer from being too comprehensive. All capital transfers must be included. Thus P and T are amalgams of current and capital transactions, in which we are not usually very interested. There may be large changes from time to time, not only in the prices of securities but also in the amount of turnover taking place in the stock exchanges. It can be argued on the other side that this will not gravely impair the usefulness of the equation since the velocity of circulation in financial transactions is exceptionally high; thus a great upsurge in such transactions would be offset by the very high value for V related to them. This might happen when prices, transactions and velocities in current account operations remained fairly stable.

I have referred to the necessary truth embodied in the equation as tautological. I do so with a slight misgiving, being profoundly dissatisfied with the existing state of deductive logic. The question is how a proposition that is strictly tautological can give rise to and be indispensable for fruitful lines of thought. Thus, if we are in a position to know what changes have occurred in the values of M, P and T, and there has been a net change in PT/M, we can infer that a countervailing change must have taken place in V. This seems to be a constructive proposition, and may lead on to various interesting lines of inquiry. Why has there been a change in V? A tautology of this type, if what we have here should indeed be called a tautology, which leads to fruitful constructive knowledge, has to be distinguished from an infinity of other tautologies which serve no such purpose. Have our deductive logicians been able to establish what are the special qualities of some tautologies that render them capable of leading on to constructive knowledge, while others remain perfectly barren?

An alternative approach to the quantity theory was made by Alfred Marshall in his lectures in Cambridge and popularised by his disciples. This is commonly known as the Cambridge version of the quantity equation. It was rendered in its simplest form by Keynes in his *Tract on Monetary Reform*, thus:

$$n = pk$$

or

$$n = pkr$$

n is the quantity of money, p the price level and k, in the shorter version, the amount of value in *real* terms that people wish to hold in the form of money. In the longer form k is a fraction and r stands for the amount of real resources entering transactions. The four terms in the longer form are the counterparts of the four terms in the Fisher equation, and thus the Cambridge equation might seem to be merely dressing up the Fisher equation in new terminology.

The object of the manœuvre was to bring monetary theory into closer harmony with the general theory of value. The concept of velocity, with its mechanical and *ex post* connotation, strikes one as an alien morsel in general economic theory. k on the other hand is defined in terms of demand, volition, or, if one likes, an indifference curve. The use of the symbol k may be a little tendentious, since its usual associations suggest that the value in question is a constant. If k were constant, this would mean that the elasticity of the demand for money, expressed in real terms, would be equal to one; but Keynes, and other authors, hasten to add that the elasticity might deviate from this value from time to time, and, if there were such deviations, k would not be constant.

It is a curious thing that it appears that the Cambridge equation is more tautological than the Fisher equation. This is another nice question for deductive logicians. If the quality of being tautological is an absolute, how can it be said that one proposition is *more* tautological than another? The point is that computations designed to illustrate the Fisher equation will not show that the facts agree with it, if the weights used in the index numbers are inappropriate. There will only be an exact correspondence between the equation and the figures designed to illustrate it if the index numbers have correct weights. By contrast, the Cambridge equation will be 'verified' whatever index numbers are used. Taking it in its simplest form, $n = pk$, let us work in terms of basketfuls of commodities, the basketful representing the implied index number. k is the number of basketfuls, purchasing power over which people desire to hold in the form of money. n is the total quantity of money and p is the price of a basketful. This equality must be correct whatever commodities we stuff into the basket. The Cambridge equation could never be used as the Fisher equation can be, to verify, or falsify, an actual set of figures. Pigou in his essay[1] went to the

---

[1] 'Value of Legal Tender Money', *Quarterly Journal of Economics*, 1917; reprinted in *Essays in Applied Economics* (1930).

extreme length of putting into the basket just simply a bushel of wheat. Of course, the equation works out correctly, even if we suppose that people decide how much money they want to hold by reference to its purchasing power over a bushel of wheat. By such a formula p would be simply the price of a bushel of wheat.

Of course, if one seeks to use this formulation sensibly, one will put into the basket the kinds of things, properly weighted, to buy which people normally hold money. Keynes has an interesting description of this in the *Treatise on Money*.[1] He points out that if we are working with the Fisher equation the components of T should be weighted in accordance with the amount of money that changes hands in relation to them. In the Cambridge equation, on the other hand, the components of k should be weighted in proportion to the amount of cash balances held in preparation for purchases of each component multiplied by the time for which they are held. This will, of course, require quite different weighting. The Cambridge formula has the advantage of largely rubbing out stock exchange transactions as elements in the equation.

To complete this notice of the Cambridge formulae, it may be well to set out Pigou's equation in its more complicated form:

$$P = \frac{kR}{M} \{c + h\,(1 - c)\}$$

Pigou, rather perversely, since he was writing after Irving Fisher, used P to stand for the purchasing power of money, namely the reciprocal of the P in the better-known Fisher equation. R stands for real resources and k for the proportion that people wish to hold purchasing power over. M is the quantity of legal tender money, c is the proportion of kR that people wish to hold in the form of the legal tender money and h is the fraction of their deposit liabilities that is constituted by the banks' holdings of legal tender money. The purpose of this formulation, the expediency of which may not seem too obvious in these days, is to show what values we assume to be constant if we are to establish a direct proportional relation between the price level and the quantity of legal tender money. Like the

[1] Vol. I, pp. 78–9, 237–9 (1930).

simpler forms, this equation is necessarily true, so that if we happen to know of changes in certain terms, we can infer that there must have been offsetting changes in other terms. At the time when these matters were more discussed, I offered an alternative formulation thus:

$$P = \frac{R}{M} \{kl + k'h(1 - l)\}$$

The terms here stand for the same things, except that l is the fraction of all payments that people choose to make by legal tender money (rather than by cheque), and k is the fraction of all legal tender money payments during the period that people choose on average to hold in the form of legal tender money, and k' is the fraction of all cheque payments during the period that people choose to hold in the form of bank deposits. While both these equations are tautological, I submit that mine is more useful – again one comes up against the question of the usefulness of a tautology. Pigou's c seems to my mind to relate to no wishes that people actually have. Motives for the holding of coins and notes at any one time and the motives for holding a bank balance are somewhat different, and I doubt if anyone ever decides that he wants to hold a certain proportion of money in the wider sense in the form of notes and coins and the residual in the form of bank deposits. On the other hand, I would suggest that my l is operational. The kinds of things one chooses to pay for by legal tender and the kinds of things that one chooses to pay for by cheque are fairly constantly determined, anyhow for a short period, by institutional arrangements and customs. Pigou's overall k is consequentially split in my equation into k, the converse there of the velocity of circulation of notes and coins, and my k' the converse of the velocity of circulation of bank deposits. Equations of this kind can of course be multiplied.

It is necessary to grapple with the status and validity of the quantity theory. So far as the quantity equation is concerned, in whichever of a number of possible ways it is formulated, it is a necessary truth, not to be challenged. It is also a valuable truth, constituting a criterion for the testing of empirical propositions, whether of a general or particular character.

2. *Essence of 'Quantity Theory'*

Acceptance of the quantity equation does not make one a 'quantity theorist'. An extreme form of the quantity theory, to which no one actually subscribes, would be to say that V and T are always constant, so that, by consequence, the price level varies directly with the quantity of money. That quantity might depend primarily on the cost of gold production or, in the modern world, on the action of a central bank, working through certain established relations with member banks in determining the 'money supply'. A proposition nearer acceptability would be to say that V and T are exogenous variables, the former depending on habits in regard to the average time interval between receipts and expenditures, the services provided by banks, etc., and the latter on such things as population and productivity. Thus one would show that the price level depended on the money supply, along with exogenous variations in V and T, and one could also then say that a given increase in the money supply would cause the price level to be proportionally higher *than it would otherwise be*.

But a quantity theorist is usually prepared to go farther than this and to allow that both V and T may have a functional dependence on the value of M, anyhow in the short period. For instance, an increase of M might cause the expectation of a rise in prices, and this might cause a rise in V on the ground that money would be *pro tem.* a depreciating asset, and that it would be worth altering one's habits, in order to hold somewhat less of it. Professor Milton Friedman has argued in relation to conditions in the United States before the Federal Deposit Insurance Act that V might be affected by a prevailing lack of confidence in the banks. Such induced changes in V would presumably be expected to be reversed in the long period, so that the more rigid form of the quantity theory would come into its own again. Or again, a rise in M might cause an increase in T either (i) to the extent that the anticipation of rising prices stimulated production, or (ii) because, during the course of an upward movement of prices, the prices of goods might be more sensitive and rise more quickly than the prices of factors of production, thereby temporarily widening profit margins.

Whereas the characteristic changes in V would enhance the effect of a rise in M in raising P, the characteristic reactions in T would presumably have a damping effect. Within the general framework of the quantity theory, opinions may differ about the duration of likely variations in V and T in consequence of changes in M.

I would suggest that the essence of the quantity theory, whether in a rigid or modified form, is that the value of P is the resultant of changes in M, along with exogenous or induced changes in V and T.

3. Another View

I should be departing from the spirit of the quantity theory if I suggested that the rise of prices in recent years in Britain (1968) had been due to the successes of wage earners in getting, by collective bargaining, wage increases in excess of current increases in productivity. I might point out that in the period in question the banking system had increased the money supply by less than PT, which in this context one might regard as roughly represented by the money value of the G.N.P., and that consequently, by the quantity equation, the velocity of circulation must have been rising. It could be held that in this period there was a spontaneous desire by the average person to circulate his money more quickly, i.e. to hold less real value in his cash balance. I know of no reason why this should have been so. I should be inclined to argue, as a matter of common sense, that, since producers had had their costs raised by the agreements for excessive wage increases and were therefore bound to put up prices if they were to stay in business, the rise in P was due quite directly and simply to the excessive wage bargains and that this has had a consequential effect in raising V.

Quantity theorists would not be likely to allow this analysis to be valid. If V had indeed risen in the period, as can readily be shown, this must have been due, they would argue, to a change in people's desire to hold the money, e.g. owing to a fear of inflation. If only governments had abided in their old habits and the banking system had remained firm as regards money supply (which in fact it did), prices just could not have gone up, whatever wages might be granted.

Which then was the basic cause of the tendency to rising prices in Britain – the excessive wage increases, or a change in the propensity to hold money? This question seems to bring the issue to a head. I confess that I believe that it was the wage increases that caused the price increases, and by this confession I suppose that I should disclaim being a 'quantity theorist', although recognising the eternal validity of a correctly formulated quantity equation.

I would hold that V in the Fisher sense, which is the sense meant in this discussion, is very plastic for quite a long period. In objection, quantity theorists, such as Professor Milton Friedman, might ask – why should people alter their ideas about how much money they want to have in hand? Why should people voluntarily choose to push out money received more quickly (increase of V), just because trade unions have secured wage increases in excess of productivity? What has this last-mentioned fact got to do with their needs and wishes as regards the amount of money that they want to hold? The answer to these questions is written large in Keynes's analysis of liquidity preference. If he is properly understood, there remains no problem.

7

THE KEYNESIAN REVOLUTION

1. The 'Treatise on Money'

THERE were, of course, in the nineteenth century, and afterwards, objectors to the quantity theory. But these consisted
mainly of members of the 'historical school', who were allergic
to any strict form of theory whatever. Within the great tradition
of classical and neo-classical economics there was probably a
greater consensus of opinion about the truth of the quantity
theory of money than about any other economic tenet, except
for those of the utmost generality.

In the sense defined at the end of the last chapter, Keynes
departed from this long-lasting tradition sometime in the
middle of the 1920s. And he departed, not on the lines of the
historical school or by raising certain amorphous doubts, but
by constructing a new theory of his own of great precision,
which could be offered, as an alternative to the classical scheme,
to the strictest adherents of the supremacy of pure theory.

His new views were given formulation in *A Treatise on
Money* (1930). I will move directly to his 'fundamental equations':

$$P = \frac{E}{O} + \frac{I' - S}{R}$$

$$= \frac{W}{e} + \frac{I' - S}{R}$$

$$\pi = \frac{W}{e} + \frac{I - S}{O}$$

P is the price level of consumer goods, *E* the total money income
of the community, *O* is the total output of goods, *I'* the part of
E which has been earned by the production of investment
goods (=the cost of production of new investment), *S* is savings,
R is the volume of consumer goods and services, *W* is the rate
of earnings per unit of human effort, *e* is the coefficient of

efficiency (output per unit of effort), π is the price level of output as a whole and I is the value of the increment of new investment.

We thus have two expressions on the right-hand side of the equations, jointly determining the value of the price level. Neither expression brings in M (money supply) as a direct determinant of the price level.

This does not mean that Keynes thought that the money supply had no effect on the price level; rather he thought that its effect was devious and had to operate indirectly through its effect on one or other of the terms in the fundamental equations, as set out. Still less did he think that the money supply was unimportant in relation to the behaviour of the economy as a whole. Throughout his life he was a firm believer in the importance of money and a passionate advocate of monetary reform. He continued to believe that monetary policy could have a potent influence, although he did not believe that the great world slump could be cured by monetary weapons alone. I cannot find anything in his *General Theory* to suggest that he did not continue to be a keen believer in the importance of money, although that work was more concerned with other economic relations. And then at the end of his life we find him busy (at Bretton Woods) endeavouring to improve the international monetary system. The report of the Radcliffe Committee on the Working of the Monetary System (Cmnd 827, 1959) was indeed far removed from the spirit of Keynes in belittling the importance of the money supply.

There are two reasons for reverting to the *Treatise on Money*, in addition to the general one that it is far richer in content relating to monetary theory and practice than the *General Theory*. The latter was written somewhat in haste after Keynes had achieved in his own mind a wide theoretical synthesis, comprising far more than merely monetary matters. He was anxious to get this before the public quickly. The *Treatise*, by contrast, contains all his gathered wisdom about monetary matters, resulting from intense thinking and observation, and indeed practical experience, over more than twenty years. It is, I would submit, impossible to have an understanding of Keynes in depth, if one has not read the *Treatise*.

The first of the two special reasons for reverting to the *Treatise* is that the equations given above set out in a very clear way the distinction between cost inflation and demand inflation. Of the two forces set out as determining the price level, the first represents the ratio of wage increases to productivity increases and the second represents what in the *General Theory* is called aggregate demand, which will tend to raise prices if I' exceeds S and to depress them when S exceeds I'.

There has been argument about the appropriate use of the two expressions, cost inflation and demand inflation. I believe that for conceptual clarity it is best to stick to the definitions implicit in these equations. It has been argued that, if a demand inflation is the cause that actuates an excess increase of wages, this increase, or that part of it due to the high level of demand, should be regarded as a part of the demand inflation itself, and not as an independent force. This is to introduce causation. I believe that for conceptual clarity it is better not to proceed in this way. It must be remembered that there can be a cost inflation, even if no demand inflation is present at the time. It may sometimes be due to an earlier demand inflation that had raised the cost of living. Or it may occur when there has been no demand inflation operating for a long time, as between 1929 and 1939. As regards policy, if demand inflation and cost inflation are proceeding simultaneously and if the former is the cause of the latter, it may be appropriate to kill two birds with one stone by terminating the demand inflation. But it is not appropriate to deflate when demand inflation is not in present operation, whether the present cost inflation is due to an earlier demand inflation or to something quite different.

It often happens that a cost inflation occurs when positive deflationary forces are operating on the side of demand (S is greater than I'). Furthermore, one single act of policy may be demand inflationary and cost deflationary, or conversely. A classic instance of the former were the British food subsidies during the Second World War which were unquestionably demand inflationary, while being cost deflationary.

The second special reason arises from the treatment of investment and saving. The validity of the expression representing aggregate demand depends on a special definition of income, which Keynes abandoned in the *General Theory*. By any ordinary definition of income, for example as used in national accounting, investment is always and necessarily equal to saving. In order to obtain an inequality, Keynes gave a special definition as follows: 'For my present purpose I propose to define the "normal" remuneration of entrepreneurs at any time as that rate of remuneration which, if they were open to make new bargains with all the factors of production at the currently prevailing rates of earnings, would leave them under no motive either to increase or to decrease their scale of operations.' This is an unhappily static definition, but it can be readily dynamised by substituting for the last clause, 'would give them a motive to increase their scale of operations by no more nor less than their normal growth rate'. For establishing total income, the remuneration of entrepreneurs is assumed to be normal, whether in fact at the time in question it is super-normal, normal or subnormal. It is this exclusion of a certain species of income, which in national accounting would certainly be reckoned as part of the national income, that makes it possible to have an inequality between investment and saving.

There are two points to be noted here. Although Keynes gave up his special definition of income and in his later volume insisted rather strongly on the necessary equality of investment and saving, there has been felt to be a continuing need since then for having some definition of investment and/or saving, by which it becomes possible to allow an inequality. One may use the term coined by Myrdal of *ex-ante*, or one may talk of 'planned' investment and saving. These may of course be unequal. I personally prefer the Keynesian concepts, because they refer to what is proceeding currently, rather than to past decisions, which may have no more than a historic interest.[1] Another virtue of this approach is that it draws a strong distinction between personal and normal company saving on the one hand, and, on the other, company saving, or dis-saving, relatively to the norm, that occurs as a result of the inflationary

[1] In my growth equations I have used concepts analogous to those of Keynes. C refers to the amount of capital actually produced in a given period (divided by the increase of total output) while C_r refers to the amount of capital that entrepreneurs would like to find themselves with, and this amount may be defined in a way analogous to Keynes's definition of normal remuneration given in the text. C_r is emphatically not an *ex-ante* concept. Entrepreneurs may have planned to have something quite different from what they *now* find it convenient to have, since when they made their plans it could not be foreseen what the demand for their products would be.

or deflationary process. This dichotomy of saving into two fundamental kinds is lost from view in the *General Theory*; but it is a distinction of the utmost importance for the understanding of many matters both in cycle theory and in growth theory.

The above equations specify determinants of the price level, which contain no reference to the quantity of money. We may be sure that there can be variations in the two right-hand expressions, causing proportionate changes in the price level, even if M/T does not change, or has some quite different change. But, since the quantity equation must be true, it must be supposed that V has accommodating changes, when P changes under the influence of the forces specified out of line with any change in M/T. The accommodating changes in V are explained by Keynes's theory of Liquidity Preference, which occurs in the *Treatise* as well as in the *General Theory*. The idea of the possibility, as postulated by Keynes, of *accommodating* changes in V, i.e. when there are *no* changes in the schedules representing the desires of individuals to hold money, is entirely contrary to the spirit of the quantity theory.

2. The 'General Theory'

It is necessary to give a brief outline of certain elements in the *General Theory*, although this covers some matters that are not within the area of monetary theory proper.

Perhaps the most central idea in the *General Theory* is that it is possible to have an equilibrium in which there is unemployment in excess of what can be attributed to frictions and lack of mobility and in excess of any unemployment that could be regarded as 'voluntary'. Many of the unemployed might be perfectly willing to work at the going rates of pay, or even, in *real* terms, somewhat below them, if only the jobs were available.

The total demand for goods and services springs from the propensity to invest and the propensity to consume. Both these propensities are conceived in real terms, and not in money terms. Understanding of this is absolutely necessary for a comprehension of Keynes and of the nature of his breakaway from the quantity theory. The investment requirement should be conceived of as a quantity of physical objects – factories, houses, etc. The size of this quantity depends on certain forces, such as the expectation of the yield of the capital goods in ratio to their cost of production and the current rate of interest; it is not necessary to explore these matters here. The propensity to consume is conceived of as a certain fraction of people's real incomes. This propensity is conceived to be quite independent of the money value of their incomes; people want to set aside 5% or 10%, or whatever the case may be, of their real incomes. The investment demand for goods and services is related to the total demand for goods and services by the 'multiplier', which is the reciprocal of the propensity to save:

$$Y = \frac{I}{s}$$

Y is the total demand for goods and services, I is the demand for investment goods and s is the fraction of income saved. The total demand for goods and services may be above or below the supply potential – call it Y^s – of the economy. In the former case there will be inflationary pressure, and in the latter case unemployment. One may put this in another way as follows: Suppose the sum total of factories, houses, etc., which those responsible for investment decisions wish to bring into being would take 20% of the productive resources of the country to produce; and suppose that consumers want to spend on consumption 90% of their real income; we then have a total demand for goods and services in excess of what the economy can supply. We have no reference to money here at all. The houses, factories, etc., are physical objects that are needed; the consumption propensity is expressed as a fraction of income, and has no reference to money.

The effect of the two propensities on the price level may be expressed very schematically as follows: If an increase in either propensity occurs when unemployment is present, it will be met by an increase of activity. When there is full employment, any further increase in the propensities will be met by higher prices. This is too schematic, because, when activity proceeds upwards from an unemployment level, some prices may move up before full employment is reached. This may be owing to sectional bottlenecks, or monopolists taking advantage of higher demand, or simply because prices had previously been at a depressed level, allowing in many cases an insufficient margin for normal profits. The improving employment may also stimulate wage increases, and these may affect prices, as shown in the left-hand terms of Keynes's *Treatise* equations. (Keynes tends to assume that improving employment will cause wage increases, but this cannot be accepted as a universal proposition. It appears that the Phillips curve, which embodies it, has not been valid for the United Kingdom since 1921.)[1]

Thus we have the idea of two major forces operating directly on the price level, both expressed in real terms, namely investment demand and consumer demand. And to this we may add, on the lines of the *Treatise*, any tendency of wages and other non-profit incomes to rise more than in proportion to productivity. If, at a time when these forces are making for price increases, bankers adopt a conservative attitude and allow no increase in the money supply, or an increase not commensurate with the rise in prices, this rise will be carried by an increase in the velocity of circulation, which thus plays a passive role. Such an idea seems to be quite inconsistent with the quantity theory in any recognised form.

3. Liquidity Preference

It is accordingly necessary to examine Keynes's concept of Liquidity Preference.[2] What follows is not intended as a precise exegesis of Keynes's ideas at the moment when he put them on paper in writing the *General Theory*. It is more useful to give a broad, and even sometimes critical, treatment, emphasising those aspects which may be considered durable and continuously useful. This is especially appropriate in the case of Keynes, whose own mind was very adaptable; he would not have regarded his own book as a sacred text, and might well have brought out a fresh edition, had he not been the victim of illness and war-time preoccupations for the remainder of his life.

Liquidity preference takes up the age-old historic idea that one of the functions of money is to be a 'store of value'. This was somewhat lost to view in the more mechanical formulations of

[1] Cf. A. G. Hines, 'Trade Unions and Wage deflation in the United Kingdom, 1893–1963', in the *Review of Economic Studies*, October 1964; 'Wage Inflation in U.K. 1943–1962: a Disaggregated Study', in *Economic Journal*, March 1969.

[2] Cf. p. 4.

the quantity theory. It also takes up the concept of k of the Cambridge formulations. We have seen that k was used to express desires or volitions, thus bringing monetary theory more into line with general value theory. The liquidity preference theory provides a more elaborate analysis of those desires and volitions. The careful student should note, however, that whereas k was expressed in real terms, i.e. represented so many basketfuls of goods, the elements in the liquidity preference theory consist of money itself.

This theory also serves to explain the passive variations in V, which are so painful to the quantity theorist. In using it for that purpose, I may deviate somewhat from the actual wording of Keynes. In the last phase he seemed, on the surface, to treat velocity in rather a cavalier way. This was perhaps a pity. It is one instance of a tendency he had, in the ardour of his own exposition and in the desire to express everything by his own terms, to brush aside as unimportant concepts which had received great consideration by the many fine minds who had over many generations put together what we regard as economics. It is essential to treat velocity with respect. I do not know if it was the influence of Keynes, wrongly interpreted, that caused the Radcliffe Committee to give such scant and superficial treatment to velocity.

We shall also be involved in Keynes's theory of interest. This was another case where he broke away. This seemed to be rather a violent break. A patient and sensible interpretation of Keynes's thought shows that it is perfectly capable of being accommodated to the classical theory of interest, and indeed that, words apart, the classical theory is deeply embedded in Keynes's theory.

Keynes gives three reasons why people want to hold money – for the transactions, precautionary and speculative motives. Thus we may write:

$$M = M_t + M_p + M_s$$

M is the total quantity of money in existence in the system. Of this total, the amount that will be taken up by the transactions motive will depend, roughly, on the money value of the national income. When its volume goes up, or the price level goes up, or both, more money will be needed for the transactions motive, and less will be available for the other two motives.

This explains how, if the money value of the national income goes up, while the banking system is conservative and does not allow any increase in M, or not a fully proportional increase in it, a higher price level can none the less be sustained. This higher price level may be solely due to excessive wage or salary increases and have nothing to do with the money supply. M being constant, replenishments for M_t can be found by drawing money from M_p and M_s. Then the transactions-circuit velocity may well remain constant, in accordance with people's habits and institutional arrangements, which are so much stressed by the quantity theorists. Keynes actually says in one place that he thinks that the transactions velocity of money is likely to be constant.

But V, as it figures in Fisher's equation, by no means remains constant. Fisher's V is an overall average. If, as a rough approximation, we find V by dividing the money value of the national income by M, we will find that it rises in the circumstances envisaged, viz. an increase in the volume of the national income, or a rise of prices, whether due to a demand pull or cost push inflation, or to both, if the banking system does not increase M in proportion.

The fraction of the total M that finds employment in the transactions circuit goes up. The effect of this is to raise the value of V in the Fisher equation. The rise in the average overall velocity is due to the fact that a larger proportion of the total money supply is circulating and a smaller proportion is stagnant, for precautionary or speculative motives. This rise in V is perfectly compatible with people retaining the same habits and arrangements, as regards the time interval between receipts and payments, as they had before. Thus the requirement of the quantity theory that insists that the whole non-bank world has certain habits that they will not have interfered with, and the requirement of the Keynesian theory than an excessive wage increase can cause prices to rise, even if there is no increase in M, owing to there being enough plasticity in V, are perfectly reconciled.

We next have to consider the effect of a fall in the quantity of money available for the precautionary and speculative motives. This, according to Keynesian theory, will send up the rate of interest. That in turn could have, although it would not in all circumstances necessarily have, some damping effect on *P*, a matter to be considered presently. But this damping effect would not normally be nearly sufficient to prevent *P* rising more than *M* in the case of excess wage and salary increases.

Meanwhile a word should be said about the precautionary motive. Money is held for the precautionary motive when the holder has some out-payment in prospect, of which he may not be sure of the precise date, or even of the precise amount. In these circumstances he may refrain from investing the money in question in securities, lest their capital value falls and leaves the cost of the project incompletely covered. He may be committed to the project by some contracts or some assurance, so that it would be gravely embarrassing to him to come to the date at which it had to be executed and have insufficient money in hand. It is true that by buying securities he might increase the value of the corpus of his capital, if the securities rose; but he is willing to waive that possible advantage, as well as the interest on the money meanwhile, in order to avoid the risk of the opposite state of affairs. That is why Keynes uses the word 'precautionary'. The holder is unwilling to take a line about the future trend of security prices; his sole motive is to avoid risk of loss when he has a commitment in prospect.

The holder under the speculative motive, by contrast, does take a line. He believes that the prices of securities will come down within a reasonable period, and that, by waiting and sacrificing interest meanwhile, he will be able to get a better yield on the securities when he does buy them for an indefinite period. That again, if it eventuates, may well be of far greater value than the loss of interest during the interval. It is an essential part of his position that he thinks he knows better than the market. If the market as a whole thought that the prices of securities would shortly fall, they would fall almost to that level immediately. Indeed, I think that the best definition of speculation as such – whether in commodities, currencies, etc. – is that the speculator is pitting his judgement against the market. Thus speculation covers a much smaller category of actions than risk-taking. We all have to be risk-takers from time to time in quite a variety of ways, but we may go through life without ever speculating at all.

In my opinion Keynes does not give nearly enough weight to

the precautionary motive, and is wrong in saying, as he does in one place, that the precautionary motive is not interest sensitive. Thereby he gives far too much work, in relation to the whole system, to the speculative motive. Professor J. Viner has argued that the funds held for the speculative motive are not large enough to have the great influence that they are made to have in Keynes's system.[1] In conversation, he remarked to me that it would be just as reasonable to argue that the price of cigars is regulated by the utility function of female cigar smokers.

On certain occasions the speculative motive can be very important indeed. The classic case was in Britain in the autumn of 1946. The Chancellor of the Exchequer (Dr Dalton) thought that, if one had been able to run a very burdensome war at 3%, one ought to be able to run the peace-time economy at $2\frac{1}{2}\%$. If it was argued that the low interest rate had not caused inflation during the war because of the universal prevalence of controls, it was open to Dr Dalton to reply that he intended to maintain controls. And that was done to some extent, but not nearly so severely as in the war-time. There were heavy investment demands, for replacing equipment, rebuilding stock and building houses, which had not been allowed during the war. People just did not believe that it would be possible to maintain $2\frac{1}{2}\%$ in these circumstances. Advice by brokers to clients to keep any money accruing in hand and postpone buying securities was widespread. There was a great build-up of money held in this way, and this is precisely what Keynes meant by the speculative motive. Even at that time, however, the majority view must have been that Dalton would get his way. One could argue, 'Well, he is the Chancellor, is he not? He has all the power in his hands.' If the majority had not thought this, security prices would have come down right away. But the number taking the opposite view was also big. It seems likely that there was a large build-up of money for the speculative motive in the months before the Wall Street crash of 1929. Doubtless the majority still thought that everything would continue on the up and up; but there were also wiser heads who foresaw the trouble and sold out some at least of their securities for money. But I am inclined to agree with

[1] R. Lekachman (ed.) *Keynes's General Theory: Reports of Three Decades* (1964), pp. 250–61.

Professor Viner that the amount of money held for the speculative motive in *ordinary* times is not very great.

I would suggest that, on the contrary, there is at any time a large amount of money held for the precautionary motive. At the time of writing I can readily think of two instances, one for a large sum and one for a small one, in my own immediate environment, and I can think back to many instances in the past. It is true that at the time of writing this money is put into the short-loan market, where interest rates are very high. I shall return to that presently.

Keynes makes the amount of money required for the precautionary motive a function of the money value of the national income, like that required for the transactions motive itself, and argues that it is interest insensitive. This is paradoxical. If interest rates are high, the direct loss from not putting money into securities is greater, and the chance of capital loss, if one occurs, owing to the fall in the prices of securities before the given date, less. While it would seem sensible to suppose that, although some holders, namely those a long way inside the margin, would feel it absolutely necessary to hold money in any case, there may be others who would balance the certain loss on forgoing interest against the risk of loss on the securities, and decide one way or another according to the circumstances of the case. There will be a much stronger case for caution if the loss of interest is moderate (owing to its rate being low) and the risk of a loss of capital value, if securities are bought, correspondingly high.

The overemphasis of speculation, as against precaution, has been instanced in an entirely different field, by the frequent reference to 'speculation' against sterling or the dollar in recent periods. Doubtless there was some speculation in these cases, but this was probably of minor importance compared with the vast movement of funds, due to the precautionary motive. This was described in Chapter 3, Section 5.

4. Interest Theory

We now come face to face with Keynes's theory of interest. He did his own cause great harm by his attacks on the classical theory and by underlining the difference of his own theory from it. The classical theory is not only not inconsistent with Keynes's theory, but is even an essential part of it, if one interprets the latter in a rational manner and is not put off by some exaggerated observations by Keynes.

Keynes's theory is primarily concerned with the actual or 'market' rate of interest. Whereas in the classical scheme the actual rate, as well as the natural rate, is determined by the flows of new savings and new requirements for capital formation, in the Keynes scheme it is determined from day to day by the whole mass of existing capitalists. Every day it is their economic duty, which is doubtless carried out by the more active-minded among them, to review their asset-mix and to consider whether it corresponds to their needs and interests. If their view on balance is that the asset-mix of yesterday contained too many bonds and not enough money, this will send the rate of interest up, and conversely. This has been characterised as a stock theory and been contrasted with a flow theory. Doubtless there are alternative possible ways of approaching this subject, but I submit that Keynes was unquestionably right in holding that the whole mass of capitalists influence the rate of interest every day, and not only the puny band of new savers. Furthermore, some writers recommending the flow approach have got themselves into hopeless confusion by supposing that bank lending can add to the aggregate of saving coming into the market. These rightly raised the ire of Keynes, and it was with reference to such writers that he made the famous analogy with the duck which dived deeply into the weeds and mud at the bottom of the pond. So far as the provision of saving is concerned, the banks are pure intermediaries. But they can alter the asset-mix by buying or selling securities, by withdrawing bonds from the non-bank pool of assets in exchange for money (bank deposits); and conversely, their lending operations may be similarly analysed.

The apparently unsatisfactory part of Keynes's theory is the lack of provision of a theory of a 'natural' rate of interest. We are told that the reason why people require interest on bonds is to compensate them for the sacrifice of liquidity, which sacrifice consists essentially in the risk that, when they want to realise their assets, the bonds may have fallen in capital value, i.e. that the rate of interest may have risen.

Keynes thus exposed himself to the criticism of Professor J. R. Hicks that he has 'left the rate of interest hanging by its own boot straps'. And D. H. Robertson has the following amusing passage:

> While there are hints here and there of a broader treatment, in the main his plan is to set the rate of interest in a direct functional relation only with that part of the money stock which is held for what he calls 'speculative reasons', i.e. because it is expected that the rate of interest will subsequently rise. Thus the rate of interest is what it is because it is expected to become other than it is; if it is not expected to become other than it is, there is nothing left to tell us why it is what it is. The organ which secretes it has been amputated, and yet it somehow still exists – a grin without a cat. Mr Plumptre of Toronto, in an unpublished paper, has aptly compared the position of the lenders of money under this theory with that of an insurance company which charges its clients a premium, the only risk against which it insures them being the risk that its premium will be raised. If we ask what ultimately governs the judgements of wealth-owners as to why the rate of interest should be different in the future from what it is today, we are surely led straight back to the fundamental phenomena of Productivity and Thrift.

It is impossible to make sense of Keynes without assuming that his scheme contains a 'natural' rate of interest, and that this natural rate is determined in exactly the way in which it is determined in the classical scheme. In this respect the difference between Keynes and the classicists is that the latter held that there would be a constant tendency in the market for the natural rate to be achieved, while Keynes did not.

As this matter is of central importance, it may be expedient to quote two passages. The first is taken from the *Treatise on Money* (p. 154):

> Following Wicksell, it will be convenient to call the rate of interest which would cause the second term of our second Fundamental Equation to be zero the *natural-rate* of interest, and the rate which actually prevails the *market-rate* of interest. Thus the natural-rate of interest is the rate at which saving and the value of investment are exactly balanced, so that the price-level of output as a whole (π) exactly corresponds to the money-rate of the efficiency-earnings of the

Factors of Production. Every departure of the market-rate from the natural-rate tends, on the other hand, to set up a disturbance of the price-level by causing the second term of the second Fundamental Equation to depart from zero.

Here we have a natural rate *à la* Wicksell. It is to be regretted that there was an unfortunate shift in emphasis in the *General Theory*. The analysis of the *Treatise* in this area is mainly concerned with the price level, although it is not implied that the level of activity does not move up and down. The most important difference between the *General Theory* and the *Treatise* is that the former contains a theory of what governs the level of employment (cf. its title!). What Keynes came to perceive is that one might get an equality between saving and investment (even in the *ex-ante* sense) at any level of employment, so that there would be as many 'natural' rates in the sense defined above as there are possible levels of employment, and so he wrote as follows in the *General Theory*:

> In my *Treatise on Money* I defined what purported to be a unique rate of interest, which I called the *natural rate* of interest – namely, the rate of interest which, in the terminology of my *Treatise*, preserved equality between the rate of saving (as there defined) and the rate of investment. I believed this to be a development and clarification of Wicksell's 'natural rate of interest', which was, according to him, the rate which would preserve the stability of some, not quite clearly specified, price-level.
>
> I had, however, overlooked the fact that in any given society there is, on this definition, a *different* natural rate of interest for each hypothetical level of employment. And, similarly, for every rate of interest there is a level of employment for which that rate is the 'natural' rate, in the sense that the system will be in equilibrium with that rate of interest and that level of employment. Thus it was a mistake to speak of *the* natural rate of interest or to suggest that the above definition would yield a unique value for the rate of interest irrespective of the level of employment. I had not then understood that, in certain conditions, the system could be in equilibrium with less than full employment.
>
> I am now no longer of the opinion that the concept of a 'natural' rate of interest, which previously seemed to me a most promising idea, has anything very useful or significant

to contribute to our analysis. It is merely the rate of interest which will preserve the *status quo*; and, in general, we have no predominant interest in the *status quo* as such.

If there is any such rate of interest, which is unique and significant, it must be the rate which we might term the *neutral* rate of interest, namely, the natural rate in the above sense which is consistent with *full* employment, given the other parameters of the system; though this rate might be better described, perhaps, as the *optimum* rate.

The neutral rate of interest can be more strictly defined as the rate of interest which prevails in equilibrium when output and employment are such that the elasticity of employment as a whole is zero.

All this makes good enough sense, if we waive the grossly exaggerated and unrealistic concept of an equilibrium with the elasticity of employment at zero. We may allow that there could be a multiplicity of natural rates in the Wicksellian sense. But now we have a 'neutral' rate, and this is what we need. (The idea of an 'optimum' rate is something entirely different[1] and is intrusive in this passage.)

The fault of the passage is that, instead of stressing the central importance of the idea of a *neutral* rate, Keynes seems inclined to pooh-pooh it. It clearly is of central importance, as has always been plain to me ever since I read the *General Theory* in proof. If the rate of interest is below the neutral level, aggregate demand will exceed the supply potential of the economy, and there will be inflationary pressure; and if it is above the neutral level, there will be unemployment.

And now we have to ask the vital question – what *determines* the level of this all-important neutral rate, viz. the rate that is consistent with an equilibrium of full employment? The answer is the propensity to invest and the propensity to save, namely precisely the same forces that determine the natural rate of interest in the classical scheme.

Thus Keynes was under an illusion when he supposed that he had somehow divided himself from the classical school in this regard. His treatment of the classicists is poor in a number of places in the *General Theory*.

His radical departure from the classical school is at another

---

[1] See p. 201.

place, namely, as already described, as regards the determination of the *market* rate of interest. The further point of difference is that he does not suppose there to be any built-in tendencies for the market rate to move to the natural, or, as he calls it, neutral, level.

Thus for Keynes the market rate of interest is governed by liquidity preference and the money supply. But there is all the time in the background a natural rate of interest – he calls it 'neutral' – which equates investment demand to saving at its current level, *when there is full employment*. The determination of this natural rate is in line with classical thinking, viz. the balance between the use that can be made of savings and the savings that people want to make. (In accordance with the *Treatise* we exclude here super-normal or sub-normal savings made by businesses in *consequence* of an inflationary or deflationary process currently under way.)

Keynes departs from the classical scheme by denying that there is any regular tendency for the market rate to become equal to the natural rate in the way, for instance, that the market price of a commodity tends in the long run to become equal to its natural price (in perfect competition, its cost of production). Consequently, if we want to have the market rate equal to the natural rate, as we surely do, it is needful for the monetary authority to regulate the money supply deliberately in such a way as, having regard to current liquidity preference, will secure this rate.

If the world money supply is governed by the volume of current gold production and the national supply is governed by this and by the national balance of payments, the resulting national money supply may not be of the amount required to get the market rate of interest, given current liquidity preference, to its natural level.

It is essential to maintain solvency on external account. If the primary instrument for doing this is the regulation of the amount of domestic money supply, this may be inconsistent with the amount of money supply required to establish a natural rate of interest and thereby full employment. And so we have a contradiction. This is the quintessence of Keynes.

In his account of what governs the market rate of interest, Keynes concentrates on the relation of cash to bonds. What these two assets have in common is that in their denomination there is no reference to anything but money. A bond is a promise to pay money at a later date. We take the pure case of governmental bonds, supposed to be more or less without risk of default. By contrast real estate, equities, etc., do have a reference to non-money objects. Thus the only difference between a bond and cash is that the former lacks liquidity and carries interest. Keynes's position is that these characteristics are causally related to each other, in the sense that the interest yielded by bonds is the compensation for their lower degree of liquidity.

Keynes does not say enough in the *General Theory* about the spectrum of interest rates, of which he was of course well aware. This may have been because short-term interest rates were so microscopic at the time of writing that they may not have seemed worth bothering about. At the time of my writing this book (1968), by contrast, they are quite exceptionally high in Britain (and elsewhere also). So high are they, that one must suppose that almost the whole of M has been drawn off into the transactions circuit. Who would hold pure cash for the precautionary or speculative motives, when such very high interest can be gained on safe short-term lending?

There is one point of central importance in the Keynes scheme to which attention must be drawn. A large array of economists of the highest standing have in the past propounded the view that the prospect of inflation tends to raise the rate of interest. And this view is still widely held by distinguished economists, by expert journalists and, doubtless, by many knowledgeable practical persons. In the Keynes scheme the prospect of inflation has no tendency to raise the rate of interest. This springs from his contention that to understand the nature of the market rate, one must fix one's spotlight firmly on the relation between cash and bonds (including promises to pay of varying maturities). The point here is that cash itself is as liable to erosion by inflation as promises to pay cash. If the choice is between holding cash and holding promises to pay cash, there is no difference whatever as between these two assets in regard to the prospect of inflation.

What the prospect of inflation does affect is the comparative yield of bonds on the one hand and equities and real estate on the other. Equities and real estate are hedges against inflation, and, in periods when inflation is expected, the rate of interest on bonds should be higher than the yield on equities of comparable standing. And a decline in the yield of equities relatively to that of bonds owing to fears of inflation is precisely what has been happening in recent years when people have been gloomily settling down to the prediction that inflation is likely to continue.

But the fact that the prospect of inflation causes the yield of equities to fall relatively to the yield of bonds does not entail that it causes the yield on bonds to rise absolutely. According to Keynes it is impossible for it to have that effect.

This is a difference of view that needs more ventilation and discussion than it has had. Keynes throughout his life gave his most concentrated thought to security values, both in relation to theory and also in relation to practical operations, to which he devoted much time, not without success. It would surely be lacking in sense of proportion to say that his considered view that the prospect of inflation did not tend to raise the rate of interest can just be ignored, indeed, the fact that no large spread between long and short rates has recently developed *proves* that current high interest rates are not due to inflation fears.

This matter is of no little practical importance in Britain at the present time (1968), and in the United States also. When one raises the question in Britain why we now have to have such high rates of interest, the answer often is that the prospect of continuing inflation makes this inevitable. This is opposed to Keynes's doctrine. I would suggest, on the contrary, that the reason why rates of interest are so high is that the money supply is so low relatively to PT.

Whether the *natural* rate is itself at present (1968) high is an altogether different question. Some argue that the pressure of investment demand is now very great. But in Britain, anyhow, personal saving has been rising relatively to investment demand during the last decade.

Keynes's analysis rests on the assumption that there are some money balances held on precautionary and speculative accounts. But it may be that after a period, like the last twenty years in the U.K., when the ratio of the money supply to G.N.P. has been reduced so drastically, there are, to all intents and purposes, no money balances held on these accounts.[1] Cash and bonds then cease to be, so to speak, competitive with one another, since there is no longer any spare cash, i.e., not urgently required for the transactions circuit. The anticipation of inflation requires that top grade equities yield less than similar grade bonds. What determines the yield of the top-grade equities? Do we have to 'concede' that this may depend on the ratio of the growth of all non-cash assets to that of aggregated savings to date less that part of savings which the authorities permit to find a haven in extra cash? The general level of the yield of top-grade non-cash assets being thus governed, the rate of interest on bonds in particular could conceivably be slightly governed by inflation fears; and of course it would be influenced by the asset-mix in the supply of non-cash assets.

This 'concession' does not imply that the authorities could not quite easily make the rates of interest come tumbling down, in line with Keynesian doctrine, if they provided a money supply just a little in excess of that required for the transactions circuit.

We may now make a comparison between the quantity theory and that of Keynes. The quantity theory, in its more moderate form, envisages that an increase in the money supply will, after time lags and, perhaps also, subject to distortions due to the business cycle, e.g. velocity changes, have a *direct* effect, on the price level. This will also be a proportional effect, subject, however, to autonomous changes in the value of the exogenous variables shown in the quantity equation, namely velocity of circulation and level of transactions. This traditional theory did not concern itself much with the possible effect of changes in the quantity of money on the level of transactions: indeed, its implication was that in the not too long run there would be no such effect. Writers did sometimes allow that there might be a short-term effect (see p. 159).

In the *Treatise* Keynes was primarily, although not wholly, concerned with the effect of what he regarded as the determining factors in price situation, *not* the quantity of money, but the level of efficiency wages, the amount of saving and the amount

---

[1] Between 1950 and 1968 the ratio of 'money supply' to G.N.P. fell by 44%. Leaving out the note circulation, which is passive, the ratio fell by 48%.

of investment. In the *General Theory* the emphasis shifts, and his primary concern is with the effect of the determining factors on employment or, in other words, on the level of transactions. He does not march with the quantity theorists in deeming these effects merely transitional. But, of course, he continues to be concerned with prices also.

It should be continually stressed that he regarded the quantity of money as of great importance. But in his view a change in the quantity did not operate on prices directly but only indirectly. It is expedient to trace the chain of indirect causation.

According to him the direct effect of a change in the quantity of money is on interest rates. How large the effect will be will depend upon the elasticity of the liquidity preference schedule. It is likely to be more elastic than it would otherwise be, if it is widely believed that the existing trend, whether towards an abnormal increase in the money supply, or towards a decrease, will presently be reversed.

The next step is the effect of a change in the interest rate, or, as I should prefer to say, in the facility for borrowing, on investment. The change in this depends on the elasticity of the demand for funds to finance investment. In this case the *less* elastic the investment schedule, or, as Keynes puts it, the less elastic the schedule of the marginal efficiency of capital, the less effect will a change in the rate of interest have on investment. In the extreme case, if prospects were very bleak, as in the United States in 1932, the schedule might be absolutely inelastic downwards. Then there would be a block in the chain of causation by which an increase in the money supply affects prices; the increase would have no effect on prices. Or this schedule might be inelastic upwards for the opposite reason, if future prospects were roaring. This is the case in which the monetary authorities find it difficult to check inflationary pressure by their unaided efforts; they may be powerless without a little help from the fiscal authorities.

Next, if investment is indeed stimulated by an increased money supply, the total effect on the economy will depend on the current value of the 'multiplier'.

Finally, if unemployment is high in the opening position, the expansion of investment and activity generally may have its main effect in increasing transactions and have little effect on the price level. But, if the opening position is one of fairly high employment, the increase of demand will have a stronger effect on prices. Even in these circumstances there will be no proportional relation between the amount by which the quantity of money has been increased and the amount of price increase. In certain circumstances the price increase might be much more than in proportion to the increase in the quantity of money; in other circumstances it might be much less.

We may summarise regarding the rate of interest. Keynes's neutral, or, as it is really better to call it, natural, rate of interest, is of central importance. It is the rate consistent with full employment without over full demand. The level of this rate is governed by the level of investment requirements and planned saving, as in the classical scheme. But the market rate of interest is governed from day to day by the whole body of capitalists, reviewing their asset-mix. There will be an actual asset-mix in existence. If this asset-mix does not correspond exactly to what capitalists want to have at the given rate of interest, then the rate of interest will move, up or down, according to the case. There are no tendencies of the market rate of interest to move towards the level of the natural rate. But the central bank can deliberately cause this to happen by altering the asset-mix available to the non-bank world.

Fisher's velocity adapts itself, not by any accommodating changes in the habits of people – why should there be such? – but by a release of money from, or absorption of money into, precautionary and speculative accounts. Even holders of money in those accounts need not alter their conceptions about what money they *desire* to hold in them, conceptions which are embodied in their elasticities of demand for money in those accounts. Given those elasticities, the absolute amount of money that they choose to hold in their 'inactive' accounts, depends on how much they can earn by swapping that money for interest-earning assets, taking into account also expectations about what they might lose at a later date by having made such swaps. This 'absolute amount' will normally vary, in response to interest rate changes, *without* any change in the schedules representing the desires of people to hold money in precautionary or speculative accounts. The traditional quantity theorists are wrong in supposing that the Fisherine velocity cannot alter without a change in the points of view of people in respect of their demand-for-money schedules. If those powerful forces, propensity to invest and propensity to consume, change, while the monetary authorities hold the quantity of money constant, money, under the influence of interest rates, will flow into or out of the precautionary and speculative pools, and thus alter the Fisherine velocity of circulation, without there being any change whatever in the points of view of people about how much money they ought to have in hand in respect of any one of the three motives.

One final point should be made. There is no hard-and-fast line between money held for the transactions motive and that held for the other two motives. If an individual is asked under *which* of the three motives he is holding the bank balance that he actually has, he may not be able to give a precise answer. They are not three water-tight compartments. Very high interest rates may cause individuals and, still more, great corporations with potent financial advisers, to let their money balances fall below the level at which they would in other times think it convenient to maintain them just for ordinary transactions purposes.

Thus the size of the money supply remains of central importance in the Keynes scheme of things. It is especially important in regard to the effect of changes in it on the level of activity of the economy. But the effect of changes in it on the price level on the Keynes theory works through an indirect chain of causes; the change in the price level need not be proportional to the change in the quantity of money, and, in the extreme case, it may be nil.

8

GROWTH THEORY

1. Full Employment versus *Growth*

WE have found in Keynes the sketch of a monetary policy designed to ensure full employment. Problems have arisen about whether this is compatible with price stability also. It is alleged that the condition of full employment will cause a tendency for excessive wage increases. If so, this would entail rising prices, in accordance with the equation set out on p. 162. Keynes recognised that there was a problem here, but did not go deeply into the matter.

In the last twenty years a growing amount of attention has been given to the economic policy, including monetary policy, requisite for ensuring that the economy will grow in accordance with its potential. It might be held that if full employment is ensured, growth will look after itself. If every employable person is at work all the time, then, it is held, the economy will grow in accordance with the increase of population, and the ordinary profit incentives will also ensure that this growing population will be employed in the most advantageous way in accordance with the advance of technology.

Two main reasons may be given why this might not necessarily be the case, and why an economic and monetary policy for full growth may have to be regarded as something not quite the same as a policy for full employment:

1. Although fully employed, the population may not be supplied with the optimum amount of up-to-date capital equipment. Investment may flag, either because entrepreneurs may find borrowing too difficult for them to install all the improved equipment that they would otherwise like to have, or because there is not enough prospect of rising demand to give them an incentive to do so. Improved equipment used in conjunction with a given quantum of labour will yield a rising output of goods. But if entrepreneurs do not anticipate a com-

mensurate increase in the demand for their products during the period in which the new equipment will be used, then they may judge that this installation is not worth while. It is sometimes argued that they will always have an incentive to introduce all improved equipment available, and even to spend adequate sums on research and development, on the ground that this will reduce unit costs of production and therefore be profitable. But what is profitable when a rising demand is in prospect may not be profitable in relation to a static demand.

This may be set out schematically. When a more modern piece of equipment is introduced, it is not usually solely for the purpose of looking after extra output. It is more likely that it will be expected to take over some part of the pre-existing output; it would be unrealistic to suppose otherwise. Let us call the output that it is expected to produce $A + B + C$, where A is the additional output that the firm expects to sell, to meet a rising demand, B is a take over of the output from existing equipment that is nearing the end of its working life and C is a take over of the output of existing equipment that is not nearing the end of its working life. It is assumed that the modern equipment reduces cost per unit (or improves quality) by comparison with the old equipment, and that therefore in respect of $A + B$ there will be a clear profit on the introduction of the modern equipment. But this will not necessarily be the case with C output. There, on the contrary, it may be more profitable to continue using the old and less efficient equipment, on Marshall's principle that the depreciation and interest of already existing equipment should not be reckoned as part of the cost of production incurred in using it. But for the projected equipment not yet ordered these charges must be included in cost accounting. Thus the producer may reckon that he will make a clear profit on A and B, by comparison with the use of more old-fashioned equipment, but that he may make a loss in respect of C. Consequently he is more likely to make a net profit on his modernisation plan, the higher is the ratio of $A + B$ to C, or more simply, since B may be predetermined, the higher is A. Thus a higher prospective growth rate is likely to constitute an incentive for prompter modernisation.

There is a virtuous circle here. Particular firms will be induced to modernise by the prospect of a higher growth in their own sales. The more firms that do this, the greater will be the growth of output that can be achieved by the economy as a whole. But this high growth potential will not be achieved unless the authorities are committed to policies that give confidence that they will allow aggregate demand to continue to grow at this rate, i.e. one equal to the growth potential, as defined, within the relevant time horizon.

Thus the fact that there is full employment at a given point of time is *not* evidence that the growth potential of the economy is being realised. Employers may continue to employ an existing labour force on old-fashioned equipment because their estimate of the prospect of rising demand is not sufficient to justify them in going to the cost of introducing more highly productive methods. It is idle to expect them to devote capital to increasing efficiency, i.e. to introducing methods that will raise the productivity of an existing labour force, if they foresee no sales for the extra product resulting therefrom. I believe that the comparatively slow growth rate of the British economy from 1955 to 1968 was due to the policy of the authorities in not allowing demand to expand sufficiently to make enough investment in higher productivity seem likely to prove worth while.

A lapse from optimum output should not be regarded as a once-over event only. If the incentive to invest is insufficient, there may be a widening gap between the growth that could take place and the growth that does take place, even although full employment is maintained all the time. New kinds of process usually have teething troubles. There is what is called the process of 'learning'. An economy which does not keep up to date in zero year may find itself getting progressively more out of date in the following years, despite the existence of full employment.

2. Insufficient aggregate demand may cause underemployment inside factories, even when there is no noticeable dip in employment. It is true that this would not by itself cause a widening gap between potential and actual growth, since underemployment inside factories is unlikely to grow progressively. But underemployment may lead to the failure by the authorities to diagnose the existence of insufficient demand, and thus exacerbate the troubles mentioned in the foregoing paragraph. It seems probable that this phenomenon of underemployment

inside factories is a fairly new phenomenon, at least to the serious extent to which it has recently obtained. The phenomenon is well established in the British case, but may not yet have become so prominent in other countries. In the period from 1953 to 1965 there were oscillations in the rate of growth, with amplitudes of sometimes up to 10% or more. Of these oscillations in growth about three-quarters consisted of oscillations in the increase in output per person and only about one-quarter in the increase of employment. It is obvious that in the trough periods there must have been considerable underemployment inside factories. Study of these figures suggests that not as much progress has been made as is sometimes supposed in overcoming the trade cycle. The maintenance of fairly full employment all the time has masked the cyclical movement. Fairly full employment should now be regarded as an institutional feature of the British economy, so that unemployment figures have ceased to be a good indicator of the level of demand prevailing.

Three reasons may be given why this has happened:

1. There has been a change in the social conscience in these matters. In earlier times it was considered to be a man's own responsibility, and his only, to get a job. So far as public policy was concerned, a change in attitude was registered by the famous White Paper on employment of 1944, which was sponsored by the three principal parties then forming the war-time coalition government. This idea that there was some collective responsibility for seeing that fairly full employment was maintained may have spread to employers and made them more inclined than they would have been in earlier times to make their own contribution towards realising the social objective.

2. The growing strength of trade unions and shop stewards may have had its influence. In many cases more trouble may be caused now than would have been the case in earlier times when redundant hands are stood off.

3. Much the most important reason, however, is that fairly full employment seems to have a self-sustaining property. When employment is high, employers are much more reluctant to stand off men, especially skilled men, rendered temporarily redundant by the state of trade, for fear that they will be unable to replace them, as needed, later on. In the days of high unemployment there was naturally less anxiety about whether

it would be possible to recruit labour in accordance with need. Thus in the new circumstances an employer may feel that he loses less by temporarily paying the wages of employees not strictly necessary than he would lose if, at a later date, he found himself unable to meet profitable orders owing to the difficulty of recruiting the labour required.

Some have taken an unfavourable view of this state of affairs, and have used the pejorative word 'hoarding' to designate this attitude. The idea is that, by rendering labour less mobile, it renders the whole productive system less efficient. While some 'hoard' labour, there may be others who would have a more profitable use for labour, if only they could obtain it. Futhermore this state of affairs may lead to more wage-price spiralling than would otherwise occur. In a condition of labour shortage, there may be more firms thinking it worth while to offer wages above the prevailing rates, as established by collective bargaining. This in turn may lead to another kind of spiralling, namely between earnings and established rates. As the prevalence of earnings in excess of established rates becomes more widespread, there is a greater pressure to raise established rates, by the principle of comparability. And then the firms determined to secure their labour supply may have to make still higher offers.

Despite these troubles, which have been partly responsible for the idea that in conditions of full employment there is the need for an 'incomes policy', ordinary humane and moral considerations suggest that we ought to welcome this development. After it was recognised that there was a public responsibility for ensuring full employment, there were agonised discussions in official circles and elsewhere as to whether there were sufficient weapons available in a market economy to achieve the target. The self-perpetuating tendency of high employment has come in as a very unexpected bonus, which the economists of an earlier generation did not foresee. And this has been a bonus of powerful operative effect. If one looks at the oscillations of demand in Britain referred to above, one may well infer that there would have been quite serious bouts of unemployment from time to time in Britain, had the self-perpetuating mechanism of high employment not been in operation.

With the further development of the social conscience, it may well be that, by a change in certain institutional arrangements, absolutely full employment will be permanently built in. Greater security of tenure of jobs may be arranged; the public authorities may assume the responsibility of finding jobs, not only by way of a general monetary policy conducive to full employment, but by the direct handling of each individual case; special arrangements can be made for the sub-normal. Future generations may well regard even the amount of unemployment that is still tolerated, and still more the higher rates of former times, as barbarous. A man has a right to a job. And society has the right to enjoy what he is able to produce.

If this state of affairs comes about, policy-makers will not have unemployment figures available as an indicator of the pressure of demand. Even in existing conditions in Britain, it is a very feeble indicator.

In the Keynes scheme there is in principle a 'neutral' rate of interest that is consistent with full employment; this rate, according to him, will not come into existence under the influence of market forces. The central bank will have to regulate the money supply deliberately with a view to bringing it into existence. It is also within the scheme of Keynesian thought that, if the circumstances are obdurate – very elastic liquidity preference schedule or very inelastic marginal efficiency of capital schedule – variations in the money supply may be unable to achieve full employment (or, in the opposite case, to prevent an inflationary level of aggregate demand,) and that in such obdurate conditions the monetary authorities will have to seek the co-operation of the fiscal authorities. Keynes thought mainly of Public Works on borrowed money as the fiscal weapon for raising aggregate demand to the full employment level. In the opposite case one could presumably reduce existing Public Works programmes; Keynes did not *say* so much about a reduction, because throughout the period in which he was evolving his seminal ideas there was heavy unemployment in Britain, and, for much of the time, in the rest of the world also. Nowadays we tend to think of the matter more broadly than in terms of Public Works on borrowed money, and refer more simply to governmental deficits and surpluses as the fiscal agencies for promoting reflation or disinflation.

When we go once from full employment theory to growth theory the story becomes more complicated. It must be added that there is as yet no settled theory of growth that has had the benefit of authentication by a number of distinguished economists.

2. Warranted Growth

The following growth equation is a truism like Fisher's $MV = PT$:

$$G = \frac{s}{C}$$

G is the percentage rate of growth per unit of time, s is the fraction of income saved, C is the ratio of the capital (fixed or circulating) accruing during the period divided by the increment of income, i.e. an *ex-post* capital output ratio. This equation is a sort of dynamic version of the identity that *ex-post* saving is equal to *ex-post* investment.

We entertain the notion that there is a certain level of savings that people desire to make and denominate this as a fraction of their income. Call it s_d. This should include company saving, but company saving broken down on the lines of Keynes's *Treatise on Money*, i.e. 'normal' company saving only. Company s_d is conjugated with company profit and should exclude saving as swollen by windfall profit; company s will, on the other hand, stand below s_d when on balance companies are making Keynesian 'losses', in the sense defined in the *Treatise* on page 124 (vol. I), but dynamised on the lines proposed on page 165 of this volume. In other words, average company s (i.e. *ex-post*) may stand above or below company s_d in consequence of an inflationary or deflationary process in the economy as a whole. It is expedient in this connection to think of an average firm in respect of profit opportunities; some companies may not be able to save so much as they desire or to make the profit margin that they desire, simply because they are inefficient or because their particular markets are laggard; others may go zooming ahead because of their high efficiency. So far as 'persons' are concerned, what they desire to save will depend on their general circumstances – family responsibilities, insur-

ance arrangements, prospects of inheritance, etc., and of course
on their level of income. Expressing desired saving as a fraction
of income is done for the convenience of exposition and does
not imply that desired saving is a constant fraction of income.
A divergence of desired from actual saving in the case of a
person may occur owing to various causes; for instance, in a
time of rising prices, with his income rising in less proportion,
he may find at the end of the year that he has to borrow from
the bank to pay for his insurance premium. He will then probably decide that he must make a cut in his standard of living.
Or his income may rise more than prices, and he may then
decide, probably after a time lag, that he can afford some
amenities that improve his standard of living.

I next define C_r (required capital/output ratio) as the
capital/output ratio that producers (and distributors) of goods
and services find convenient. They find themselves working
their fixed equipment to capacity or to that percentage of
capacity that avoids bottle-necks, and they find their stocks just
where they want them to be. C_r and s_d are conceived as *net*
figures. Replacements as such do not draw on current savings.
But if, on the occasion of a replacement, a producer introduces
a more capital-intensive method of producing some of the pre-
existent output we must reckon the extra capital required for
that purpose as part of C_r; any extra output due to the improved method will, of course, be part of the growth of output.

The term G_ω is defined in the following equation:

$$G_w = \frac{s_d}{C_r}$$

I have called G_w the 'warranted' rate of growth, and in recent
years have sometimes added 'in an undiluted capitalist
economy'. The reason for this is that in this equation the
equilibrium rate of growth of the economy is governed by what
individuals happen to be prepared to provide by way of saving;
this may 'warrant' a growth rate below what current technology
might render possible. 'Why are we not introducing on to our
production lines all the new findings of science?' 'Well, people
are just not saving enough to allow us to do all that (without
inflation).' And so one frames the idea that in certain cases one
ought not to sit back and limit one's targets because of the savings

decisions of persons, but supplement their savings, e.g. by budget surpluses. That might be especially important in less developed countries. Of this more hereafter.

One point may be got out of the way quickly. There is an implication in the above formulation that all new capital is required for the increase in current output. But some may be geared to long-range projects having no immediate return; some indeed, like public parks, may have no products that enter into the market system. This is a technical point; one can meet it by subtracting from s_d in the numerator of the equation a figure representing the value of capital formation of this type.[1]

The values s_d and C_r are both dependent on the rate of interest.[2] More will be said about this. The preliminary trouble is that the static theory of economic equilibrium does not, and cannot, have anything satisfactory to say about the rate of interest, while dynamic theory is still undeveloped.

I next set out what I have called the instability principle, which is highly relevant to the theory of monetary policy. This principle has been discussed by various writers. I believe that the balance of opinion is in its favour.

Let us suppose that there is a *chance* deviation of G (actual growth) away from G_w owing to the many uncertainties confronting those who place orders. Let us suppose that $G > G_w$; then by the tautological equation *either* s will exceed s_r *or* C will fall short of C_r or both. If $s > s_r$ individuals will tend to revise their spending plans upwards or companies will distribute more dividends or undertake capital expansion that they would not otherwise have done. If $C < C_r$, producers will be short of fixed capital or stocks and place extra orders accordingly. Either way the excess value of G, by comparison with the G_w of equilibrium, will cause a further upward departure, viz. a further increase in the value of G. I will not presume to attempt to assess how far the runaway movement is likely to go; this would take one on to very difficult terrain. For a certain distance the upward departure of G is likely to lead to what is called an 'overheating' of the economy. Saving, probably particularly company saving, will tend to excess, while stocks will run down and production press ever harder against existing capacity, leading to inefficiencies and delayed deliveries. All applies in

---

[1] R. F. Harrod, *Economic Journal*, March 1939.   [2] Ibid.

reverse when there is a chance downward deviation of G from G_w.

This would seem to call for a corrective monetary policy. A tightening (or easing) of the money supply would operate mainly, if not exclusively, in the first instance, on G, i.e. on the current flow of orders placed. Some firms, finding it more difficult to get finance, would slow down their rate of increase of orders, or even reduce their orders below the previous level. This would have a multiplier effect also.

In the converse case some firms on the advent of 'easier money' would take opportunities that they would have liked to take at an earlier date, but could not take for lack of sufficient finance.

It is not relevant that many firms normally have adequate finance for all projects judged by them feasible; they will be left unmoved by the action of the monetary authorities. It suffices that a certain number of marginal firms should be affected by the ease or tightness of money. But the firms with adequate finance will be caught up in the upward or downward movement also, owing to the multiplier effect on the whole economy of what the marginal firms do.

I have here attempted to give a brief account of the essential nature of monetary policy addressed to ironing out the business cycle. Doubtless the monetary authorities cannot have cognisance of small deviations of G from G_w. The cumulative process will have to go some way before the tendency to mounting inflationary pressure or recession becomes manifest. As soon as the evidence is clear, it is up to the authorities to act promptly. But they must not overdo it. They must not maintain monetary stringency so long that G falls below G_w. And conversely.

In the foregoing I have used the concepts of desired saving and required investment, in accordance with the required capital output ratio. These will both differ, from time to time, from *ex-post* saving and *ex-post* investment. My concepts are *not* the same as those of *ex-ante* saving and *ex-ante* investment, as defined by Myrdal. I have been taken to task by Professor Shackle in his distinguished book[1] for not using *ex-ante* concepts. They are most valuable concepts, and I have no doubt that they will have an important part to play in the completed

[1] G. L. S. Shackle, *The Years of High Theory* (1967).

theory of dynamic economics. But they are not relevant to my central propositions.

Taking the case of investment, the difference between *ex-ante* investment and 'required' investment may be very simply illustrated. Suppose that the turnover of a store is growing at the rate 1% a month, and that the management holds that at any time the stock in hand ought to be equal to one month's turnover. Represent turnover in $month_0$ as 100 units. *Ex-ante* investment in $month_1$ will then be 1 unit. Suppose that sales unexpectedly increase by 2% in $month_1$. *Ex-post* investment in that month will be zero, while 'required' investment will be 2 units. If, on the other hand, sales fall flat in $month_1$, *ex-ante* investment will still be 1 unit, *ex-post* investment will be 2 units, while 'required' investment will be zero. While paying tribute to the *ex-ante* concept, I should suppose that the concept of currently required investment is more potent in relation to a dynamic analysis.

It has been envisaged that the primary objective of monetary policy will be to check cumulative movement away from an equilibrium position. The rate of interest conjugated with such a policy might be regarded as the dynamised version of Keynes's 'neutral' rate.

There is a further matter to be considered. As has been stated, the values of both s_d and C_r may be expected to be, in some degree, functions of the rate of interest. This is a point stressed by certain economists, sometimes called neo-classical. Thus the warranted rate of growth would itself be in some degree a function of interest. In this connection one ought presumably to be seeking to establish the concept of an equilibrium rate of interest relative to all the circumstances of the case. Before I proceed with this, certain other matters must be considered.

Meanwhile there is this problem. If monetary policy is ear-marked for preventing runaway movements, can it also be simultaneously used to establish an equilibrium interest rate, if such a concept can be defined, in relation to s_d and C_r? It will be recalled that we have the possibility of calling fiscal policy in aid to help us with our objectives. Would it be possible to ear-mark monetary policy for establishing the equilibrium rate of interest, if any, while fiscal policy is used to prevent runaway movements of the economy? If there could be such a division of labour, that would be how it would have to go, since fiscal policy cannot be used to establish an equilibrium rate of interest. The trouble about such a division is that for ironing out the cycle we need a quick-working weapon, which monetary policy is. About whether the reaction in the economy to a change of course in fiscal policy could be so quick there has been some difference of opinion. Even if it could be, there is a further snag. To date the authorities of most countries have difficulty in getting such a change in fiscal policy in response to a business cycle development clearly requiring it. In the United States Congress may be slow in responding to the wishes of the authorities in the matter of taxation. In the United Kingdom the Government has certain reserve powers (called the 'Regulator'), which may, however, not be sufficient; the Chancellor can also always have a special Budget and force it through Parliament. But this is a cumbersome procedure, at present only used on exceptional occasions. In Germany there have been well-known difficulties in getting prompt legislation on fiscal matters. And so it surely is in most countries.

Of course all this could be changed, if the appropriate bodies were convinced that such a change was desirable. For that to happen, we need a much more clearly articulated monetary theory of growth, and one much more widely accepted than we have at present.

3. Natural Growth

It is time to move on to consideration of a less individualistic system, i.e. less individualistic than one in which the collectivity of wishes by persons and companies about what they would like, or need, to save determines the equilibrium ('warranted') rate of growth of the economy.

I have defined a 'natural' rate of growth (G_n), as that determined by the current growth of the working population and the current potential for technical progress. Such a growth rate is not determined by the wishes of persons and companies as regards saving. The position is reversed. We ask what saving the economy must currently do, if this potential growth rate is to be achieved. A certain current rate of saving becomes a desideratum. We may write our equation

$$s_0 = G_n C_r,$$

where s_0 stands for the optimum rate of saving, as socially required.

'The current potential for technical progress' is a wide-ranging concept. It includes the current findings of science, to the extent that these are relevant, and of technology. It includes the rate of growth in the number of entrepreneurs at each separate level of proficiency as regards imagination, appreciation of what technology can offer, willingness to spend money on research and development, and sense of urgency in getting ideas off the drawing-board on to the production line. It includes the rate of growth in the cadres of qualified personnel at every level, from those who conduct the research to skilled manual workers and competent foremen. These growth potentials will doubtless depend on matters quite outside the economic system as such, namely political stability, a suitable legal system and body of law, social attitudes, the educational system, etc. What the potential is at any time in a given society will long remain a matter of fallible judgement. The essential doctrine of a natural growth rate is that there should not be a palpable failure to achieve it because Tom, Dick and Harry do not choose, from their own personal motives, to save as much as would be required to achieve the growth potential without inflation. There is also the possibility, especially in advanced countries, that persons and companies will tend to save more in aggregate than is required to achieve the growth potential, and this has to be considered.

In fine, we have to consider both the case when $G_n > G_w$ and the case when $G_n < G_w$. The former condition is likely to prevail in less developed countries and in many others also, the latter only in the highly advanced countries.

It would seem that the appropriate weapon for curing these inequalities is fiscal policy. In free market economies a budget surplus can be used to supplement private saving and bring total saving up to the socially required level (s_0). In a centrally planned economy a similar regulatory mechanism is found in the mark-up of market prices over production costs. Unhappily in many less developed countries, where private saving may fall far below requirements, fiscal policy to supplement it may be easier said than done, owing to the administrative and social difficulties of raising sufficient sums by taxation.

It may be thought that, where savings are more than sufficient to finance the full growth potential, there would be no problem. But this is not so. The actual growth rate cannot, taking one year with another, be above the natural rate, although it may be so for a time when the economy has previously been allowed to slip down and unemployed resources are being brought back into use. If the natural rate is below the warranted rate, then the actual rate must also be below it for most of the time. But when the actual rate is below the warranted rate, a cumulative downward movement sets in. This is the dynamised version of what was known among some followers of Keynes as the 'stagnation thesis'. Accordingly it is expedient in such a case that the Government should show a deficit in its accounts, in order to mop up that part of savings that are redundant to the needs of the growth potential, and which would otherwise drag activity down below its full employment, and, *a fortiori*, its full growth level. The point is a simple one. The value that persons and companies want to have on hand, to meet the uncertainties of the future, to provide a regular income from capital, to bequeath to their children, etc., may exceed the value of the total of equipment, buildings, etc., that the country needs for its production, proceeding at its full growth potential. There is no reason why individuals should be frustrated in such circumstances. Why should they not be allowed to accumulate as assets in their possession as much as they wish to? Their needs can be met if the Government issues marketable bits of paper (thus financing its own deficit), which individuals can have the satisfaction of holding and also of realising, as and when required. They are not likely ever to wish to realise an inconveniently large part at the same time.

At this point we can return to the vexed question of the interest rate. We are now envisaging that economic policy-makers are not prepared to accept the totality of decisions of individuals about how much they wish to save as the final arbiter of how much saving is to be done in the economy. This is really implied in the very existence of a 'fiscal policy' with planned Budget surpluses or deficits. The *laissez-faire* idea would be to have the Budget in exact balance, or to have a surplus sufficient to pay off the National Debt at a steady and ⟶ unalterable rate.

For the individual the demand for saving with which he is confronted has in general infinite elasticity and is represented by the going rate of interest. (The matter is somewhat different when he ploughs his personal saving directly into his own business, where the demand curve has a downward slope. Even in that case his marginal savings may often go into the security market.) There are two elements governing the individual's supply of saving, namely: (i) the rate at which the marginal utility of his income is falling owing to his growth of income, and (ii) his preference, if any, for a given quantum of present as against future utility. These matters have been set out by Irving Fisher in his *Theory of Interest*, and earlier by Böhm-Bawerk and other writers.

The question might be raised whether in a market economy one could not take the sum total of individual preferences, as governed by these factors, to represent the optimum saving for the community as a whole, just as we may take the market preferences of individuals for a commodity, anyhow in conditions of perfect competition, to represent the optimum amount of the commodity that should be produced – subject to problems concerning income distribution. The answer is in the negative. The individual's supply schedule of saving is too much influenced by institutional arrangements, which differ widely from country to country and from one period of time to another, for it to be regarded as a pointer to the social optimum. Such arrangements are the extent to which future events, such as the education of children, hospitalisation, unemployment and old age are provided gratis by the state, the level of death duties and the expected opportunities for children to advance themselves by their own efforts in due course. As regards companies, including family firms, much will depend on the level of organisation of the capital market in which they might raise money from outside at a given time and place. Furthermore, it is not usually a primary concern of boards of companies, in framing their policy of dividend distribution, to consider carefully the preferences of their miscellaneous collection of

shareholders as between present and future consumption. They
have other important matters in mind, like keeping the market
sweet for new issues.

If the policy-makers are to have a savings target designed to
secure optimum growth, it is implied that they must have in
mind some notional optimum rate of interest, since C_r may
depend in part on the rate of interest, and we have seen that
optimum saving is equal to G_nC_r.

Opinions differ about how important a part the second factor
mentioned above, preference for present over future utilities,
called by Pigou 'lack of telescopic faculty', plays in the individual's saving schedule. I would suppose it to play an unimportant part, except in the case of very poor, and thereby
improvident, societies. I would suggest that policy-makers
should have no lack of telescopic faculty and rank the future
equally with the present. They ought to be 'far-sighted states-
men'.

The all-important factor in regard to interest is the prospective decline in the marginal utility of income owing to its
growth. In a society in which income per head was perfectly
static and known to continue to be so, there would be no rationale
for interest at all. The criterion for the choice among methods
of production would be that that method be chosen, which
showed the highest output per unit of input after allowing for
the amortisation of capital, but not for interest on it.

I do not see that any progress can be made in this area unless
we allow the concept of a community indifference curve. That
is a concept that has proved useful in other branches of
economics.

The rate at which future income should be discounted then
becomes the rate that is equal to the prospective rate of growth
of income per head divided by the elasticity of the community's
diminishing utility of income curve at the margin (discounting
formula).

In market economies investment, if it is to be undertaken,
must be expected to yield a certain minimum rate of return on
capital. We have already noted (p. 64) that this appears to run
very much above the rate of interest in the market on first-rate
bonds, even after allowing for the risks of the investment. The
discounting formula given in the last paragraph relates to the

minimum acceptable rate of return on investment and *not* to the market rate of interest. Consequently, if policy-makers are to get the minimum acceptable rate of return (which governs C_r) to the optimum level, they must secure a market rate of interest that is substantially below the rate shown in the formula.

We have now moved into a very rarefied atmosphere. The values of some of the concepts would be difficult to establish statistically. I have referred elsewhere, however, to efforts that have been made to evaluate the elasticity of the income utility schedule.[1] More work could be done on the relation of the market rate on first-class bonds to the minimum rate of return on their own capital outlays that first-class firms find acceptable.

The fact that the true analysis of the optimum leads one into the use of difficult concepts does not mean that it should be ignored. If it is ignored, there is great danger that a false analysis may be accepted in its place. It may be possible to narrow the uncertainties involved in the true analysis by the use of common sense.

In my citation of Keynes (p. 177) I noted, with dissent, that, after defining his 'neutral' rate of interest, an interesting concept within its limits, he added that 'this rate might be better described perhaps, as the "optimum" rate'. Keynes's 'neutral' rate of interest has nothing whatever to do with the 'optimum' as defined by me in the last few paragraphs.

On two occasions (pp. 193 and 195) I have boggled at the task of defining an equilibrium rate interest, to be conjugated with a warranted growth rate, namely an equilibrium rate of interest in an economy in which policy-makers allow the total amount of saving to be governed by the collectivity of individual wishes.

Keynes's concept of a 'neutral' rate is clear enough. It presupposes the use of monetary policy to secure full employment, and it is defined as the rate consistent with the monetary policy that secures full employment. We can dynamise this by saying that it is the rate consistent with a monetary policy that secures a growth of demand, neither more nor less than is required to ensure that the economy grows at its optimum potential growth rate. As I have already explained, monetary policy designed to

[1] *Economic Journal*, December 1964.

ensure that demand is at a suitable level operates mainly through the ease or difficulty that people have in getting finance for investment outlays (as well as through the multiplier effect of changes in the outlays). There will be a certain rate of interest in perfect markets conjugated with the right amount of ease or difficulty in borrowing as required by the stated objective. So far all is clear. It is to be noted that the right degree of ease or difficulty in borrowing, as required to secure this result is partly determined by psychological factors, including the 'animal spirits'[1] of entrepreneurs and the influence of expectations about an uncertain future.

What has all this to do with an 'equilibrium' rate of interest as required to determine the capital intensity (C_r) of methods of production chosen in a given situation? The determination of the equilibrium rate as required to give an equilibrium value for C_r is clearly important in the context of *laissez-faire* capitalism.

I must now reveal my position. I have thought, hard and to the best of my ability, over many years, about how to name the factors that determine an equilibrium rate of interest, as conjugated with 'warranted' growth. I have totally failed in my endeavour. This intellectual failure is a matter of regret to me, but it must be put on the record.

But does it really matter? Now that fiscal policy has been widely recognised, from the United States leftwards, as appropriate and necessary, we need no longer concern ourselves much with defining what the equilibrium rate of interest, as conjugated with a warranted growth rate, would be, in countries still so *laissez-faire* as to consider 'fiscal policy' an illegitimate device.

We have established an optimum level for the minimum acceptable rate of return (which governs C_r) as conjugated with the natural growth rate. And this should suffice.

4. Theory of Monetary Policy

So where do we now stand in relation to the theory of monetary policy? Three problems have been distinguished:

[1] This expression was applied to entrepreneurs by Keynes (*General Theory* 1936; new edn 1960), (p. 161), and has also been used by Professor Joan Robinson.

1. Policy may be directed towards preventing run away movements above or below the warranted growth rate. This is the familiar terrain of ironing out the business cycle. It may be thought that both monetary and fiscal measures would come in handy. If only it were possible to get more fiscal flexibility, it might be argued that fiscal policy, as against monetary policy, should be stressed.

2. There is the somewhat longer-term problem that arises when the warranted growth rate is not equal to the natural growth rate. There will be recurrent embarrassments, if these cannot be brought together. It was suggested that fiscal policy is the appropriate method for dealing with this. If the warranted rate is below the natural rate (capital shortage) a Budget surplus can be used to supplement private saving and thus raise the warranted rate towards, and to, the natural level. In the opposite case Budget deficits are required to mop up redundant savings and obviate a tendency towards stagnation.

Are there likely to be conflicts, if fiscal policy is employed *both* for ironing out the business cycle *and* for altering the warranted rate? There probably will at times be such conflicts in the short period. But on the whole it seems likely that there will more often be agreement than conflict. If the warranted rate is above the natural rate, there will be a prevailing tendency towards stagnation and recession, so that the ironing-out criterion will more often call for fiscal stimulation, while fiscal expansion is *also* needed in order to reduce the warranted rate towards the natural rate. But, of course, tendencies towards overheating may develop at times, and fiscal restraint will then be required. What such a state of affairs seems to call for is an average Budget deficit, taking one year with another, but a readiness to reduce or eliminate it on occasions of overheating.

When the warranted rate is below the natural, which is, perhaps, the more common case, Budget surpluses are required in order to raise the warranted rate. Such an economy will have a chronic tendency to overheating (unless the entrepreneurs are very sluggish), and this also will call for fiscal rigour. In some less developed countries it is to be feared that entrepreneurs are very sluggish. The natural solution seems to be, and is in fact often adopted, for the State to take the initiative in undertaking investment and financing it from its surplus.

Finally, under this heading, we may ask if monetary policy
has a part to play. It is always objectionable to postulate an
asymmetry, if this can be avoided. But I believe that there is
truly one in this case. It may be noted that fiscal policy designed
to close the gap between the natural and the warranted growth
rates operates on the latter, not on the former. Measures of
fiscal restraint do not reduce the natural rate. But measures of
monetary restraint might do so, and that would surely be undesirable. Take the (more common) case where the warranted
rate is too low. Fiscal restraint (budget surplus) tends to raise
it. Monetary restraint (high interest) would also tend to do so.
It would presumably increase the propensity to save (s_d) –
although this is not absolutely certain – and this would have the
same effect as a budget surplus in raising the warranted rate. But
it would have further effect, unless the production coefficient
were absolutely inelastic. It would tend to reduce C_r and that
would affect the *natural* rate adversely. The natural rate is
normally an increasing function of C_r.

Well, it might be argued, would not that contribute towards
bringing the two rates together, which is our objective? High
interest, to the extent that it affected C_r, would tend to raise the
warranted rate and to reduce the natural rate and thus have a
double effect in bringing the rates together. On the contrary, I
submit that it should not be an objective of policy to reduce the
natural rate. What is needed is to bring the warranted rate up
to the natural rate and not the other way round.

In the case where the warranted rate is above the natural
rate and an expansive monetary policy is accordingly required,
it would bring them together by lowering the warranted rate
(decrease of s_d and increase of C_r) and by raising the natural
rate (increase of C_r); and that is quite all right. This is where we
have an asymmetry.

We get this result. Fiscal policy is appropriate in both types
of case. Monetary policy (low interest) is appropriate where
saving is redundant, because, as well as lowering the warranted
rate, it raises the natural rate. But one should be chary of using
tight money to bring the two rates together in the opposite
case, because it might do so partly by lowering the natural rate.

3. Finally, we have the question whether monetary policy
should be used in order to establish the minimum acceptable

return on capital (MARC) at its optimum level relatively to present and future utilities. It may be held that the MARC may be rather insensitive to short-run changes in the market rate of interest. This suggests the idea that, if one wishes to get the MARC down, one should maintain a consistently low rate of interest over a rather long period. This might not be inconsistent with occasional and *short-lived* sallies into a higher rate, to deal with overheating.

The trouble is that we are now in an area of statistical incalculables. The optimum MARC depends on the future growth rate, about which we are uncertain, and on the elasticity of the community utility schedule, calculations of which are only in their infancy.

None the less common sense may suggest that values of the MARC around 15, 20 and 25%, as often reported, are above the optimum, even after allowing for risk, and that the high market rates of interest that have recently been prevailing are not helpful for getting a downward revision of the MARC. (If the prospective growth rate were 5% per annum and the elasticity of marginal utility schedule 2, the optimum MARC would be 10%.)

It ought to be possible for the authorities, holding in nice balance considerations relating to ironing out the business cycle, the longer-term trend of the balance between saving propensity and investment requirements, and what should be done to influence the level of the MARC in relation to the balance between present and future income, to rough out an appropriate policy from time to time.

We have still to consider the theory of the international equilibrium. A few economists, but a much greater number of 'experts' at the central banking level, have advocated that the domestic equilibrium should be maintained by the use of fiscal measures only, while monetary policy should be ear-marked for maintaining the international equilibrium. It is to be hoped that readers who have read the introduction that I have attempted to supply, provisionally, into the complexity of the domestic problems, will hesitate to accept such a doctrine. We must now proceed to the theory of the international equilibrium.

9

EXTERNAL EQUILIBRIUM THEORY

1. Balance on Current Account

THE classical view was that the balance of payments adjusted itself under the gold standard in an elegant manner. We may begin by ignoring capital movement and concentrate upon the income account, and particularly on the merchandise part of it. We assume that the income account has to be kept in balance. The arguments relating to this apply also if there is what may be called a normal or 'autonomous' outflow or inflow of capital proceeding, the requirement for the income account then being that it should have a corresponding surplus or deficit.

We may start with the earlier economists' thought about specie. If there is a deficit on external account, this causes an outflow of specie. As the quantity left behind is thus diminished, its value will rise, i.e. prices will fall. The fall in prices makes domestic prices more competitive, both for foreign markets and at home. Thus the adverse balance is corrected.

This account does not imply a rigid form of the quantity theory. It rests on the more general proposition that if an article becomes scarcer, its value will tend to rise.

The same mechanism will work if specie is supplemented by notes and deposits. The total money supply is reduced by the outflow of specie, and gradually the prices will fall; but, if the ratio of notes and deposits in circulation to specie is high, the outflow of specie may not reduce the money supply sufficiently. The country might become altogether denuded of specie before the adverse balance was corrected. Accordingly it came to be recognised that the central bank might have to take action to reinforce the effect of the outflow of specie by reducing the quantity of notes and deposits. This might be in accordance with legal reserve requirements, or, more generally, be needed to enable the Bank to maintain convertibility. With a sufficient restriction of the total money supply, the external balance would be bound to come right owing to the fall of domestic prices. All would work in reverse in the event of a favourable balance. Domestic prices would rise. All this doctrine sprang from the basic proposition of Adam Smith that the precious metals tend to get distributed among countries in proportion to the wealth (income) of each country.

The early economists did not generally uphold the view that an increase in the money supply will tend to reduce interest rates (and conversely). That became established doctrine somewhat later. A fall of interest rates would reinforce the effect of higher commodity prices on the external balance by causing an outflow of capital to centres wherein interest remained higher; and conversely. The rather important effect of a change in the interest rate was much stressed by the practical authorities in the United Kingdom in the later part of the full gold standard period. Indeed, in the United Kingdom irregularities in the balance of payments on current account were largely offset by capital movements, when changes in commodity prices might play a minor role or none.

The idea that changes of interest rates and changes of commodity prices worked together to produce the same equilibrating effect on the external balance was a further instance of the elegance of the system. It was the classical economists' interpretation of how it actually worked.

In this field also Keynes marked an important turning-point of thought. We may focus our attention on the reinforcing action required by the central bank, as noted above. For the later classical economists this was part of the machinery whereby commodity prices were reduced (or raised in the requisite case), of a reduction of lending, by open market operations or otherwise. But might not this contraction of credit have a side effect, in the form of a contraction of business activity? And, if one looked at the matter closely, might not this side effect be more important than the primary effect on prices? Might not this side effect really be the main effect?

If this were so, it would not imply that the mechanism was any less effective than the classicals supposed in correcting an adverse balance. And again conversely. But it would operate in a different way, namely, by causing a contraction of business activity, thereby reducing the requirements for imported materials, the incomes of citizens and the amount that they would want or be able to spend on imports. One might express the difference of view by saying that the classicals relied on the *price* elasticity of the demand for tradable goods to rectify the balance, while Keynesian thinking relied on the *income* elasticity of demand to rectify it. The two views are naturally not mutually inconsistent. The two effects may both operate and reinforce one another. But Keynes laid stress on the income effect.

The failure of the classicals to take note of the income effect was connected with their assumption that full employment would normally be maintained. On that hypothesis the whole effect of the contraction of credit by the central bank would be on commodity prices; the volume of production would remain as before. By Keynesian thinking the contraction would cause a certain amount of unemployment.

And now we come to a divergence, in addition to the difference of opinion about how the system worked. If it worked by causing a certain amount of unemployment from time to time, then it was clearly not so elegant and beautiful as the classical economists claimed. We move now from pure analysis to normative thinking. Keynes held that we must condemn the gold standard mechanism if in its normal working it creates unemployment from time to time.

It has been suggested that a contraction of credit would exert all its influence on commodity prices if only wages were flexible downwards. As soon as any little bit of unemployment began to occur, wages would be reduced, so that the amount of unemployment generated would be negligible. It may be inferred from the account of Keynes's thought given in an earlier chapter that he would not agree that a downward plasticity of wages would suffice to prevent unemployment developing. In relation to how the system actually worked in the nineteenth century, we should note that decreases in wages were very rare and that very heavy unemployment often developed. While the wages problem has presented greater difficulties in recent years, it would be wrong to suppose that in the nineteenth century there was normally a downward movement of wages whenever unemployment occurred or increased.

To return to the normative question, it must not be supposed Keynes thought that all contractions of credit are bad; they are to be approved when used to correct inflationary pressures in the economy. They are to be condemned when used to create unemployment. But a deficit in the external account, although it can on occasion be caused by inflationary pressure in the economy, is by no means always, or even not more often than not, thus caused. Changes of taste at home and abroad or technological developments in the various countries cause changes in their external balances from time to time. It is not an acceptable principle that, on every occasion when such a change is adverse from the point of view of the country's external balance, unemployment should be created. It was on this ground that the semi-automatic working of the gold standard stood condemned in Keynes's view.

It is desirable to relate the mechanism of the foreign balance on current account to the general theory of income. We may first present the foreign trade multiplier in its simplest form:

$$Y = \frac{1}{m} X$$

X is the value of exports, m the fraction of income that people choose to spend on imports and Y is income. To get this simple formulation, we must assume that no saving or investment is taking place. X is the base of the 'foreign trade multiplier' and the reciprocal of m is the multiplier. The level of income is thus determined. Trade balances automatically. Subject to the assumption about saving and investment, there is no problem as regards the balance of trade.

The values of X and m will be governed by the relative prices, and, of course, qualities and prompt availabilities, of goods at home and abroad. If prices at home are uncompetitive by world standards, this leads not to an adverse balance of trade but to heavy unemployment at home.

Y, as thus determined, might be above, equal to, or below the supply potential of the economy (Y^s). But, as we cannot suppose an income above the supply potential, for Y we may substitute Y^d, this being total demand, as determined by the foreign trade multiplier. If Y^d exceeds Y^s there will be an inflationary situation. It might be that the classical mechanism would then get to work, prices rising, and having an appropriate effect on exports and imports. If Y^d is below Y^s there will be unemployment.

Next we introduce saving and investment. We may write:

$$Y = C + X + I = (c + m + s)\, Y$$

C is the amount of income derived by the sale of consumer goods at home and I the amount of income derived from the domestic sale of goods on capital account (*ex-post* investment). The small letters stand for fractions of income, s being the fraction of income saved. It is evident that

$$C = c(Y)$$

consequently, $X + I = (m + s)\, Y$

But we can no longer say that X is necessarily equal to mY. What we can say is that

$$X - mY = sY - I$$

i.e. the excess (or deficiency) of exports compared with imports is equal to the excess (or deficiency) of savings compared with domestic investment.

There has been some tendency for experts concerned with policy to jump to the conclusion that, when a country is in external deficit and by consequence its domestic investment exceeds domestic saving, this is a condition in which a deflationary policy should be adopted, in order to eliminate the domestic excess of investment over saving. This prescription, taken by itself, has no validity. A more throughgoing analysis is necessary.

If we have regard to the truism that investment must be equal to saving, this is fulfilled in the case in question by the fact that the excess of domestic investment is offset by an external disinvestment of an amount equal to the external deficit; thus total investment, domestic and foreign, remains equal to saving. The state of the external balance cannot be used to indicate that domestic investment is excessive or the reverse.

There are two different types of disequilibrium which must be sharply distinguished. If we suppose that the normal, or 'autonomous', inflow and outflow of capital is nil, a deficit or surplus on current items is a disequilibrium on external account. Quite different is the disequilibrium that exists when the propensity to consume, the propensity to invest and exports together give an aggregate demand that exceeds or falls short of the supply potential of the economy. Reasoning will falter and maxims of policy will go far astray unless the entirely different nature of these two kinds of disequilibrium is kept in the forefront of the mind.

There are four possible combinations of these two kinds of disequilibrium. It is necessary to consider them each in turn.

We may take first the two simpler kinds of case. There may be a combination of an excess of aggregate demand at home with an external deficit. Such was the position of many European countries in the decade after the Second World War. The undoubted remedy in this case is to deflate domestic demand, by monetary and/or fiscal policies. This will at the same time reduce the excess of aggregate demand over the supply potential of the economy and tend to remedy the external deficit. Of course an equilibrium may be achieved on one side, say on that of the elimination of excess aggregate demand, before it is achieved on the other, the external deficit. In that case the condition of the country passes over into one of the other three categories.

Secondly, there is the case when a country has domestic unemployment and an external surplus. This was true of the United States for most of the thirties. Here the sovereign remedy is to reflate, as was recognised at the time. This reduces both domestic unemployment and the excess of exports.

But then we come over to types of case in which both these remedies are inappropriate. A country may have unemployment and an external deficit. This was true of some European countries in the thirties. If there is unemployment, domestic deflation of demand would make matters worse, while domestic reflation would intensify the external deficit. In this case the right remedy is to get a downward realignment of domestic costs and prices relatively to those obtaining abroad. This realignment will, subject to a proviso to be discussed below, serve to promote exports and retard imports and thus remedy the external imbalance. And this same process will serve to increase aggregate demand, and thus correct the domestic deficiency of demand. It may happen that the external balance is brought into equilibrium, before the domestic deficiency of demand is fully corrected. Subject to the external condition having become strong enough, some domestic demand reflation may then be required. If from the start it happens to be evident that the measures taken to restore the external balance are not likely to raise aggregate demand sufficiently to restore full domestic employment, as was the case, for instance, in the United Kingdom in the thirties, then one might well adopt domestic reflationary measures right at the beginning, simultaneously with the measures designed to rectify the external deficit.

Finally, there is the case of a country which has domestic inflationary pressure accompanied by external surplus. Germany in certain years recently has provided an example of this. Deflation of the domestic demand would tend to increase the external surplus; while reflation, though tending to rectify the external imbalance, would make the domestic inflationary pressure worse. The point about a country in this position is that it is in effect too competitive! It can afford to have an upward realignment of its own costs and prices relatively to the outside world.

Whereas in the first two (easy) cases a reflation or a disinflation will serve simultaneously to correct both the disequilibria, in the two last-mentioned cases neither reflation nor disinflation are appropriate, because they will make one of the two disequilibria worse. What is required for the last two cases is a realignment (upwards or downwards) of domestic costs and prices relatively to those obtaining outside the country.

It may be noticed, however, that if one of the two disequilibria is much more serious than the other, it may be expedient to adopt a mixed policy. For instance, a country may have very heavy unemployment and a small external deficit; the recipe for such a country is to get a downward adjustment of its costs and prices so as to correct its deficit; this, by increasing exports and import-competing production, will serve to stimulate the economy and reduce unemployment. But, if the deficit is moderate only and the unemployment severe, it may be expedient to take steps right away to reflate the economy, although this will have the wrong kind of effect on the external balance.

What is required here is a really effective policy for getting a realignment of costs and prices, of sufficient strength, not only to correct the existing deficit, but also to offset any tendency towards increased deficit caused by the reflationary policy.

There are two ways of getting a downward adjustment of costs and prices. One of these may now, perhaps, after some decades of discussion, be called the 'orthodox' remedy. This is a devaluation of the currency. It must be hastily added the high-powered central bankers of the world will take great exception to the devaluation being called an 'orthodox' remedy in any connection; but the fact of the matter is that these high pundits have not provided any orthodox remedy of their own for a country suffering from underemployment and external deficit. Yet this is a very common case indeed. There is nothing in theory or economic history to suggest that it is less common than the other classes of case. We have here a lacuna in the thinking of the pundits,[1] and it may well be that it is this lacuna that has been responsible for sundry disorders in the international monetary system in recent years.

The other method for getting a downward adjustment is what is known as 'incomes policy'. The concept here is entirely different from that of putting pressure on wages by means of deflation. As a country in this class of case is by hypothesis suffering from underemployment, it is not desirable to have another turn of the screw of deflation with a view to putting a downward pressure on wages or at least to prevent their rising too quickly. In this case one is seeking to avoid deflation; and it may indeed be needful, as explained above, to have some reflation. The idea of an incomes policy is to exert an influence on wages, etc., not through market forces but by going to the grass roots and influencing decisions taken at the bargaining table. It is proposed to do this by a nation-wide campaign of persuasion and education. But it may prove to be impossible to effect such a policy by these methods alone, and in this case legal sanctions may be required of a kind acceptable in a democracy.

There is still a good deal of lack of understanding of the point that deflation and incomes policy are in many respects of opposite tendency. In the United Kingdom in 1968, for instance, where deflation and an incomes policy were being pursued simultaneously, they were widely thought of as two facets of one 'package deal' designed to secure 'austerity'.

[1] Cf. The report of Working Party No. 3 of the Economic Policy Committee of the O.E.C.D. on The Adjustment Process (1966).

H

The United Kingdom was probably at this time a country requiring a downward adjustment of costs and prices. Deflation was certainly not called for by the actual position, since there was considerable underemployment at the time. It might conceivably have been justified as a precautionary measure, designed to offset in due course what might possibly be an excessive amount of stimulation, on a highly optimistic view about the effect of the recent devaluation combined with the incomes policy, on export and import-competing industry.

It is true that a different point of view has been held, i.e. that deflation, by causing more unemployment, might help to bring success to the incomes policy itself. This is very doubtful psychologically. Since the war there has been in the United Kingdom no tendency for the upward movement of wages to be greater in times of good employment than in times of less good employment.

The United States and the United Kingdom have both made experiments with the incomes policy (in the United States called guide-posts), in the United Kingdom with greater determination and with some mild legal sanctions in the background for part of the time. In neither country is there yet an assurance that these policies will be successful.

The advantage of the other way of getting an adjustment of costs and prices, i.e. devaluation, is that it can be done by a stroke of the pen, instead of requiring a vast campaign of propaganda and far-flung negotiations. But there is a disadvantage in that it surrenders one of the prime objectives of economic policy, namely price stability. This was set out on page 2 of this volume as being *the* objective of monetary policy, anyhow in the narrow sense. If one has a 'measure of value', it ought itself to have stability of value. Unless the devaluing country comprises more than half the world, import prices, as denominated in its own currency, are bound to rise. This will have an arithmetical effect on the cost of living in the country; but this is not likely to be the end of the matter. There is almost certain to be a push for greater wage increases than would occur in absence of a rise in the cost of living; such increases must affect the prices of home-produced goods also, and this in turn will cause further wage demands. There is a danger of a spiralling between wages and prices. If 'in due course' (for more about this, see below) costs rise more than they would otherwise have done by the full amount of devaluation, then the effects of the devaluation will have been totally frustrated!

There is a further trouble. If devaluation is recognised as the regular remedy for the case now under discussion, then the anticipation of it is likely to cause one-way precautionary and speculative movements of short-term funds on a large scale.

Advisers will know which way the cat is likely to jump. This would not matter if countries generally had reserves of really massive dimensions, so that they could deal with the leads and lags in trade payments out of their reserves without much bother. But world reserves are not in the least likely to be made available on such a scale, as will be explained later. It may be that this trouble could be avoided by having exchange rates float downwards gently, but regularly, over a period of time. It is more appropriate to deal with this alternative when we come to the dynamic aspects of the international balance.

Such being the problems for a deficit country, we may raise the question whether the surplus countries cannot help. They can certainly help very much if they are suffering from under-employment. The unambiguous remedy for them is to reflate their own economies, thus reducing their own unemployment, reducing or eliminating their external surpluses, and thereby helping the deficit countries. But suppose that the surplus countries, or, anyhow, the more important ones, belong to the fourth class of case, with the tendency to the domestic inflationary pressure. They have their own difficulties. The standard remedy for them is an upward realignment of wages and costs. But in this world, with its post-war tendency for a universal upward movement of money wages and prices, no country is likely to be willing deliberately to give its own costs and prices an upward push, merely to help deficit countries abroad. In the deficit countries it is the devaluation alternative that means surrendering to price inflation, whereas in the surplus countries it is the incomes policy alternative, which in this case consists in an upward revision of incomes, that means surrendering to price inflation. The most that one could hope for by way of mutual assistance between the two groups of countries is that the deficit countries should pursue with great vigour a grass-roots policy for checking wage increases, while the surplus countries would have a more relaxed attitude. The surplus countries will not deliberately arrange for wage increases.

Or should the surplus countries use the other method of getting a realignment, i.e. up-valuing their currency? This was done by Germany and Holland in 1961. This was an appropriate remedy in relation to the analysis we are giving. But in general it has its difficulties. There is bound to be heavy pressure in industrial circles against a measure for deliberately making them less competitive in foreign trade. It is also natural for the authorities to be chary of taking this step in an uncertain world. All might suddenly change. We have experience in the past of great changes coming in very quick time. Then the country which had up-valued prematurely might be faced with all the trials and tribulations of devaluation. It is understandable that the authorities should prefer to play for safety.

The surplus countries also have their own troubles about leads and lags in trade payments. If upward valuation is regarded as a regular remedy for surplus countries, those countries will experience a heavy inward flow of short-term capital, as the Germans did before February 1961 and after it also, and again in 1968. The trouble after February 1961 was because many thought that the Germans would have a second upward valuation, just as many thought that the British would have a second devaluation after November 1967. The Germans claimed that this inflow of short-term capital made their economy excessively liquid and thereby increased the domestic inflationary pressure from which they were suffering.

Friendly critics suggested that they might have offset the effects of the inflow of capital by deflationary open market operations. They pleaded that it was not practicable for them to do so fully; and there may have been something in their contention.

It was stated above that the curative effect of a realignment of costs and prices was subject to a condition. This is that the elasticity of the foreign demand for a country's exports and the elasticity of her demand for imports should be sufficiently great. The formula is that the sum of those two elasticities must be greater than one. If the country has at the outset a surplus of imports, as we may suppose if it is trying this remedy, the condition is a little less severe. The elasticity of the United Kingdom demand for imports is low, because so large a proportion of them consists of materials that cannot be produced in the country, of fuel, and of food, the domestic production of which cannot readily be increased in large proportion. The United States elasticity is probably somewhat higher. On the side of exports, the prices of primary products are apt to be sensitive to changes in supply. Conditions are likely to be most elastic in relation to finished products. But in regard to these it must be noted that they are marketed in conditions of imperfect competition, and that the effects of a price reduction (e.g. owing to devaluation) on the amount demanded is slow-working. There is the need to follow up a price concession by effective marketing, advertisement, etc., and all this takes time.

It is generally believed by the experts that in the long run the sum of the two elasticities mentioned above is greater than one. But there is not very much confidence about the short-run elasticities, and here an important point is to be noticed. We have mentioned the possibility of the rise in the cost of living due to devaluation leading 'in due course'[1] to a spiralling between wages and prices. If it takes too much time for the elasticities to become favourable, there is danger that, if spiralling sets in meanwhile, it may frustrate the beneficent effect of the devaluation altogether. This malign result will not be present if the required realignment is effected by an incomes policy.

The elasticity condition applies *both* to a devaluation and an incomes policy, however effective the latter may be. It is no good getting a favourable relation between productivity increases and income increases, and thereby the opportunity to quote more favourable prices, if the elasticities are not sufficient.

What then has to be done? Must one say that, if the elasticities are insufficient, we have to fall back, in the case of deficit countries, on creating more unemployment? There remains the possibility of interfering with the free flow of trade. This is very much frowned upon, especially in political and official, as distinct from academic, circles. It is said that any tendency to condone protection as a regular adjustment mechanism will open the floodgates to pressure groups and vested interests. Feather-

[1] Cf. p. 214.

bedding will become widespread, and the keen edge of competition will be blunted. But ought it not to be possible to distinguish between a legitimate and an illegitimate use of this weapon? From the point of view of economics, let us say from the point of view of human welfare, cutting off marginal items from the flow of international trade is likely to involve much less loss than the creation of unemployment or holding growth down below its potential. Interference with trade is much to be preferred to deflation, save as the latter may be required to hold aggregate demand down to the supply potential of the economy.[1]

It ought to be possible to place the whole question of interfering with trade on a rational foundation, and to secure an international consensus about the underlying principles. If it is thought that we can give effect to monetary and fiscal policies on rational principles, without too much interference from pressure groups – and this seems to be implied in much discussion – why should we not be able to do the same in relation to interferences with the free flow of trade? Before this book is concluded, it will have been observed that I take a somewhat unsympathetic view of 'multilateral surveillance', as it at present operates. This is because there seems to be a tendency in the high circles in question to prefer deflation to import control.

2. Capital Movements

In the analysis of the foreign trade multiplier, a deficit was defined as a condition in which a surplus on current account fell short of the simultaneous outflow of capital or when the deficit on the current account exceeded the inflow of capital. Thus the movement of capital was taken to be something 'autonomous', and the adjustment mechanism was taken to be one which would make the balance on current account conform to capital movement. There would be fundamental equilibrium if the current balance and the capital balance offset one another. We have still to consider whether we ought to include among

---

[1] I have been a lifelong *Free Trader* and was not fully sympathetic to Keynes during his protectionist period in the thirties. I hope that my little book on 'International Economics' made some contribution to the cause.

the recognised adjustment mechanisms available some interference with the free flow of capital.

If we are taking the movement of capital to be autonomous,
this capital should include short-term capital flows, to the
extent that these occur under the influence of ordinary commercial requirements. Short-term capital movements constituting leads and lags in trade payments should not be included;
nor, of course, should precautionary or speculative movements
connected with anticipated exchange rate changes, whether
these are helpful or perverse. Nor should a flow of capital
attracted by high interest rates, if these have been deliberately
raised by the authority in the country, to deal with balance of
payments embarrassments. It would make no sense to say that
because of an inflow of capital deliberately attracted by the
authorities to deal with a deficit position, there was, after all, no
deficit! There may, however, be a margin of ambiguity here,
namely if the authorities think it a normal condition for their
country to have interest rates high enough to attract a certain
quantity of short-term capital year by year.

The theory of the international capital flow presents great
difficulty, and it may not be possible to say much that is sensible,
until we proceed from static to dynamic theory.

Should policy be fashioned to tailor capital movements to a
current account surplus or deficit? President Johnson's policy
in this respect (1965–68) may have been the best that could
have been achieved in the circumstances. But we have to
review it in the light of general principles. In particular we have
to ask whether it is less bad to interfere with the free flow of
capital than it is to interfere with the free flow of trade.

A capital outflow is normally regarded as a debit item in the
overall balance of payment. The correctness of doing this
depends upon our time span. It would be possible to regard the
prospective estimated yield eventually to be brought back home
in consequence of an investment abroad as part and parcel of
the act of making the investment in question. In that case we
should usually find that a capital outflow was a favourable item
in the balance, if our time span were ten years or even less. One
year is merely an accounting convention. What time span should
our policy-makers have, when deciding upon the need for
adjustment measures? One could argue that capital movement

should be excluded altogether in determining whether a country was in surplus or deficit and whether an adjustment was required. The justification for this would be that, although, given the relevant time span, a capital outflow should presumably be regarded as a favourable item, the outcome is too dicey to enable a figure to be put down. In fact the authorities cannot look at the matter in this way, because they have to find means for financing a deficit as it occurs within a short time span; they cannot lay their hands on future reverse-flow accruals. Yet the likely occurrence of those is relevant to wise policy formation. In the sphere of industry one may often have to take quite a long time span, as in the development of a power project, or the production of an aircraft. It is arguable that the monetary authorities should normally have sufficient reserves to enable them to take a much longer view than is at present possible for them.

Relevant to the consideration of whether public policy ought to take into its sphere the question of influencing the international capital flow is the intrusion of 'fiscal policy' into what is now considered to be the domain of public policy.

Of course fiscal policy may be regarded in a narrow way, that is to say, as a mere jiggering, to iron out the business cycle. But we may take a wider view of it, i.e. as designed to ensure, by means of budget deficit as well as surplus, that the domestic capital supply matches the requirement for it. Private savings, by individuals or corporations, may be supplemented by a budget surplus, especially in the less developed countries, or be in part offset by a budget deficit, when these savings are redundant to need and in danger of causing economic stagnation. If this matching comes more and more to be conceived of as part of the duties of the authorities, can they ignore what is happening by way of investment abroad by corporations and individuals?

One might devise a highly simplified model. Let us suppose that in year o a country is in balance internally and externally. Let us suppose that in year 1 capitalists are attracted by certain foreign prospects and that the capital outflow is increased by a hundred units. Let us suppose that the authorities, in compliance with the idea that an international capital movement must be regarded as an autonomous datum, ensure, e.g. by devaluation, that the current account improves by a hundred units.

If the capitalists, having good 'animal spirits', proceed with their previous plans on the side of domestic investment, there will be excessive aggregate demand; or if, at the other extreme, they reduce their domestic investment by a hundred units, there may not be enough domestic investment to keep the domestic economy growing at its full potential. In either case it will be incumbent on the authorities to increase the budget surplus (or reduce the deficit), in the former case to prevent overheating, and in the latter to ensure sufficient domestic investment to maintain growth. What this in effect means is that tax-payers will be supplying the funds to enable the capitalists to finance their foreign investment, or, in other words, to enable the country to increase its external surplus on its current account by a hundred units. Is this right?

The essential point is whether, once it is admitted that it is a responsibility of the authorities to secure a balance between the saving and the investment requirements of a growing economy, they can turn a blind eye on what is happening in relation to capital export.

3. Some Recent Discussions

The essentials of the income ('multiplier') theory of the foreign balance of trade were fairly well understood by the time of the Second World War. They were subsequently elaborated with great thoroughness and given formal shape in Professor James Meade's magisterial volume on the Balance of Payments. Mention should also be made of the work of Professor Fritz Machlup.

For a time there then seemed to be a pause in further thinking about this matter. More recently there has been a renaissance in which Professor Harry Johnson was a prominent pioneer. The matter has been carried forward among the younger generation of economists by Professors Robert Mundell, Richard Cooper, Peter Kenen, Ronald McKinnon and Mr Max Corden.

An important stimulant to the new lines of thinking was the famous proposition by Professor Tinbergen that in economic policy one must have at least as many instruments as objectives. This gives an edge to thinking. It is clearly not good enough to say that monetary policy, the details of which are not fully specified, should aim at giving us full employment, optimum growth, stable prices and an equal balance of external payments. It has been ingeniously pointed out that, if each of 'n' countries has two instruments to achieve two objectives, namely internal balance and external balance, there will be one instrument going begging and available for some other use, since there are only $(n-1)$ external balances.

In an interesting article (*Quarterly Journal of Economics*, May 1960) Professor Mundell sought to establish the principle of 'effective market classification'. He argued that a weapon will be more effective, if those who operate it use, as their criterion for action, movements in the balance which the weapon influences directly rather than only indirectly. For instance, under fixed exchange rates, those who operate on interest rates will normally use as their criterion the external balance of payments. The effect of such action on the external balance will be the stronger, the more internationally mobile capital is. If the international mobility of capital is only low, the main effect of interest rate changes will be on internal prices and its main effect on the external balance will be indirect, namely via the effect on that balance of changes in internal prices. Under flexible exchange rates the criterion for interest rate manipulation switches to the state of the domestic economy, the external balance being looked after by the movements in the exchange rates themselves. If capital is in fact highly mobile internationally, the adoption of flexible exchange rates means that interest rate policy is deflected away from the criterion (balance of payments) by the use of which it could have a stronger effect. But if capital is immobile, then the use of the domestic condition as the criterion for interest rate movements becomes as good as the use of the external balance.

Professor Mundell carried his views one stage further in a classic article published in *The International Monetary Fund Staff Papers*, March 1962. There he deals with the two 'difficult cases' specified on pp. 211–12. He makes what is really a heroic claim that these cases can be dealt with by monetary and fiscal policies only, and without the use of an additional instrument of policy, such as some direct method for getting a realignment of domestic costs and prices. He holds that fiscal policy should be guided by the state of the domestic economy and monetary policy by that of the external balance. Thus for a country with domestic unemployment and an external deficit an expansionary fiscal policy should be used to cure the unemployment, and a tight monetary policy to cure the external deficit. The tight monetary policy will, it is true, tend to intensify the domestic depression, thereby working against the expansionary fiscal policy; but if the positive effect of the interest rate policy on the external balance is more powerful than its negative effect on the domestic balance, all will be well. The argument turns on there being international mobility of capital; high interest rates will attract an inflow of capital and cure the external balance in that way. For a country which has domestic inflationary pressure and an external surplus, a deflationary fiscal policy should be combined with easy money. The former will cure the internal inflationary pressure, and the latter the external surplus, by stimulating the outflow of capital. Thus in both cases the international mobility of capital plays a crucial part.

There remains the background question whether policy-makers should seek to tailor the international movement of capital to the condition (surplus or deficit) of the overall external balance. If in fact the external balance is weak because domestic costs and prices are high by international standards – Professor Mundell was subjecting himself to the hypothesis of fixed exchange rates – ought policy-makers to be content to correct the external disequilibrium by deliberately influencing the flow of capital in the direction required? If the answer to this question is in the negative, that need not be taken to imply that the policy-makers should never seek to interfere with the international flow of capital. But it may be that they should use quite different criteria for influencing the capital flow.

Further to this, it seems that the nature of the capital that moves should be examined rather carefully. It is to be understood that we are considering the case where there is a 'fundamental disequilibrium' that needs correcting. The use of interest rate adjustment to influence the flow of *short-term* capital has long been recognised as an appropriate and effective method of dealing with surpluses and deficits due to seasonal, cyclical or random causes. It is to be assumed that when short-term causes of this kind cease to operate, as by definition they will, the state of the external balance will be reversed; then the short-term interest rate differentials can be removed and the short-term capital will flow back. If, on the other hand, there is a fundamental disequilibrium, an increased outflow (or inflow) of capital for the cure of this disequilibrium will have to go on indefinitely. This seems an inappropriate role for short-term capital. And it is doubtful whether high interest rates in a particular centre will go on attracting more and more short-term capital year by year; rather one would expect them to pull in a certain lump of short-term capital and then cease to have a further effect. Maybe one would have to envisage the short-term interest rates in the centre in question going ever higher and higher, year by year, in order to attract a yearly inflow of short-term capital.

So we must suppose that Professor Mundell's proposed remedy operates mainly through other kinds of capital. First we may take portfolio capital. In this connection it is to be noted that the influence of monetary policy on long-term interest rates is much more slow-working than it is on short-term interest rates. The influence will depend in part on expectations. This is not a fatal objection to the scheme, provided that each country has an ample reserve to carry it through the period in which the long-term interest rates are being slowly adjusted. Further-more, it must be noted that this recipe applies to a limited group of countries only, since many countries do not have good portfolio securities denominated in their own currencies.

Finally we come to direct investment. Here two points must be noted:

1. The markets are imperfect, and the flow of capital will be influenced not only by the going rate of return in a given country but also by the number of feasible projects at a given point of time.

2. It is doubtful if 'monetary policy' has a substantial in-fluence on what we have previously called the MARC (mini-mum acceptable rate of return on capital) in each country. There are problems here that have already been noted; in fact it seems that the MARC is very insensitive to changes in mar-ket rates of interest. To explain this we need to explore the theory of decision-making in the firm, and that would take us too far away from the subject of this volume.

Paradoxically, a high interest rate policy in a given country might, so far from attracting an inflow of direct investment by raising the MARC, which it would probably not do, discourage the inflow of direct investment by reducing the number of feasible projects owing to the consequent depression in the economy. Professor Mundell can in principle counter this by pointing out that the number of feasible projects will be maintained by the expansionary fiscal policy which he postulates as being simultaneously enforced. None the less the symmetry of his scheme is disturbed, because it is then the expansionary fiscal policy and not the high interest rate policy that is attracting foreign capital. This is obviously a point of wide implications.

The conclusion surely is that, when we are dealing with a fundamental disequilibrium, the scope of monetary policy for influencing the capital flow is somewhat limited. And we may revert to the deeper question of whether the state of the external balance at any time is really the right criterion for policy makers to use in influencing the capital flow.

Mr Jerome L. Stein (*American Economic Review*, June 1963) suggested an intriguing criterion by reference to which a country might make the choice between having a flexible or fixed exchange rate. A flexible exchange rate would be helpful, if the country in question tended to be in deficit in a period of general contraction and in surplus in one of expansion. The deficit would cause a downward movement in the flexible exchange rate and thus exert a stimulating influence on the economy in the depression period. In the period of expansion and surplus, the exchange rate would move up and this would have a valuable damping influence on the domestic economy, counteracting any tendency to inflationary pressure. But, if the country tends to have a surplus in periods of contraction and a deficit in expansion, a flexible exchange rate would have a perverse effect, making matters worse during the depression and tending towards overheating during the expansion. Accordingly such a country should opt for a fixed exchange rate. This seems convincing as far as it goes.

But what of the rest of the world? There are, it is true, occasions when one country's depression is accompanied by expansion elsewhere, and conversely. The more usual case is for most countries to be booming at the same time and to be in recession at the same time. If country A has a flexible exchange rate with the rest of the world, the rest of the world has a flexible exchange rate with it. If country A is in deficit with the rest of the world in a period of recession, the rest of the world is in surplus with it. Accordingly, if the flexible exchange rate had a stabilising effect on country A, it would have a de-stabilising effect on the rest of the world. Thus Mr Stein's doctrine becomes unacceptable, if we look at it, not simply from the point of view of national self-interest, but as one that can be embodied in an international code of good behaviour.

In an article[1] prior to that in the I.M.F. Staff Papers already quoted, Professor Mundell raised the question of what ought to be regarded as an 'optimal currency area'. This was followed by an article by Professor Ronald McKinnon,[2] on the same subject. In discussions about whether fixed or flexible foreign exchange rates are expedient, it is commonly assumed that the unit which has these fixed or flexible rates is a nation. The reason is that there is an authority in each nation responsible for monetary management. But there is no *a priori* reason why, if there be need for flexible rates, the areas which they bound should be co-terminous with those of the national governments. One might envisage larger areas, like a dollar area, or a sterling area, or the E.E.C. group. In the well-known report of the Brookings Institution on the United States Balance of Payments in 1968, it was suggested that sterling and the dollar should come together and be allowed to fluctuate against the E.E.C. group. Or one might go in the other direction, and decide that the ideal boundary was around a region inside a nation.

Professor Mundell holds that a region should be defined by reference to the mobility of the factors of production. And he suggests, by way of example, that there might possibly be more mobility between the eastern parts of the United States and of Canada than there is between the eastern regions of the United States and Canada together and the western regions of those two countries. Would it then be expedient to have a flexible rate, not between the United States and Canada, but between the eastern areas of the United States and Canada and the western areas?

[1] *American Economic Review*, September 1961.
[2] Ibid., September 1963.

If in a given currency area there is less than full mobility between the regions within it, it may be impossible, on the occasion of a switch in demand from the products of region A to the products of region B to prevent unemployment in A, and therefore some degree of overall unemployment in the whole area, without having overall demand inflation. If the monetary and fiscal policies are sufficient to secure full employment in the adversely affected region A, they will cause excess demand in the favourably affected region B, if there is not mobility of factors between them.

There will, of course, be a question of degree. One would have to interpret immobility in a broad sense. There may be some immobility as between producers of each and every commodity. If this was held to justify flexible exchange rates between each, there might be as many currencies as there were commodities. This would greatly impair the usefulness of money as a measure of value and medium of exchange.

Professor Mundell further argues that the effectiveness of flexible exchange rates implies a 'money illusion', i.e. that, when the exchange rate depreciates factors of production become willing to accept lower *real* incomes. If they did not do so, then the exchange rate depreciation would be without avail in the external balance. The necessary degree of money illusion becomes greater, the smaller are the currency areas.

If labour and capital are insufficiently mobile inside a currency area, flexibility of its currency will not be a safeguard against *both* unemployment *and* inflation.

Professor McKinnon stresses a somewhat different point, namely the ratio of tradable goods to non-tradable goods inside an area. He regards this distinction as more important than that between 'exportables' and 'importables', and in particular the ratio of the prices of the tradables to those of the non-tradables.[1]

If the proportion of non-tradable goods is high, then, with fixed exchange rates, it will be needful to have rather heavy unemployment in order to improve the external balance, when this has got into deficit. It would be better, according to this view, to use monetary policies to ensure stability in the domestic

---

[1] If Prof. McKinnon is right, the U.K. Government erred in two respects in 1968, namely (i) by its undue stress on exports and (ii) by raising the relative prices of non-tradables by its Selective Employment Tax.

price level of the body of non-tradable goods and change the domestic price of tradable goods by altering the exchange rate. This would ensure a shift in the price level of the non-tradable goods to that of the tradable goods, and that is what is needed to restore equilibrium.

On the other hand, if the ratio of non-tradables to tradables is low, then he suggests that a fixed exchange rate would be better. Large movements might be needed to ensure equilibrium through flexible rates; these would have a heavy effect on the *general* domestic price level and therefore tend to undermine the liquidity value of individual currencies for residents. If this is undermined, there may be an undue tendency for nationals to attempt to accumulate foreign bank balances. Strict foreign exchange controls might then be needed.

Professor McKinnon states at one point that, if an area is small, the ratio of tradable to non-tradable goods will be large, without making the reasoning behind this proposition altogether clear.

4. Growth

The theory of growth *policy* inevitably presupposes a certain amount of prognostication, which is of course fallible. For instance, policy-makers – assuming them to have optimum growth as their main objective – in deciding upon the right level at which to maintain aggregate demand, must predicate that their country is capable of such and such a growth rate. If the economy seems to be going slack, the relative authority should put his foot on the accelerator. The estimate of growth potential has to be tentative and provisional. If potential growth is over-estimated, overheating in the economy will become manifest. Overheating must not be judged by the course of prices, since an upward movement of prices may be due to cost-push, but by such phenomena as a pile-up of unfulfilled orders. Although the matter may sometimes be doubtful, we may note there have been repeated periods in the United Kingdom, and also in the United States, in which the use of common sense could indicate that growth was clearly lagging below potential. But growth policy went by the board.

Some have thought that it would be expedient to supplement

the verdict of common sense by what has been called 'indicative planning'.[1] This consists in making forecasts of the growth potential of the economy for a number of years ahead. It is necessary, first, to compile input–output tables for determining what rates of growth in the different sectors are mutually consistent. Secondly, it is needful to refer the sectoral rates of growth thus determined to representative firms in each sector to ascertain if each rate of growth is greater (or less) than what each sector thinks it reasonable to expect it to be able to achieve. If negative answers are received, the planning authority will have to revise its input–output tables accordingly, so as to ensure that what is achievable in each sector is consistent with the plan as a whole. And then there should be further references to and fro.

This planning has two purposes: (1) It should provide a basis of feasibility for a given growth target, and for laying down and implementing programmes in the public sector that are consistent with that. (2) It may be needful to reinforce (or damp down) the 'animal spirits'[2] of the entrepreneurs. In placing orders or undertaking investment projects, they cannot be guided by the current state of demand alone, as influenced by monetary and fiscal policies, but need to have some confidence about what the future will bring. They may lack confidence that the existing rate of growth of demand will be maintained, perhaps owing to some unexpected difficulties in the country's balance of payments. It is needful for the authorities, as was done in France, to give the entrepreneurs an assurance that the objective of growth has top priority and that they are determined not to deal with any balance of payments difficulty by damping growth down, but will find some other method for dealing with it. The authorities will assure the entrepreneurs that monetary and fiscal policies will be directed to ensuring growth of demand at the agreed upon rate, and also that outlays for which the public sector is responsible will be maintained at appropriate rates.

It may well be the case that it is not possible to define the right principles of adjustment to international imbalances or to determine the right kind of interferences, if any, with the

---

[1] See also Ch. 10, Section 3.
[2] See above, p. 202.

international capital flow, without the aid of some indicative planning of world-wide scope. This is indeed a formidable project, but, given goodwill, it should not be impossible to make some headway, in view of the rapid increase in the statistical data becoming available, the vast apparatus for economic research that now exists and the number of computer-aided national forecasts that are already being made in various quarters.

A greater difficulty is that of getting acceptance in the right places that the growth objective has top priority. So long as the personnel of indicative planning have an outlook biased in favour of deflation (puritanism) or in favour of unfettered liberty of international dealings (Adam Smith), there is danger in entrusting them with the task of getting together machinery for world indicative planning. Before that is done it is needful for the effective heads of state in a number of the most important countries to adopt the *credo* that growth has first priority. In France, the scene of the greatest success of indicative national planning, there were certain dominant personalities who carried the thing forward.

An indicative plan would presumably reveal that there were some countries, notably the less developed countries, that, given existing parameters, were likely to have increasingly adverse balances if they insisted on having domestic full-growth programmes. The alternative possible adjustment policies for dealing with external imbalance should be considered in the light of future trends. We have also to assess the right amount of capital flow, as well as of soft loans and aid. It does not make good sense to prescribe methods of adjustment for deficits, even if these have lasted for a number of years, without reference to the likely long-run trends. One may endeavour to assess these in the light of trends to date and given existing parameters, but a more fruitful result would be obtained by assessing them in the light of an indicative plan of world scope.

A sharp distinction should always be drawn between an existing fundamental disequilibrium (which is a static concept) calling for some kind of once-over adjustment, and a dynamic disequilibrium calling for a continuing adjustment policy. Different recipes may be appropriate in these two cases. The United Kingdom has recently been in this double position. The removal of what remained of the war-time import controls in the late fifties created a gap. If a reimposition of some of the controls was disallowed, this gap constituted a static 'fundamental disequilibrium'. Aside from that there has been a *moderate* tendency for this disequilibrium to get worse, i.e. a moderate dynamic disequilibrium.

In the indicative plan of the Labour Government (1965) developments in the foreign balance were postulated that would bring the country into full balance at the end of the period. This approach conflated the two problems and required a steeper rate of growth of exports during the plan than would permanently be needed. Whether this was the right approach it is difficult to judge. In the event, the various growth rates laid down were not achieved.

Reference should be made to a piece of pioneering work by Professor Harry Johnson.[1] This is the first study with which I am acquainted in which dynamic concepts are systematically applied in foreign trade theory. He presents a series of equations in which the rates of growth of productivity in each of two countries and the rates of rise (or fall) of the price levels in each country figure as terms.

He conjugates these with the income- and price-elasticities of demand for the traded goods in each country. These are treated as constants. I believe that this is correct procedure; it is analogous to the treatment of the saving ratio as a constant in my fundamental growth equation. It was not thereby implied that the saving ratio will normally be constant (or even that saving is a function of income).

Professor Johnson's elasticities may of course change through time. For instance, the income elasticity of demand for food may decline with rising income, and price elasticities generally may have some tendency to fall. It may be that in the analysis of dynamic equilibrium, elasticity changes should be conjugated not with growth rates but with changes in growth rates. This relates to methodological principles, which still lack precise analysis and formulation.

Among other interesting points, Professor Johnson reached

[1] 'Increasing Productivity, Income Price Trends and the Trade Balance', *Economic Journal*, September 1954; reprinted in *International Trade and Economic Growth* (George Allen & Unwin, 1958).

the elegant conclusion that, if elasticity conditions are such –
but they may *not* be – that a superior rise in productivity in
country A compared with country B and a consequent lower
rise (or greater fall) of prices there, causes A's balance to
improve progressively, the resulting disequilibrium can certainly be rectified by a devaluation of B's currency.

More attention ought perhaps to be given by writers on this
topic to the possibility of demand curves having a 'Hall–Hitch
kink' in the wide field of imperfect competition at exchange
rates prevailing at a given point of time. With growth, the kink
might move steadily rightwards.

There has been much discussion about the great gulf between
rich and poor countries and for its tendency to widen, rather
than the other way round. This tendency, which from a
welfare point of view we may deplore, may be inevitable owing
to the richer endowment of the already advanced countries
with technical know-how. Of course they have helped the less
developed countries by providing them with know-how as well
as aid, and men of goodwill have urged an acceleration of this
assistance. It seems unlikely that, within the limits of what is
feasible, the amount of qualified personnel can be made to
increase in the less developed countries at the same rate that it
will increase in the ordinary course of things in the advanced
countries. The existence of large cadres of qualified personnel
in certain countries is a hard fact, like the existence of gold-
mines or oil deposits, and the increase of this personnel through
education, training, etc., gathers its own momentum.

There is another factor which may also be unfortunate from
the point of view of the less developed countries. We may suppose that in a rough sort of way the division of labour as
between countries conforms with the classical principle of
comparative costs. As growth occurs, the world demand for all
products may be expected to increase. But the income elasticity
of the demands for some products may be greater than those for
others. It seems likely that the income elasticity of demand for
more advanced products, e.g. consumer durables, will for
some time be greater than that of the demand for primary
products. If it so happens that the more advanced countries
have a comparative advantage to start with in the products for
which income elasticity of demand is great, this will give them

a cumulative advantage. It is to be hoped that a progressive readjustment of the pattern of comparative advantage will occur, so that the less developed countries take over some production formerly undertaken by the more advanced countries, the take-over beginning at that end of the spectrum where the need for highly qualified personnel is less. But this process of shift will have to go a long way before the tendency to a worsening of the terms of trade for the less developed countries ceases. It is fair to add here that some workers on historical time series conclude that there has not been a secular worsening in the terms of trade for primary product producers to date.

But let us suppose that such a tendency develops. How should this affect monetary arrangements? By one line of 'orthodox' thinking one would suppose that the exchange rates of the less developed countries would have to decline.

Do we have to accept this mechanism of readjustment as the best? May there be some other possible and perhaps better mechanism for getting a change in the pattern of production without the less developed countries having to suffer a worsening in the terms of trade? For many years there have been discussions about the buffer stock plans designed to iron out the oscillations of prices to which primary products are especially subject. But more recently some have proposed to carry the matter one stage farther and sustain primary product prices at their existing level for a longer and unspecified period. This would mean *not* allowing them to fall to their 'economic' level. Presumably some joint restrictions on production would be needed. If we revert to the idea of indicative planning on a world scale, then perhaps the readjustment of production could be carried out, without the less developed countries having to suffer the terms of trade going against them and their exchange rates falling as a necessary part of the adjustment process. *Ultimately*, we may suppose, primary product prices would be allowed to fall to their economic level, but this might be delayed for a substantial time, namely until the less developed countries had more widely based economic systems and produced as many commodities the demand for which was income elastic as those of the other sort.

The principles of dynamic policy in relation to international capital movements undoubtedly present great difficulties. The

question of the appropriate time span has already been noted.
It has also been noted that the optimum MARC depends on
the rate of growth of income per person. Consequently different
countries will have different optimum MARCs. We may think
broadly in terms of three categories of countries. There are
those on the frontier of advance whose output per person can
grow only to the extent that their technological knowledge
advances; they are entirely dependent upon new discovery and
invention. Then there is the middling group of countries which
are already fairly well-endowed with qualified personnel and
can incorporate into their industrial set-up techniques already
known in the most advanced countries. One would expect this
middling group to have a higher growth rate and therefore a
higher optimum MARC. And then there are the unfortunate
less developed countries which are bogged down by lack of
personnel. The optimum MARC for these countries is likely to
be lower than that for the middling group.

It is very widely held that countries which are ill-endowed
with capital should, in their planning of projects, go for labour
intensive methods of production. This dictum is lacking in
authority. If the maximum obtainable achievement in the rate
of increase of output per person is low for reasons of personnel,
then their optimum MARC will be low. Although these countries are short of capital per head compared with more advanced
countries, it does not follow that their MARC should be high.
The effect of the scarcity of capital per person is outweighed by
the effect of the limitation of their growth for personnel
reasons. They will not in any case use so much capital per
person as the middling countries; their methods of production
should be chosen by reference to a low MARC.

An exception must, however, be mentioned. If the introduction of a development plan, e.g. on the initiative of the Government, causes an *inflection* in the growth rate, so that there is a
once-over rise in the level of investment requirements and the
need, if this were to be met, for an actual *fall* in consumption,
then the definition of the optimum MARC would have to be
revised upwards. But this would be a temporary phase only,
during which the 'inflection' was casting its shadow forward.
After a certain period the optimum MARC as defined by the
formula should be restored.

Perfect mobility of capital would tend to equalise the MARCs in different countries. This does not, on the face of it, conform to the optimum arrangement. It may be counter-argued that, if we take the case of a country with a high relative MARC, it would be quite all right if certain investments in it were made with lower returns, provided that all the capital required for these lower-yielding investments belonged to the nationals of some other country where the domestic MARC was lower. This seems all right as far as it goes. But we have to consider what is happening in the countries losing capital. This brings us back to the difficult question raised during our static analysis. If the authorities in the countries losing capital subscribe to the maxim that fiscal policy should ensure the optimum amount of capital domestically, it will be their duty to ensure that there is enough capital available for all investments justified by the low MARC proper to the country itself. A flagrant case would be if some rich citizens of a less developed country were attracted by the higher MARC actually ruling in a richer country, which might even be the optimum MARC for that country, and invested their money abroad accordingly. There do seem to be very difficult contradictions in relation to the idea of a free flow of capital between countries and the establishment in each country of investment at its optimum level.

I have not found it possible to reach firm conclusions. I believe that we can hold with confidence that it cannot be accepted as a principle of policy that the external capital account should be tailored to comply with a *de facto* current account. I believe it also to be true, although this can be said with less assurance, that it cannot be assumed as a fundamental principle, from a world welfare point of view, that an unfettered international movement of capital should be allowed.

PART THREE

Present-day Institutions and Policies

10

DOMESTIC POLICIES IN THE UNITED STATES AND UNITED KINGDOM AFTER THE SECOND WORLD WAR

---

1. Revival of Monetary Policy (1951) in the United States and United Kingdom

BOTH in the United Kingdom and in the United States the Second World War was financed at a low rate of interest, around 3%. This is in contrast, of course, with the high rates of interest that obtained in the First World War. In the United Kingdom, this difference was due to the thinking, advocacy and advice of Keynes.

By earlier thinking, the need for the Government to borrow large sums for the finance of the war, it not being feasible to have taxes so high as to preclude the need for borrowing, would inevitably entail high interest rates. The demand for savings would outrun the supply. By Keynesian thinking, on the other hand, interest rates would not rise if a sufficient supply of liquidity was provided. Since the rate of interest depended on the supply and demand for liquidity, the authorities could by monetary policy keep the rates of interest wherever they wanted them to be. Shortly before the war Keynes reminded those concerned of this point of view by important articles in *The Times* newspaper. Doubtless, he also gave advice to this effect when he was taken on by the United Kingdom Treasury as an honorary consultant in 1940. Liquidity was, in fact, supplied in ample quantity, and, in accordance with Keynes's prediction, interest rates did not rise.

In the case of the United States, where Keynes was not then held in as high esteem as he was in the United Kingdom, there was already the British example of how to run the war on low interest rates, and there were also 'back-room boys' in the United States Administration, who were disciples of Keynes.

One advantage in holding interest rates down was that it contained the service charge that would be due on the National Debt when the war should be over, thus reducing the burden on the tax-payer. The interest charge due to servicing the United Kingdom National Debt was only about half as high, in ratio to the size of the Debt, after 1945, as it had been at the conclusion of the First World War. But holding down the rate of interest does not by itself solve the problem of war finance. One function of a high rate of interest is to check investment demand, which, when government borrowing is included in that demand, runs at a high level in a major war. If investment demand is not contained, severe demand inflation will ensue and prices will tend strongly upwards. Investment demand was in fact contained by severe controls. Private citizens were just not allowed to make investments not conducive to the war effort. Even so, government borrowing would alone be conducive to demand inflation; this occurred; but its effect on prices was largely prevented by price controls and rationing. Despite low interest, prices in both countries rose very much less during the Second World War than they did in the First World War, when interest rates were high, and this despite the fact that the economic strain and effort of the Second World War were much greater.

This war-time experience had a post-war effect. In both countries it was argued that, if one could run a war of vast dimensions at 3%, one ought to be able to run a peace-time economy at no higher a rate. In both countries it was desired to contain interest rates owing to the large size of the National Debt and to the severe increase of taxation that would be needed if interest rates rose. In the United Kingdom there was the further motive that the Government intended to nationalise a number of industries; Government Bonds would be issued by way of compensation to their owners, and it was therefore desirable that the going rate of interest on Government Bonds should be as low as possible.

When the war was over, accordingly, both countries aimed at a $2\frac{1}{2}\%$ interest rate on long-term Government Bonds. This target was achieved for six years in the United States, but in the

United Kingdom the policy began to fail some two years after the war; none the less, rates of interest were probably lower there than they would have been if a low interest policy had not been pursued.

But how about demand inflation? Investment demand was likely to continue high, although not so high as during the war, owing to the needs of post-war reconstruction. The policy of the British authorities was to contain investment demand in precisely the same way as they had done during the war, namely by direct controls. These were in fact maintained but, owing to pressing needs, reconstruction programmes and a more relaxed attitude in the post-war world in regard to the danger of inflation, controls over private investment were not exercised with sufficient severity to keep aggregate investment down to a non-inflationary level.

The United States Administration had similar ideas in the period immediately after the end of the war. Plans of this sort were, however, frustrated by the action of the Congress in 1946 in having a holocaust of war-time controls. But the low interest rates were maintained in the United States, and inflationary pressure rapidly built up. This led to a rise of dollar prices, not only in the United States itself, but also, owing to the great influence of the United States on primary product markets, in the world as a whole. This development reflected back on the United Kingdom. While it is by no means the case that domestic demand inflation was absent in the United Kingdom, the rise of world-wide dollar prices probably had a greater effect on the course of prices in the United Kingdom than domestic inflationary pressure, as is suggested by Table 1:

TABLE I

World Inflation, 1945–48

Percentage increase

	U.K.	U.S.
Import prices	46·0	51·7
Wage rates	18·0	31·7
Cost of living	14·5	33·6
Wholesale prices	30·3	55·3
Export prices	31·0	39·1

This table shows that domestic price inflation was better

contained in the United Kingdom than in the United States during the three years after the war. Wage rates, the cost of living, and even wholesale prices, rose much less than in the United States. But import prices rose strongly and this rise was the most important cause of domestic price inflation. There was no holocaust of controls at this time in the United Kingdom, although there was a considerable relaxation.

The United Kingdom authorities did not succeed in holding down long-term bond prices so well as the United States. The reason for this was what may be called a 'credibility gap'. The pressure of demand was somewhat greater in the United Kingdom than in the United States, partly because there was a larger pool of unemployment and under-utilised resources before the war in the United States than in the United Kingdom, so that the war-time and post-war demands did not put so severe a pressure on aggregate productive resources in the former country. The British people just did not believe that the authorities would succeed in holding the long-term interest rate at $2\frac{1}{2}\%$ in the face of the very great pressure. There was a conviction in many quarters that interest rates were likely to rise and a large liquidity preference on speculative account built up, which was more than could be countered by any feasible increase in the money supply. The course of bond and bill rates in the two countries is shown in the following table:

TABLE II

Bond and Treasury Bill Yields in the United States and the United Kingdom

	Bond yields		Treasury Bill yields	
	U.S.	U.K.	U.S.	U.K.
1946	2·19	2·60	0·38	0·51
1947	2·25	2·76	0·60	0·51
1948	2·44	3·21	1·04	0·51
1949	2·31	3·30	1·10	0·52
1950	2·32	3·54	1·22	0·51
1951	2·57	3·78	1·55	0·56
1952	2·68	4·23	1·77	2·20
1953	2·92	4·08	1·94	2·30

This table shows that the Federal Reserve System was markedly successful in holding down bond yields prior to 1951, while in the United Kingdom they had come up by about 1%. On the other hand, we see the greater discipline imposed by the Bank of England, as compared with the Federal Reserve System, on Treasury Bill rates. In the United States the main target was the maintainance of a low bond rate. The interplay between the Federal Reserve policies as regards bills and bonds has been well described by Mr Fforde.[1]

Meanwhile, the British Chancellor, Sir Stafford Cripps, decided to supplement the system of price controls and rationing, which still continued, by what we now call an 'Incomes policy', executed on a voluntary basis. For the two years, wage rates rose at 2% per annum, only. This was well below the increase of labour productivity. This policy was undermined by the premature and excessive devaluation of sterling in 1949. This devaluation was not a voluntary act of policy, any more than that of November 1967, but was forced upon the country by outside pressures. In 1949, but not in 1967, these included official opinion in the United States which had the mistaken hope that a devaluation of sterling would enable the United Kingdom to relax its import controls. This did not prove to be the case in the period immediately after devaluation.

The large devaluation made it impossible to maintain the incomes policy. Some writers have tended to place undue stress on the Korean War in this connection. That war certainly inflamed the situation for the United Kingdom by causing a world-wide rise in prices. It is possible that the Korean War and its aftermath would alone have defeated the Crippsian Policy, but this is not quite certain. At the peak of the Korean price inflation, which occurred early in 1951, United States import prices had risen by 30·6%, while United Kingdom prices had risen by 53·4%. In 1953, when world prices had relaxed somewhat, United States import prices were only 17·6% above their pre-Korean level, while United Kingdom import prices were 37% up. These figures show clearly that the devaluation of sterling had already had its major effect on United Kingdom import prices in 1951. The fact that the superior rise of United Kingdom import prices compared with United States import prices was not in full proportion to the devaluation of sterling

[1] *The Federal Reserve System, 1945–1949* (1954), by J. S. Fforde.

was due to the fact that many other countries devalued along with the United Kingdom in full or partial proportion.

The United States and United Kingdom both abandoned their rigid policies of easy money and returned to 'monetary management' in the year 1951. One may wonder whether this simultaneity was a coincidence, like the abandonment of bimetallism by the United States and the Latin Union in 1873. Were the motives quite independent, or was there some identical underlying force operating in both countries?

Hitherto, the Federal Reserve System had been restrained by the financing needs of the United States Treasury, and had worked to the understanding that it would keep the bond rate at $2\frac{1}{2}\%$. Some argued that this more or less guaranteed bond rate in effect turned United States Government Bonds into part of the 'Money Supply'; there seemed to be no risk of loss of value by holding these bonds rather than cash.

This system was terminated by the famous 'Accord' between the Federal Reserve System and the Treasury in March 1951. The reason for the 'Accord' taking place at this time was the threat of inflationary pressure due to the Korean War and to the large new defence programme of the United States. I may make the matter vivid by referring to a Conference at White Sulphur Springs in West Virginia, which was held at the time when negotiations for the 'Accord' were proceeding, but in ignorance of them. I was one of the only two foreigners at a large meeting of well-known American economists, bankers, industrialists and members of Congress. The debate there concerned whether an event of the dimensions of the Korean War must entail, if inflation was to be prevented, all the paraphernalia of war-time controls. Some held that these would undoubtedly be needed. Most hoped that it should be possible to contain inflation by monetary and fiscal policies. But fiscal policy would be rather under a handicap owing to the large defence expenditures, so that it seemed to be up to the monetary authorities to play the major role in curbing inflation. Surely that could be made to do the trick.

Doubtless, the Federal Reserve officials were deploying these same arguments to Treasury officials. Again, to make the matter vivid, I may refer to a dinner that I had a week later with Mr Rieffler, chief adviser to the Federal Reserve Board, and he showed me a studio in his back garden where the authorities of the two great institutions had met together without knowledge of the general public. This was perhaps a better method of proceeding with delicate negotiations than by much publicised meetings in Basel or in Bonn!

By the 'Accord' it was understood that the Federal Reserve should continue to have Treasury needs very much in mind, but should no longer be expected to hold the bond rate fixed at $2\frac{1}{2}\%$. The 'Accord' signalised the revival of monetary policy in the United States after eighteen years in which it played a very minor part. The Federal Reserve was to attempt once more, as in the period from 1922 to 1929, to iron out the business circle, including the consequences of wars that were not on a world-wide scale.

The revival of monetary policy in the United Kingdom, also after a lapse of eighteen years – except to the extent that one should regard easy money as a 'policy' – came after the advent to power of the Conservative Party in the later part of 1951. This may have been largely due to the thinking of the Conservatives, who hoped to exert policy by less *dirigiste* methods than those used by the Labour Government. It should be noted, however, that the latter had already abandoned controls on a considerable scale before losing office.

But, apart from this changed outlook, the United Kingdom had also been subject to inflationary pressure and to a bad adverse balance of payments in consequence of the Korean War, and it is quite possible that the Labour Government itself, if returned to office, would have turned its attention to the possibility of using monetary policy. In the United Kingdom case, there did not have to be an 'Accord', since the Bank of England had become formally responsible to the Treasury since its nationalisation in 1946.

The British also had defence expenditure related to the Korean War, but not so much in proportion as that of the United States. The United Kingdom was badly hurt on the side of its balance of payments by the rise of world prices. This reached its peak in the early part of 1951, but it was generally believed, e.g. at the White Sulphur Springs meeting already mentioned, that the pause, and even slight down turn, was only a 'lull', and that the mounting heavy United States defence

I

programme was bound to cause a further climb in world prices. In accordance with this expectation, there was a good deal of super-normal stock building in the United Kingdom during the rest of 1951, which further exacerbated the balance of payment problem.

A deflationary policy was pursued by the Conservative government in the United Kingdom, including a rise of Bank Rate and a very large funding of Treasury Bills. This soon became untimely and was followed by a recession in 1952 which was shared by most of Europe. Engines were in due course reversed. The United States was exempt from the recession of 1952, owing to the effect of the large defence programme and especially of the capital investment necessitated by it. The recession came there in 1953, when the capital expenses of the defence programme had passed their peak. In that year the Republicans had been returned to power, and we may find a parallel with the British case. They encouraged the monetary authorities to step up their restraining measures when things were already cooling off. This led to quite a crisis in the Government Bond market in the summer of 1953, and engines had to be reversed. In 1954 there was a revival, while booming conditions developed in the United Kingdom.

Monetary policy was back at work in both countries.

2. 'New Dimensions of Political Economy' (United States)

There was rather a sharp recession in the United States in 1957/58. It was, however, short-lived. A recovery came quickly. It seems that this was mainly due to Federal Reserve policy. There are various yardsticks for measuring the degree of monetary ease or tightness. One may take a simple one, the size of demand deposits. These were increased during the year from $109·5 billion to $115 billion, after an average increase of about 1% p.a. in the preceding three years.

Although the recovery came quickly, it did not persist in strength. Two points may be mentioned: First, the authorities of the Federal Reserve System had in mind that there would be negotiations for wage increases in the steel industry in the first part of 1959. It was important that this leading wage settlement should not be of an inflationary character, and so it was thought expedient to pursue a cautious monetary policy, in order to prevent the economy becoming too lush and easy while the negotiations were proceeding, since this might encourage large demands on the Labour Union side and reduce the determination of employers to resist an inflationary settlement. Furthermore, the possibility that an agreement might not be reached would inevitably lead to heavy stock-piling prior to the date of a possible strike, and this would be a factor in itself making for high aggregate demand, so that there would be no need for strong help to expansion on the monetary side. It may be noted that the triennial wage settlements in the steel industry have become quite an important event in the American economy, both in relation to the domestic side and to the balance of payments. Similar phenomena occurred in 1968 when the stock-building of steel had a significant effect on the internal conditions which were approaching those of boom in the first part of that year, and on the external balance, owing to large imports of steel.

Meanwhile a heavy deficit in the balance of payments had come on towards the end of 1957, and, as things turned out, this was destined to continue for many years. It is very difficult, even for Americans, to judge how far the presence of these deficits has deflected the Federal Reserve System away from a monetary policy that would have been ideal in relation to the domestic business cycle and caused them to be more restrained than they would otherwise have been. It may certainly be said that American deficits have deflected monetary policy much less in the United States than in the United Kingdom, mainly, doubtless, because the United States deficits in the sixties, although larger in ratio to its external trade than those of the United Kingdom, have been far smaller in ratio to United States national income. Furthermore, United States public opinion would be much more rebellious if it were known that domestic growth was being seriously hampered by the external deficits, owing to American pride in its productive potential and achievement, and to a sense that it would be monstrous for this great country to be hamstrung in its progress by what was a minor event (the external deficit) in relation to the whole scene. There could be pressure, especially in Congress, for solving the external problem in another way, e.g. by increased protectionism; there was such pressure in 1967/68, but it was unsuccessful. That pressure had other causes also, but the existence of the deficits gave it an extra arguing point. The American Administration, for long pledged to a policy of securing more liberal trading relations in the world, would be most reluctant for the United States to take a backward step in this matter.

During 1959, the year of caution, demand deposits dropped from $115 billion to $114·4 billion.

It may be interesting to set out the growth rates of the G.N.P. of the United States at constant prices in the period from 1950 to 1967:

TABLE III

United States Growth Rates of G.N.P. at Constant Prices

	%		%
1950	9·6	1959	6·4
1951	7·9	1960	2·5
1952	3·1	1961	1·1
1953	4·5	1962	6·9
1954	−1·4	1963	4·0
1955	7·6	1964	5·3
1956	1·8	1965	6·0
1957	1·4	1966	5·4
1958	−1·2	1967	2·6

In the early fifties the Korean War and the defence programme caused a great upsurge, as already noted, which was followed by a period of substantial expansion until we come to the recession of 1953/54. After this recession we have a year of strong revival followed by a continuing expansion but at a subnormal rate. (These are merely annual figures and monthly figures would be needed to show the precise dates of the various inflections in the growth rate.) We find a similar pattern after the recession of 1957/58. Indeed the pattern after the 1948/49 recession is not entirely different, but modified by the important expansionary effect of the defence programme.

But in the years following the moderate recession of 1960/61 the pattern is substantially different. A high rate of expansion was maintained for a longer period. The heading of this section of this chapter consists of the title of a book by Mr Walter Heller, which narrates his experiences and economic philosophy during the time in which he headed the Council of Economic Advisers to the President. This consisted of the period of office of President Kennedy and the first year of President Johnson. The different pattern after 1960/61 may be attributed, in part at least, to a new line of policy. For this Mr Walter Heller, doubtless aided and abetted by other distinguished economists of modern outlook, has the principal responsibility. 'Fiscal' policy comes into its own in this period in a big way.

A considerable degree of persuasion was needed. For this purpose the concept of a 'full employment budget' was brought into service. The Federal Government was running deficits in 1961 and 1962. The idea in the fresh thinking was to look aside from these actual deficits and consider what the state of the Budget would be, given existing rates of taxation and expenditures committed, if the economy was fully employed, e.g. so as to have not more than 4% unemployed. It was ascertained that, although there was an actual deficit, there would be a surplus if only the economy were fully employed, owing to the larger incomes on which taxes are levied. The actual deficit pointed to the need for raising rates of taxation (or reducing expenditures). The full employment budget surplus pointed in the opposite direction, namely to the desirability of reducing tax rates. This reduction would be a fiscal 'reflator' and cause the economy to move towards full employment. Thus, paradoxically, moving tax rates in the opposite direction from that suggested by the Budget deficit, namely downwards, would improve the state of the Federal finances, as actually happened in the years 1965 and 1966. It was thinking of this kind that caused President Kennedy to ask for a large reduction in the rates of direct taxation in 1963, and the reduction was put through Congress under the auspices of President Johnson in early 1964. This was quite a landmark in the history of world fiscal policy, and it caused the American economy to have a period of strong expansion of record duration. The success of the experiment was thought to have weaned average American business opinion away from the doctrine that, whenever there is an actual deficit in the Federal Budget, it is needful to adopt measures of fiscal deflation, whether tax raising or expenditure reduction, in order to get rid of the deficit. If there was a high unemployment rate, the deficit was curable by reflation, not deflation. Whether we can say that orthodox business opinion went one stage farther, and accepted the view that a country of a certain maturity, like the United States, should tolerate having continuing net Federal Government deficits, taking one year with another, is not certain. It must also be added that many who welcomed the Kennedy–Johnson tax cuts were thinking, not so much in terms of Mr Heller's argument for raising aggregate demand, as in the more orthodox terms that tax reduction was a good thing in itself, even at a cost to the Federal Budget balance, because it increased incentives and stimulated business enterprise.

Meanwhile the external deficits continued. On the home front, on the other hand, the United States was at the head of the world league table for the moderation of its wage increases. Between 1960 and 1965, consumer prices were rising at little more than the annual rate of 1%. Between 1958 and 1964 wholesale prices did not rise at all and rose by a modest amount of 2% only in 1965. But in 1966 there was a marked upward inflection in the curves of prices and this gave rise to anxiety and dissatisfaction. The unemployment rate which had been running at 6·7% in 1961 dropped below the 4% mark in 1966. It was feared that the economy was becoming 'overheated'.

It must be stressed that it cannot be stated with certainty that the phenomena reviewed were a manifestation of the 'Phillips curve'. It is still not certain whether this curve has any validity, at least within the ranges of reasonably good employment, or whether the pressure for higher wages has an independent cycle of its own. In 1966 the Federal Reserve embarked on a tight money policy. The increase in demand deposits considerably abated and interest rates rose strongly. This produced a crisis in the mortgage market in the later part of the year.

In 1967 industrial production, which had been rising so strongly since 1961, went flat, and an easy money policy was restored, incidentally to the relief of the mortgage market. But there were cross-currents. Consumer prices continued to rise. Thus there could be a divergence of view between those who regard industrial production as the most important indicator of the buoyancy of the economy and those who lay more stress on the course of prices. On the whole it was felt during 1967 that some restraint was desirable. On the other hand, there was a reluctance to revert to the tight money policy of 1966 with its distressing effect on the mortgage market. And so it began to be argued that, if restraint was indeed desirable, fiscal policy should do a little more work in this direction. This was also in line with the prevailing view among foreign central bankers, who were troubled by the international levering-up of interest rates and thought that fiscal policy should play the main part in restraining the domestic economy, when such restraint was needed. And so, early in the year, the Administration began asking for a tax increase, to take the form of a 10% surtax on the income tax and corporation tax. It was thought needful in order to reduce the upward trend of consumer prices, needful in order to take some of the load off monetary policy as a restraining weapon, and needful in relation to international opinion.

On the external side the proximate cause of the continuing deficit had been, not a deterioration in the merchandise balance, which continued to improve, but the big upsurge of capital outflow from the United States, which had started in 1956. This was accounted for mainly by an increased propensity of the Americans to invest overseas and also by an increased propensity of foreigners to use the New York market to meet their capital requirements. In 1963 President Kennedy proposed an 'Interest Equalisation Tax', to be imposed on capital going abroad, except to the less developed countries, and this was enacted in 1964. In the following year President Johnson also inaugurated a 'voluntary restraint' programme whereby industrial corporations and banks limited the amount of their net investments overseas.

This restraint programme had considerable success in relation to its sphere of operation. It did not, however, impose a severe limit on the expansion of real investment overseas by American corporations, because they discovered that, without contravening President Johnson's wishes, they could increase their operations overseas by raising local capital, especially, in due course, by the issue of 'convertible Euro-dollar bonds' in Europe. There will be a further discussion of the international situation in the following chapter. The American Administration began already in 1967 to use the international argument as an important reason for the passage of the proposed surtax.

The Secretary of the Treasury, Mr Fowler, testified to this effect before the International Sub-committee of the Joint Economic Committee of Congress in September 1967. It is to be noted that at this time economists of a liberal complexion, including Mr Walter Heller himself, began to argue that the tax would be a good thing. This was the reverse side of the great reflationary tax cut in 1964. There was no contradiction here; in business-cycle management fiscal policy may need to be exerted in a downward as well as in an upward direction. Some may have had doubts, however, whether the state of the domestic American economy really did call for deflationary measures. There are two points: (i) Was American opinion having a serious taste of the pressure of international opinion, biased as it tends to be in favour of deflation, which the United Kingdom had already experienced for so long? (ii) During the heyday of the period following the tax cut the United States was in the happy position of having a combination of strong expansion with very slight domestic price inflation indeed. But now the position was different. Industrial production was, as we have seen, stagnant, while the G.N.P. was rising at a moderate rate only but prices were rising markedly. There may be deeper problems, not brought fully into the open in Mr Heller's work, concerning the relation between the rate of expansion of real income and price inflation. Which should monetary and fiscal policies take as their primary criterion, when there is a conflict: the rate of expansion of real income or the course of prices?

There was strong Congressional resistance during the later part of 1967 and the early part of 1968 to the proposal for the surtax. This was mainly based on the more conventional view that, if there was to be deflation by tax increase, the Administration should make a complementary contribution by reducing expenditure. We had a phase, which was highly self-contradictory in terms of economics, in which it was contended that the more the Administration did by way of expenditure reduction, the more lenient Congress would be as regards the tax, in amount and date. From an analytic point of view, on the contrary, in relation to the balance of the economy, the more the Government did in reducing expenditure, the *less* would be needed in the way of extra taxation.

On the external side the authorities by this time had to think not only of the actual deficits but also of the weakness of the dollar in world opinion and the danger of outward movements of short-term capital from precautionary motives. This danger was exacerbated by the devaluation of sterling in November 1967, which brought the dollar into the first line of defence, for the time being, as regards the precautionary movement of funds. After long delays the tax was passed in July 1968. By this time the passage or non-passage of the tax had become a world-wide symbol of whether the Americans really meant or did not mean business in making sacrifices for the sake of getting their external balance straight. The pressure on the dollar had been intensified and reached its climax in the flight out of the dollar in March 1968 (see below). The passage of the tax was a bull-point for the dollar throughout the world. It is not clear, however, that it contributed anything to the more favourable U.S. balance of payments on capital account in 1968 which offset the grave decline in its merchandise account.

The economy was booming in the first half of 1968, partly owing to the stock-building of steel, which has already been mentioned, and partly owing to delayed purchases of cars in consequence of the Ford strike in the later part of 1967. The passage of the tax in the summer did not apparently produce an abatement in consumption, as expected. Persons began by paying the tax at the expense of savings. This might have been anticipated, having regard to the 'Duesenberry effect', whereby consumers show resistance at the first onset of a decline of disposable income in tailoring their expenditures. The effect of the tax may come later.

The foregoing suggests that in the later part of 1968, no very clear principles have yet been established for management of the domestic economy, either in relation to real growth, to price movements or to the external balance.

3. United Kingdom Experience (1955–68)

There was a good revival in the United Kingdom after the recession of 1952. On 30 November 1954 I wrote an article in the *Financial Times* called 'A Drift Towards Inflation?'.[1] On that

[1] Also published in chapter 5 of *Topical Comment* (1961). See also article in the *Economic Journal*, March 1956, entitled 'The British Boom 1954/5'.

day the gilt-edged market receded, and at a formal banquet on the same day my article was held responsible by a number of those dining for this event. I little thought that evening that Government Bonds had during the day been knocked down from a level which they were not destined to regain for the next fourteen years and probably not in my lifetime. While there was something to be said for a little monetary restraint towards the close of 1954, I regard the continuing maintenance of high interest rates since then as unnecessary and injurious. It belongs to an older tradition, and in my opinion a sound one, that a monetary squeeze, if imposed, will do its work quickly and should be reversed quickly. I recall a discussion with a Cabinet Minister at that time in which I said, giving my words a perhaps undesirable political slant, that, if they imposed a tight money policy right away (viz. towards the end of 1954), there would be plenty of time to reverse it, in accordance with sound economic policy, before the General Election that was due to take place in the early summer of the following year. Since that time the authorities have tended to think of a credit squeeze, not in terms of three or four months, but in terms of two or three years. This latter kind of policy has nothing whatever to do with ironing out the business cycle and merely serves to stunt the growth of the economy over a long period.

No restraints were in fact imposed in the autumn of 1954, and the Budget in the following year was a mild one. I judged at the time that an inflationary pressure was developing. It has been said that the authorities refrained from action because they were awaiting the General Election. There may have been a little in this, but in my opinion the comment errs on the side of cynicism. Comments in recent years have been much spiced with cynicism, which is often misplaced and certainly does harm. I believe that the repeated failure of the authorities to take appropriate action has not been because they were deflected from the stern course of duty by political motives but rather because they lacked a proper analysis and understanding of current economic events. And, in any case, there has been a preponderance of measures painful to the voters. If psychology has to be brought into the picture at all – but this is a doubtful point – one might think that the authorities have been subject to an unconscious desire to give pain. (Cf. the so-called 'sadistic' deflation of the German Chancellor Brüning in 1932, which helped to bring the Nazis into power.)

Moderate measures of monetary deflation were, however, undertaken in the early part of 1955. This may have been partly connected with the move by the Bank of England in February of that year to make sterling *de facto* convertible at a small discount through intervention in the markets for transferable sterling. The need for some measure of deflation became more widely recognised as 1955 wore on; and a worsening external balance of payments helped in this direction. The pursuance of monetary deflation during 1955 met with technical obstacles, which have been described in Chapter 2, Section 8. The normal mechanisms of restraint being obstructed, resort was had to a personal approach by the Chancellor of the Exchequer to the Bank of England and direct requests by the Bank to the commercial bankers to reduce advances.

On the external side sterling was weakened by a British statement at a meeting of the O.E.E.C. at Paris in June, to the effect that, if formal convertibility were reintroduced by the countries of Europe – and this was thought at that time to be not far round the corner – the British would like to see established a margin of 3% on either side of the parities. This was interpreted to mean that the British desired a further (slight) devaluation of sterling, and caused sterling to weaken. The situation was only partly rectified by a statement by the British Chancellor at the annual meeting of the I.M.F. in Istanbul that any such suggestion was unrealistic and irrelevant. This was followed by a special Budget in which some minor additional taxes were imposed.

The economy began to recede in late 1955, and, with the help of hindsight, one may think that engines should have been reversed then. I did not begin to advocate that until the second half of 1956. But then the Suez crisis came on, and it was some time before it became clear that this would not involve very large expenditures. Thus there was something to be said for a policy of 'wait and see' until the withdrawal of the British from Egypt.

In 1957 there was a moderate revival. There were not, however, any signs of inflationary pressure. But sterling got into difficulties during the summer for a different reason. It was held by many, including the British, that the Deutschemark ought to be revalued upwards. The French franc, the existing parity of which had been under suspicion ever since 1952, was devalued in August and sterling came under strong pressure; funds flowed out into Germany. This movement was reversed after it had been strongly affirmed by those concerned, including Dr Per Jacobsson, the Managing Director of the International Monetary Fund, at its meeting in Washington in September that there was no need to alter the existing Deutschemark parity. The sterling crisis of the summer, which really had nothing to do with domestic economic conditions, was made the excuse for a further round of deflation. It so happened that the British Chancellor of the Exchequer, and two of his junior Ministers, had rather old-fashioned deflationary views. The deflation was inappropriate and caused an unnecessary recession in 1958, which was, however, to some extent shared by Continental Europe.

Strong reflationary measures were undertaken in the United Kingdom in the second half of 1958. They did not have a quick effect, owing to climatic conditions, but resulted in a powerful expansion during 1959 and the early months of 1960. Industrial production rose from 106·6 (1954 = 100) in the last quarter of 1958 to 120·6 in the second quarter of 1960. This notable expansion shows that there was a large slack in the economy to be taken up, and that, from the domestic point of view, there had been much too much deflation in the preceding years. It has been argued by some since then that the reflationary measures of late 1958 were too powerful and that a slower rate of increase should have been aimed at. The reason for this view is not clear, especially if we concentrate our attention on the domestic economy. If productive resources were sufficient to enable us to produce at the 120·6 level, why should they not be allowed to do so? Why should the reversion to a full use of resources be further delayed? Doubtless the reason for the above-mentioned line of thinking is that the United Kingdom developed a serious external deficit in 1960. This was due in part to the increased import requirements of domestic industry, now working more fully, and to a super-normal rate of stockbuilding. The adjustment of stocks to a level appropriate to higher output was delayed during 1959.

This brings us to the central dilemma of the British position since 1955. It has seemed that, when the economy returns to a level of full activity, after a period of slackness and recession, the external balance goes sour. Is the moral of this that the authorities should never allow the domestic economy to return to a level of full activity? Does the course of events not rather suggest that some remedy for the external weakness should be found, *other* than keeping domestic activity depressed? There is no reason to suppose that, if the return to full working had been somewhat more gradual in that period, the ultimate external deficit would have been any less. Vagaries of stock building do not matter.

It is not denied that expansion could not have continued to proceed at the 1959/60 rate. It is arguable that some damping was needed in early 1960 to prevent the development of inflationary pressure. This was done. The expansion proceeded at a much more moderate rate thereafter. In the second quarter of 1961 the index of production stood at 123, showing an increase of only 2% during the preceding year. It is arguable that the economy was capable of a somewhat greater rate of increase than this.

The adverse balance of 1960 was financed by the use of the old conventional weapon, a rise of Bank Rate, which attracted short-term funds in large quantities. There was no immediate pressure on sterling. But at the opening of 1961 the situation changed. People were beginning to be aware of the large United Kingdom deficit in 1960 and were not sure how it would be rectified. The situation was again complicated by the Deutschemark. It was again thought that the Germans would have to value it upwards, especially as they seemed unable to handle their domestic inflationary pressures that were building up in consequence of the large inflow of funds. The Deutschemark and the Dutch guilder were in fact valued upwards in February. The inflow of funds into Deutschemarks continued for a while, because people argued that the Germans had not valued upwards enough, and would have to do so again. In the early months of 1961 there was strong pressure on sterling for the reasons mentioned. The funds attracted in 1960 were not all available to finance the reflux of short-term capital, since some had been used to finance the deficit of 1960. Accordingly, the central bankers got together at Basel and arranged for sufficient short-term credits for the United Kingdom to offset the outflow of short-term capital. It was put to the British that, if they could not redeem these credits out of their own resources at a fairly early date, they should transfer their indebtedness to the I.M.F. This transference was effected in July 1961 after full discussions with the I.M.F. authorities about what steps the British should take to rectify their position. Further measures of deflation were required of the United Kingdom. From a domestic point of view these were entirely inappropriate, whatever may be thought about the early months of 1960. The economy had been expanding at a very moderate pace and external payments had come into balance. Thus the dilemma of the United Kingdom was very clearly etched. Measures that were entirely inappropriate to deal with the domestic situation were required because of the earlier external deficit. I pointed this out shortly afterwards to Dr Jacobsson at the I.M.F. meeting in Vienna, and, without disrespect, I may say that he did not resolve my difficulties. The consequence of the deflationary measures was a cessation of expansion. Industrial production dropped from 116 (1958 = 100) in the quarter ending in August 1961 to the seasonally adjusted figure of 115 in October and November 1962. (I omit the seasonally adjusted figure of 111 for December, as there may have been exceptional climatic factors in that month.)

Thereafter expansion was permitted again, and between the fourth quarter of 1962 and that of 1963 industrial production rose by 8%; it had risen by 10% by January 1964. Again it is obvious that production had been held below capacity between August 1961 and the end of 1962; and we can say that this undesirable phenomenon was the result of the international 'surveillance' exercised by Dr Jacobsson. A great deal of good productive capacity had gone to seed between 1955 and the end of 1962. What was the correct cure for the external imbalance which was the cause of this unfortunate affair? It should be added that it seems likely that the United Kingdom suffered, not only by having its industrial capacity lie idle, but also by the lack of incentive for modernisation, which might have raised its productive potential to a higher level than was actually achieved in early 1964. During 1964 industrial production seemed to be flat – but there was some ambiguity in the statistics – and then had a sharp upturn in the last quarter of that year, oddly enough at the same time that a sterling crisis of unprecedented severity was proceeding. Exports were up by 4·3% in 1964.

In the last quarter of 1964 a Labour Government assumed office. This coincided with attention being drawn to the heavy United Kingdom deficit in 1964. As in the other year of strong expansion, 1959, so in 1963 imports of required materials, etc., were not increased simultaneously; the effect of the revival of 1963 on the merchandise balance was delayed until 1964, when there was super-normal stock-building, as well as a rise of imports to match the higher level of production. Imports of manufactures rose strongly and there was a deterioration in the merchandise balance of about £350 million. On top of this the net outflow of long-term capital, always a very volatile item, happened to rise also in 1964. During 1964 pressure on sterling was delayed owing to the rest of the sterling area having a favourable balance in the first half of the year, which went into reverse in the second half. The weakness in the underlying position was, however, known to the authorities by mid-year. By the autumn of 1964 a system of mutual credits had been built up between the central banks, which was also designed to help the dollar through a crisis induced by lack of confidence owing to the prolonged United States deficits. It was understood that there were likely to be flurries in the foreign exchange markets prior to the autumn General Election in the United Kingdom and after it, especially if the Labour Party should have been returned to office. These flurries occurred, and the system of mutual credits worked smoothly. But then an unforeseen event occurred. A few weeks after the General Election Mr Callaghan made a speech which shook world confidence to its foundations. This was doubtless owing to his lack of experience, as Mr Callaghan subsequently built up confidence in himself among official international banking circles, which was considerably higher than that which some of his predecessors had enjoyed.

The reason why his speech shook confidence was that it seemed to give scant attention to the rather alarming situation that had developed on the external side and was mainly concerned with additional social benefits and with the prospective introduction of two new taxes, which, whether good or bad in themselves, were totally irrelevant to the existing situation; and if Mr Callaghan seemed to think that they were relevant, that would undermine confidence in him still further. In effect the taxes probably did harm, since they tied up a great deal of the top brain power in British industry in the problems of how to adjust to them during the important year of 1965. It is true that the Government imposed a temporary surcharge of 15% on British manufactured imports; but the effect of this was problematic; in the event it proved to be rather weak.

When the run on sterling seemed to be at its height, the Bank Rate was raised to 7% on a Monday – hitherto changes in it had always been made on Thursdays. This rise in the Bank Rate was of no effect, and, indeed, the run on sterling became worse on the next day. On the following day a huge international credit of $3000 million was organised for the defence of sterling, on the personal initiative of Mr Al. Hayes of the Federal Reserve Bank of New York. This credit sufficed for the time being and had been repaid six months later.

During the General Election Mr Harold Wilson, who was destined to become Prime Minister, inveighed heavily against the alternation of permitted expansions followed by periods of prolonged stagnation or recession to help restore the balance of payments. This system had come to be known as a 'stop–go' policy. Mr Wilson made a powerful case against it.

Thus the Labour Government was faced with two basic problems, namely: (i) how to get rid of the policy of 'stop–go', and (ii) how to deal with the large gap in the external balance of payments that had occurred.

It is needful to revert to the events of late 1961. It has been seen that the United Kingdom had been driven to untimely measures of deflation. The British Chancellor, Mr Selwyn Lloyd, had some feeling that more deflation was not the real answer. His mind moved along two lines. One was to obtain a more rational policy of continuing expansion, by setting up a National Economic Development Council ('Neddy'), perhaps on the lines of French 'indicative planning', which had seemed to have had remarkable success in that country. 'Neddy' got busy with its work which was bound to take some time. The other line of thought was that something should be done about the continuing wage and salary increases, which had injured the competitiveness of the United Kingdom in international markets. In relation to the second task Mr Selwyn Lloyd set up a Commission; but his handling of this side of the business was not effective; he did not gain support from the Trade Unions. In a certain sense, however, he was a forerunner of what the Labour Government later decided to do in relation to the aforementioned problems.

A Department for Economic Affairs was set up by the Labour Government, one of the tasks of which was to deal with 'indicative planning'. It had the advantage of the work already done by 'Neddy'. In due course a number of Economic Development Committees were set up to look, industry by industry, at the specific problems that were obstacles to the improvement of efficiency in each. In due course the Department for Economic Affairs produced a 'National Plan', envisaging a growth rate of about 4%, and prescribing what performance on the external side was needful, to be consistent with this domestic growth rate.

Secondly, what we now call an Incomes Policy was pursued with great vigour. If excessive wage and salary increases could be prevented, that should make the United Kingdom more competitive and serve to improve the external balance. Before Christmas 1964 Mr George Brown, the Minister concerned, had obtained agreement to a 'Statement of Intent', by leaders on both sides of industry. They undertook to work to the target of having only such increases in pay as would be consistent with a stable price level. This policy was to be effectuated on a voluntary basis through propaganda, persuasion and education, which were to influence decisions for pay increases through the machinery of collective bargaining. Stress was at the same time laid on the need for the managements of industries to show restraint in their pricing policies, so that it could be explained to the Trade Unions that the Government was working just as hard to get restraints in 'administered' prices as it was to get restraints in wage bargains. Some time afterwards a Prices and Incomes Board was set up to supervise the implementation of the incomes policy and make reports.

We have to ask the question whether these two lines of policy, however successful they might be, were sufficiently quick-working to deal with the immediate problem of the balance of payments deficit.

In the first year and a half the Incomes Policy was not successful. Wages rose at a higher rate than they had done in the preceding years.

In fact the external balance did improve strongly in the following two years, namely from an overall deficit of £769 million in 1964 to one of £89 million in 1966, but it did not appear that this was due to policy measures on the lines proposed. The merchandise balance improved by about £300 million, but this was partly due to an improvement in the terms of trade and partly because the Government, despite its good intentions, had been prevented by the recurrent pressure on sterling from embarking on a policy of industrial expansion, so that the demand for imported materials was somewhat damped and stock-building subnormal.

In the summer of 1966 a seamen's strike occurred, which set off a new run on sterling. Advisers to foreign corporations had also perceived that the Incomes Policy was not being a success. Accordingly the Prime Minister called for a more drastic implementation of an Incomes Policy. There was to be a total freeze of wages and prices for a period of six months. Legal sanctions were enacted, but these in fact only had to be used for a very few unimportant cases. The policy was in fact implemented voluntarily. The initial six months was to be followed by another six months of 'severe restraint', in which increases were to be implemented only in certain categories. For a year this policy succeeded in securing that the amount of wage increase was very modest. There was some upsurge at the end of the year but not sufficient to restore the average movement from mid-1966 to mid-1968 to the level of increase that had been prevalent before mid-1966.

From the beginning Mr Wilson set his face against the devaluation of sterling as a remedy for the external trouble. There were from the beginning, however, a number of people, especially among academic economists, who believed devaluation was the right remedy. During 1967 the United Kingdom encountered a series of misfortunes and the merchandise balance went heavily into the red. The current balance relapsed to where it had been in 1964. The gap in the overall balance was less severe as the net long-term capital outflow had dropped, partly owing to governmental measures, from its quite abnormally high level in 1964. The misfortunes included the closure of the Suez Canal, a strong rise in the price of oil imports, a heavy (delayed) adverse effect due to the Rhodesian troubles, and the fact that world markets for manufactures, on which the United Kingdom relies almost exclusively for its exports, were not buoyant. On top of all these came a number of dock strikes which had an immediate effect on the trade returns, since in the short-term they affected exports more than imports.

There had been recurrent runs on sterling since November 1964, usually followed by returns of confidence and reverse flows. A crisis arose in November 1967 which exceeded all others in severity.

Another restrospect is needed. The 'National Plan' was abandoned at an early date. It was subsequently said to have been too ambitious. These are anodyne words in relation to the failure to execute it; the feasibility of the plan was not put to the test at the time and the anodyne words may well have been incorrect in fact. My own belief is that the United Kingdom should aim at a growth rate above 4%, such as other European countries have achieved. The real reason, however, for the abandonment of the Plan was something quite different, namely the continuing British weakness on external balance of payments account and the recurrent runs on sterling which were due to that. These runs required large official credits, if the United Kingdom was not to become totally insolvent, and its official creditors called for a policy of demand deflation on occasions of official support. This policy was put into effect.

In 1967 industrial production was no higher than it had been in 1966 and in the month before devaluation had risen only by 0·6%. Accordingly it is impossible to hold that there was any excess of demand in 1967. Industry had been furnished with much new equipment since the previous year, and we must suppose that, if it had not been held back by heavy monetary and fiscal deflation, it could have turned out substantially more goods than in fact it did. Furthermore, in 1967 industrial production was only 2·3% above the seasonally adjusted figure for the last quarter of 1964. This gives a cumulative annual rate of increase of only 1·4%. It is quite fantastic – for scholarly accuracy it is needful to use strong words – to suppose that at the end of more than two years of this very meagre average rate of increase, the industrial system could have been under any strain. What it sorely needed at that time was some reflationary stimulant.

It could, of course, be argued, and was argued, that there was not enough slack in the system to make producers ardently seek out export markets. This argument is not generally acceptable, although pressed in some quarters, mainly of a civil service character. It is counter-argued by most people with industrial experience that a rising total demand, including that of the home market, gives a better incentive for investment and modernisation, thus tends to improve competitiveness and is thus helpful for the external balance of payments. It is not needful at this point to weigh the pros and cons of these opposing views. The insufficiency of the export increase to fill the gap in the balance of payments – the annual increase was, however, quite a reasonable one – cannot have been due to undue attraction to the home market, for the simple reason that it was in the home market, much more than in the export markets, that British producers were defeated by foreign competition. Foreigners were greatly enlarging their share of the British home market for manufactured goods. The extrusion from the home market by foreign competitors gave quite enough slack in the economy for British producers to be activated to strive more strenuously to increase their exports. The fact is that British producers were not making sufficient selling effort in the home market, and it was the lack of effort in that quarter that was mainly responsible for the United Kingdom balance of payments not improving as much as was needed. The argument that it was expedient to damp down the home market in order to release productive capacity for exports in these circumstances cannot be pursued without giving rise to the most violent contradictions. The flaw in the whole course of events in the years in question was that the British producers were not making sufficient effort in the home market to prevent a strong upsurge in the imports of competing foreign goods. Would it be the right way to make British producers try harder in the home market to render it (by restraints on consumption, etc.) even less profitable than it was?

During the November (1967) sterling crisis there were discussions about credits to help sterling and large credits were in fact provided. These were conditional on the United Kingdom intensifying its deflationary policy. The details of these discussions are not known. To maintain sterling at its existing parity of $2·8 to the £ larger and longer-term credits would have been needed than were needed to see it through the troubles surrounding a devaluation to $2·4. It is understood that the larger and longer-term credits would in fact have been available – there remained a strong desire in official circles that sterling should not be devalued – if the British had been willing to take even more violent deflationary measures than would be asked of them in relation to the more moderate credits required to sustain sterling at $2·4. At long last, so it may be believed, the British Government rebelled.

It must be remembered that there were always elements who thought that devaluation at this juncture would be a good thing, and indeed, that a devaluation three years earlier would have been. Under the external pressures those elements who might have liked to resist devaluation for a further period could no longer hold out.

Devaluation is a dicey experiment, and it is impossible yet to say (December 1968) whether it has been a successful one. The experts hold that the likely course of the external merchandise balance from the date of the devaluation should be represented by a J-shaped curve. It has to be admitted that the period in which the United Kingdom remained on the downward sloping section of it was unexpectedly long. It is premature to attempt a judgement as to whether the hoped for upward movement will in fact be realised. There is still no sign of this in May 1969.

If we compare exports in the first eight months of 1967 with those in the three months from August to October 1968, and allow for the adjustment of unit values, as expressed in sterling, we find an increase of 12%; this gives an annual rate of increase of 9% and may be regarded as quite satisfactory. As against this the sterling value of imports rose by 10%, giving an annual rate of 7·2%. This is highly unsatisfactory. Devaluation is supposed to reduce the inflow of goods by giving home producers a price advantage as expressed in the home currency. In the period in question the 'terms of trade' deteriorated by about

3%, so that the slightly higher rise of exports, as compared with imports, was not sufficient to offset this deterioration, and the net position was not improved.

While there is considerable inelasticity in the United Kingdom demand for imported food, materials, etc., it is in the field of finished manufactures that the competitive advantage resulting from devaluation would be expected to show up. But imports of finished manufactures continued to climb at a strong rate despite the devaluation. Separate unit value figures are not provided for these. The total value of finished manufactures, excluding United States military aircraft, rose by 26% in the period referred to above while all imports of manufactures rose by 28%. It is understood that in fact the unit values of finished manufactures rose less than the unit values of manufactures for further processing, so that the percentages just quoted may understate the relative rise in the quantity of finished manufactures.

There was another sterling crisis of considerable severity in November 1968. This was peripheral to the European currency crisis of that month, which was concentrated on the French franc and the Deutschemark. There were thoughts that the French franc would have to be devalued owing to domestic upheavals in May/June, and that the Deutschemark would again have to be revalued upwards owing to the inflow of funds into Germany. The experts had in mind that there was no clear evidence that these two countries were in substantial fundamental imbalance and that, if a readjustment of parities was appropriate, it should be a small one only. But the advisers of international corporations, who appear to be somewhat allergic to statistics, did not apprehend this. The stand taken by General de Gaulle against devaluation was valuable in demonstrating that, on this occasion at least, France would not be forced to take action of doubtful validity by the ill-considered opinions of corporation advisers.

Sterling was involved in this crisis, because it was thought that, if there were to be any realignment of continental European countries, as it was for some days believed that there would be, sterling also would have to be realigned in a downward direction relative to the Deutschemark.

As the result of this crisis and of the fact that the British balance had not yet begun to mount up on the right-hand side of the J-shaped curve, the British authorities adopted another expedient, which, like most of those that preceded it, may be described as 'dicey', namely the requirement for non-interest-bearing deposits in relation to half each firm's imports of manufactures over a six months period. This expedient had previously been adopted by some other countries, e.g. Japan. It is by no means certain what effect it will have on the course of imports.

It might be thought that after so long a period of recurrent deficits and increasing external indebtedness, the British would at long last have decided to adopt some expedient of *certain* effect, such as the imposition of import controls. By this method they could have ensured, without any question, that there would be a sufficient overall external surplus to make possible a repayment of external indebtedness at an appropriate rate. Such controls would be legal under the G.A.T.T. and could not have been legally countered by retaliation. And, surely, after so long a period of fundamental deficit and increasing debt there would be an international consensus that the measure was appropriate to the circumstances. For a good many years I have advocated this measure as being of certain effect, to be a temporary shield while other experiments with measures to rectify the underlying deficit could proceed.

It may be said in conclusion that in the case of the United Kingdom also the general principles guiding policy in this field have been of doubtful validity.

11

INTERNATIONAL INSTITUTIONS

---

1. International Monetary Fund

DURING the course of 1941 Winston Churchill and Roosevelt
had a meeting which issued a communiqué known as the
Atlantic Charter. This constituted an agreed statement of aims
for a better world, when the war should be over. It included a
reference to economic opportunities for all peoples.

At a less exalted level, plans were being made during that
year in greater detail. The American President was sympathetic
to Britain's stand against Hitler, and had proposed a plan for
helping Britain, in the face of congressional legislation against
money loans to belligerents (cf. p. 95 above) by 'lending' or
'leasing' actual objects, i.e. weapons of war or other useful
commodities. Hardly had this idea been conceived, when it
appeared that the plan for returning what had been lent or
leased in kind, after the war was over, was not very realistic.
The goods in question would be either obsolete, like aircraft, or
redundant to America's needs, like tobacco. But it had been
agreed from the beginning that no dollar sign should be put
upon the goods sent to Britain; this was to avoid strains on her
balance of payments, uncertainties and international friction.
To resolve these difficulties there was drawn up a document
that was first known as 'The Consideration', and later became
the 'Mutual Aid Agreement', 'mutual' because Britain did in
fact supply the United States with substantial quantities of aid
after Pearl Harbor, although of course much less than flowed
in the opposite direction. Although this document did not say
in so many words that there would be no return of the lent or
leased objects – considerable quantities of silver were in fact
returned – that was the implication. The idea was that, instead,
Britain should commit itself to co-operating with the United
States in establishing a better order of things in the economic
sphere after the war. It was rather a curious kind of bargain.

But constitutional constraints, notably, in the United States, Congressional constraints, do sometimes lead to curious twists and turns.

However, the broad objectives of the bargain were good. Before the war the economic arrangements of the world had got very much snarled up. This was largely due to the great world slump. Many countries had resorted to exchange controls and trade restrictions, some of them discriminatory. Germany, in particular, was thought also to have used its bilateralist commercial policy for political ends, getting something of a stranglehold on the Balkan countries, and even stretching out its tentacles to South America. Article 7 of the Mutual Aid Agreement prescribed an endeavour to reduce obstacles to international trade and eliminate discriminations. The idea of 'elimination' was rather a sore point with the British owing to imperial preference, itself a product, so far as the British were concerned, of the Great Depression. A compromise interpretation of this was fixed up in top level correspondence.

The spearhead of the American initiative was Cordell Hull. He was a great advocate of more freedom of trade, and had already made some contribution to this on the American side before the war. There was a strong feeling in Britain that the economic havoc wrought by the war would leave her in still greater economic difficulties than the great depression had done, and the British felt that other European countries also would be in a similar plight. They were likely to need, it was felt, even more strongly protectionist and discriminatory devices in the harsh post-war conditions than they had done before the war. When the Mutual Aid Agreement was first mooted, and many months before it was signed (February 1942), Keynes addressed his mind to the problem. It was obvious that Britain, which was beginning to become dependent on lend–lease supplies, would have to comply with Cordell Hull's wishes. Keynes felt, contrary to what was still probably the prevailing opinion in official circles, that this should be possible, but subject to one condition, namely that arrangements be made on an adequate scale for an increase of international reserves, allowing each country a breathing space to tide over awkward balance of payments problems. This was in line with his previous thought. At the time of the World Economic

Conference (1933) he had proposed the issuance of international gold notes, arguing that it was perfectly futile to expect countries to reduce trade barriers unless more adequate means for international settlement were provided. The barriers had not been imposed out of sheer perversity, but because the various countries did not see how they could make two ends meet without them. Accordingly during 1941 he got busy on a scheme for increasing international liquidity on a large scale, which became known as the Clearing Union.

Meanwhile in the United States there were men in high positions of outlook somewhat different from the old-fashioned liberalism of Cordell Hull. In the Treasury there was Harry White, aided by Mr E. M. Bernstein, who has made notable contributions to international monetary affairs since the war. During 1941 White was working on an international Stabilisation Fund, without knowing that Keynes was doing similar work in Whitehall.

The two plans were eventually published and compared. There was a series of inter-changes about them, leading up to the all-important conference of Americans, British and Canadians in Washington in September 1943. This was followed later by the publication of an agreed statement of principles and by the conference (1944), at which many nations were represented, but largely by expatriate governments, at Bretton Woods, where it was agreed to set up the International Monetary Fund and the International Bank for Reconstruction and Development.

It is not necessary to compare the two money plans in detail. Keynes's plan was on a much larger scale than White's, and post-war events have shown that Keynes was in the right on this point. Keynes's plan involved introducing a new unit of account, 'grammor', later called 'bancor'. White's plan also had a new unit, called unitas, but whereas Keynes's unit would have been functional, White's was a mere piece of window-dressing, which could easily bed ropped without affecting anything in the scheme. It is probable that Keynes's bancor could also, by a little ingenuity, have been dropped, while leaving the essence of his scheme intact. One feeling was that a new name might serve as a clarion call for a new and better post-war world and truly encourage support; but it soon appeared that the

contrary was the case and that a new name was liable to
frighten such bodies as the United States Congress and, indeed,
central banks, and had better be dispensed with.

We may concentrate on the most important difference
between the two schemes. Both envisaged that countries would
be able to draw upon the Fund, up to amounts to be agreed
upon in advance. In the American plan the Fund would be
able to meet these drawings through members having initially
made subscriptions in gold and in their own currencies. In the
British plan, the ability of the Fund to honour drawing rights
rested, not on this, but on the willingness of creditor countries to
accept claims upon the Fund as a final discharge of indebtedness. Thus when a country drew, it would reduce its claim upon
the Fund, while the recipient country would increase its
claim.

The Americans pointed out that the British plan would have
the consequence that a given country, which happened to be
in credit with the rest of the world, would be committing itself
to accepting, in final discharge of debt, claims upon the Fund
amounting to the sum total of the drawing rights of all the
other countries in the world. The Americans, rightly envisaging
that they would be in credit *vis-à-vis* most other countries after
the war, held that this would involve a 'hand-out' by them of
gigantic dimensions, was more than they could be expected to
undertake, and would certainly not be acceptable to Congress.
This attitude was understandable, but not strictly logical. By
being on the gold standard, as the United States was, she was
already implicitly agreeing to accept in payment for debts due
to her all the monetary gold in the world. If gold, then why not
claims upon the International Monetary Fund? The answer
may be obvious – gold is a superior asset. This view existed
then, and still exists, despite depreciatory references to gold in
many quarters. Although it is not admitted, this deep-laid
attitude continues to hamper efforts to establish a workable
international system based on paper.

The structures of the institutions envisaged in the two plans
were different in various respects; and they were expressed in
very different language. The Americans argued that everything
that could be done under the British plan could be done under
the American plan, and the American structure was eventually

accepted by the British. But the claim was not fully correct, and at a fundamental level the American plan is not really workable. The structure of the Fund remains radically deficient to this day.

When the Americans argued that they could not be expected to accept claims upon the fund in final discharge of debt amounting to the sum total of drawing rights in all other countries, one could counter-argue that, if the Americans were not prepared to accept this, it would be impossible for the Fund to honour the drawing rights of the various countries if the world in general happened to be in debit with the United States. The Americans met this difficulty by an ingenious and generous proposal, which became Article 7 of the Articles of Agreement of the I.M.F., embodying what is known as the 'scarce currency clause'. This laid down that 'if it becomes evident to the Fund that the demand for a member's currency seriously threatens the fund's ability to supply that currency' (its supply being limited by the amount of that member's initial subscription) 'the fund . . . shall formally declare such currency scarce and shall thenceforth apportion its existing and accruing supply of the scarce currency with due regard to the relative needs of members . . .'.

'Such a formal declaration shall operate as an authorisation to any member, after consultation with the Fund, temporarily to impose limitations on the freedom of exchange operations in this scarce currency . . . The member shall have complete jurisdiction in determining the nature of such limitations, but they shall be no more restrictive than is necessary to limit the demand for the scarce currency to the supply held by, or accruing to, the member in question . . .'

There is a curious anomaly in the above provision. The Fund envisaged that, as soon as possible, all members should have convertible currencies. In such a world there would be no meaning in the reference to a particular member having a specific amount of the 'scarce' currency. When currencies are convertible the amounts of a particular currency held by the various countries at a particular time, will depend, not on the balances of payments of the countries in question but on the last bit of telephoning in foreign exchange markets. The clause really implies a world of inconvertible currencies; the authors, having been used to a régime of inconvertible currencies for some years, evidently lacked the mental energy to address their minds to how things worked in a world of convertible currencies.

The scarce currency clause has a drawback of wider scope, which is also no doubt partly due to the time at which it was drafted. It envisages that, as a regular procedure, countries should be authorised to discriminate in their monetary and commercial arrangements against a particular country, namely against the one the currency of which was scarce. Again, it may not have been then realised how far the industrial countries at least would move away from the idea of discriminatory exchange or import control as a regular and approved practice. The scarce currency clause has become very much out of line with the established modes of thought of today. It has, in fact, never been used. But this leaves a gap, both in theory and in practice, in the arrangements as set up in the Articles of Agreement of the International Monetary Fund.

In the early days the Fund was not much used. There were three mains reasons for this:

1. There was a world-wide shortage of dollars, but this was particularly concentrated in Europe. When the Americans proposed their plan of Marshall Aid, the Executive Directors of the I.M.F. decided that they would not allow drawings of dollars to any recipient country. This was reasonable enough. The dollar shortage was so great that, if the I.M.F. had been open-handed, it would, despite Marshall Aid, have soon found itself running short of dollars. Then, under Article 7, it would have had to declare the dollar scarce. It would have ill-requited the generosity of the Americans in putting forward some $20 billion to help Europe to have the recipient countries authorised by the I.M.F. to discriminate against dollar trade. Actually, the European countries were thus discriminating *de facto*; but that is a rather different matter. For the I.M.F. to have authorised such discrimination would have been, so to say, adding insult to injury.

2. The Articles of Agreement envisage a world of convertible currencies. If a nation drew an inconvertible currency from the Fund, it was obliged to repay in gold or in convertible currencies. Thus if one wanted any currency other than the dollar,

the use of the Fund's facilities was a bad bargain, since it meant acquiring soft currency along with an obligation to repay in a hard one.

3. The world dislocation after the war was so vast that the attempt to rectify matters by the resources of the I.M.F., which was intended to be a permanent institution, might have so weakened it as to disable it from discharging its proper functions thereafter. Thus the I.M.F. authorities were justified in taking rather a stiff attitude as regards drawings at that time.

In due course there was a reversal of the dollar position. This was partly due to the reconstruction of industrial capacity of Europe. Between 1950 and 1958 the United States went into a slight deficit. This was by no means considered a bad thing, but rather was welcomed as causing some redistribution to other countries of gold, of which the United States had previously had more than its proportionate share. It was recognised that it was quite legitimate to use some portion of Marshall Aid for the rebuilding of reserves, and thus putting countries into a position in which they could initiate more liberal payments and commercial policies.

After 1957 the United States went into a heavy deficit. The question of what was the 'cause' of the heavy deficits might be regarded as a question of what is now called 'semantics'. The United States has almost all the time enjoyed substantial surpluses on merchandise accounts. These have been offset by heavy overseas military expenditures, Aid and capital outflow. At the termination of Marshall Aid the United States began to direct its main attention to Aid to the less developed countries. Military expenditures (prior to the Vietnam War) and Aid did not increase in the years after 1957. What did increase was the private capital outflow. As this change was coincident in time with the serious deterioration in the balance of payments, it seems proper to attribute that deterioration to the increased private capital outflow. Actually the beginning of the big change was in 1956, but this was offset by super-normal exports in 1956 and 1957, owing to the investment boom in continental Europe leading to large purchases of marginal supplies from the United States and owing to the Suez crisis.

The British began to get into balance of payments difficulties in 1960. These have been discussed on pp. 257–8.

Meanwhile already in 1960, the third year of the United States deficit, the Americans had been receiving a similar kind of support from the central banks of Europe. Towards the end of that year there were heavy conversions of the dollar into gold in the London bullion market.

Thus in the early part of 1961 it seemed certain that the British would ask for a drawing of substantial amount, and it was by no means impossible, depending on the attitude of the other central banks, that the Americans would have to ask for a drawing also. The position had swung around completely. It was now no longer the dollar that was scarce, but the currencies of continental Europe. And precisely the same difficulties arose owing to the constitution of the International Monetary Fund. A proper interpretation of the Articles of Agreement might at any moment make it the duty of the Fund to declare the Deutschemark scarce. Any such action would seem to be quite out of line with the ideas and ideologies of the time.

Article 7 did, however, present a possible way out of this difficulty. Section 2 authorises the Fund, in the case when a currency is in danger of becoming scarce, to 'propose to the member that, on terms and conditions agreed between the Fund and the member, the latter lend its currency to the Fund or that, with the approval of the member, the Fund borrow such currency from some other source either within or outside the territories of the member, but no member shall be under any obligation to make such loans to the Fund, or to approve the borrowing of its currency by the Fund from any other source'. During the course of 1961 Per Jacobsson, the Managing Director of the Fund, conceived of the idea of getting ten important members of the Fund to be parties to a joint agreement to lend under Article 7, Section 2. The scheme was rendered palatable by being made multilateral and not confined to the members whose currencies were likely at that particular point of time (1961) to be in short supply in the near future. It thus went a little beyond the terms of Article 7, but was conformable with its spirit. Instead of an appeal to particular members whose currencies were temporarily in short supply, it secured what might be called a stand-by agreement

for members to lend their currencies to the Fund, as and when
the need should arise. This scheme was put forward at the
annual Fund meeting in September at Vienna and afterwards
ratified. The ten members were the United States, Canada,
Britain, France, Germany, Italy, Holland, Belgium-Luxem-
bourg, Sweden and Japan. The agreement was known as the
General Arrangements to Borrow (G.A.B.), and the collection
of countries in question has since been known as the Group of
Ten. The total sum of money in the stand-by amounted to
$6 billion. This General Arrangement did not, after all, have
to be used in 1961. But it was used on the occasion of the
British drawings in November 1964, April 1965, November
1967 and on the occasion of the French drawing in 1968.

It was unfortunately not possible to secure an absolutely
unconditional agreement. According to reports at the time this
was due to the attitude of the French. Lending members are
entitled to take cognisance of what is being done with their
money. The result has been, to put the matter quite bluntly,
that, to the extent that the Fund has to use the G.A.B., it is no
longer master in its own house. The Group of Ten has become
the world's monetary overlord. Doubtless members who are
actually lending have a special influence. This is a most
regrettable state of affairs. It points to the need for a fundamental restructuring of the Fund. But this at present seems
unlikely to occur. The Articles of Agreement drawn up during
the war by a limited number of people in a great hurry, who
had many other matters to think of also, have acquired an
irrational sacrosanctity.

There is no doubt that Keynes conceived of the drawing
rights being unconditional. They would be analogous, not to
the facility of getting an overdraft at one's bank, but to having a
deposit at one's bank. This idea is reflected in the wording of
the Articles of Agreement. From the early days drawings by
members have been referred to as 'borrowings'. This suggests
an analogy with getting a loan from a bank. But in the Articles
drawings are nowhere referred to as 'borrowings'; they are
referred to as 'purchases'. This points to the idea that the drawing rights were regarded by the drafters of the Articles as
deposits. If I have a deposit at a British bank and require
dollars, which I am prepared to pay for at the expense of my

deposit, I am not said to 'borrow' those dollars, but to 'purchase' them from my bank. The use of the word 'borrow' in this connecttion is a gross violation of the spirit of the Articles of Agreement – if the wording can be regarded as properly reflecting the spirit – which has had widespread practical effects.

It has been said by Americans, who are in a good position to know, that the Americans, in supporting the creation of the Fund, always assumed that drawing rights would be conditional. It has been put to me that Keynes must have known this. I am confident that at the time of Bretton Woods he did not know that the Americans would take a rigid stand on this – there were many other complex issues that had to be settled there in a hurry. He may have known that this was an American view, but may have assumed that they could be negotiated out of it in due course. It is probable, however, that at the meeting at Savannah (1946), he surmised that they would continue to take a hard line. It is known that he was bitterly mortified by the proceedings at Savannah, and, in his doctor's opinion, his sense of frustration at Savannah was the cause of his death a few weeks later. I found it hard, despite long discussions with many concerned with the conference, to pin-point all the issues that had so worried him. I had excellent evidence for some points. It may be – but I still lack sufficient evidence – that this concept of the conditionality of drawing rights, which would have been violently repugnant to him, was one of the issues, and even the most important one, that 'got him down'.[1]

By this interpretation of the Articles, drawing rights upon the Fund cannot be regarded as true reserves, but only as potential borrowing facilities. Some distinctions must be drawn, however. It will be recalled that members have to furnish gold to the Fund up to 25% of their quotas and their own currencies for the remaining 75%. The first 25% of drawing rights, corresponding to the gold previously subscribed, is known as the 'gold tranche'. It would seem that a member ought to be able to draw out an amount no greater than the gold previously put in without question. The Fund does not allow even this, but lays down that a member's application for this amount will be given 'the overwhelming benefit of the doubt'. Accordingly the

[1] See my *Life of Keynes* (1951), pp. 629–35.

K

gold tranche is usually classified as a true reserve, although it is unlike a true reserve in entailing a repayment obligation.

There is also what is sometimes called a super-gold tranche. If a member's currency has been bought by another member, so that the Fund holding of its currency is less than 75% of its quota, then a drawing can be made by the country absolutely without question up to the difference between the amount of the Fund's current holding of its currency and 75% of its quota. There is no repayment obligation.

The Fund enshrines the principle of the 'adjustable peg'. This has already been discussed. There is a clause to the effect that the Fund shall raise no objection to a change in the par value of a member's currency of up to 10%. This is a once-over right, so that, once a member has deviated from the original parity by 10%, it has lost its right of unilateral action for all time. But larger changes can be effected with the concurrence of the Fund. These must be only such as are justified by what is called a 'fundamental disequilibrium'. There can be disagreement about what a fundamental disequilibrium is. It is laid down that the Fund shall not object to a change 'because of the domestic, social or political policies of the member'. As 'social policy' has rather a wide coverage, this limitation must be difficult to interpret.

Keynes's original proposal was that there should be a unilateral right to revalue by an amount of up to 5% in any one year. At first sight this seems more niggardly than the 10% actually allowed, but was not so in fact, since the 5% right was to be cumulative. This original proposal has perhaps a greater affinity to recent proposals for a 'crawling peg' (cf. above). Larger changes were to be allowed with the concurrence of the Fund.

Keynes doubtless abandoned his original idea at an early stage. It is worth noting the contrast between it and what has actually happened. By the original idea it was supposed that it would be within the province of the national authorities to manage a system of exchange rates, variable within moderate limitations, at their own discretion. These variations should have been sufficient to correct fundamental disequilibria occurring in the normal course of events, especially as the cumulative effect of the variation over a run of years, if the changes were all one way, would be substantial. Only exceptional circumstances could have made the power thus given to national monetary authorities to regulate their affairs insufficient. In exceptional circumstances it would be proper that the matter should be given full consideration by the Fund.

Now one might consider the adjustable peg system that we have as somewhat analogous to the Keynes plan, but with the Fund playing a greater part in supervising changes. That would be so, if movement of the adjustable peg were regarded as the normal regular method of adjusting for disequilibria. One might suppose that such adjustments would have to be fairly frequent, rather like changes in the Bank Rate when these are used to regulate the external balance. But in fact this is not the way in which things have worked out. The opinion appears to have grown up that use of the adjustable peg should be regarded as a remedy of last resort, when other methods have been proved vain.

Issues of the most fundamental kind are involved here. There is no doubt that the British, and it may be that some members of the American Administration also *at that time*, envisaged fairly frequent changes of parity. The traditional gold standard required fairly frequent changes in Bank Rate in order to adjust the external balance, but these changes might be contrary to what would be required by the domestic situation for the proper regulation of the business cycle and the avoidance of unemployment. Therefore it was hoped that by the new system countries would not be compelled by their external situation to vary Bank Rate in a way that was unsuitable domestically. But something has to be done to regulate the external situation, and that not once in a blue moon, but fairly often, just as, under the old system, the Bank Rate had to be altered fairly often. Alter the rate of exchange? I am not saying that this is the right answer. But it is certainly what a great many people had in mind at the time of Bretton Woods.

All has turned out differently. The adjustable peg is not regarded as a regulator to be used as frequently as the Bank Rate was under the gold standard system. We have not got the deliverance from the tyranny of the Bank Rate that was then hoped for. Certainly during the last decade changes in the British Bank Rate have been made inappropriately from the domestic point of view, just as if the country had been on an old-fashioned gold standard.

It is not altogether clear that the adjustable peg does not do more harm than good, except for countries of rather disorderly domestic monetary systems. Everything possible is to be done to avoid its use, such as putting up the Bank Rate. But the presence of this option is never entirely forgotten, and is itself the cause of breaks in confidence and perverse capital flows that would not occur under a regular fixed exchange rate system with no adjustable peg option (cf. above, p. 90). Thus we seem to have the worst of both worlds.

Meanwhile the I.M.F. has not had its intended effect in increasing world reserves. By 1963 these had fallen from 101·7% of world imports in 1937/38 to 45·3% in 1963; if we add in conditional drawing rights on the Fund, we still get only 54·2%. There has been a very large further decline in reserves to 34·6% (and 42%). The main cause of the decline has been the shrinkage in the commodity value of gold, the dollar price of which has not been increased since 1934 although almost all other dollar prices have more than doubled. Thus Keynes's main objective in proposing a body such as the Fund has been frustrated.

2. *International Discussions (1963–67)*

Reference has been made to the Basel agreement for the support of sterling in 1961, and to subsequent international supports. Before proceeding to the discussions about the formal international system, I should mention the far-reaching arrangements that have been made for the mutual support of currencies on the occasions of breaks of confidence in them by means of large short-term credits supplied by other central banks. These have been informal, *ad hoc* and based on the mutual trust of Central Banks. On the whole they have worked remarkably smoothly, and are rightly taken to demonstrate in a striking manner the spirit of co-operation.

These support credits are intended to be used only to look after short-term capital movements and *not* to finance underlying deficits, for which resort must be had to the I.M.F., as re-enforced by the G.A.B.

Mention should also be made of somewhat different and additional methods for supporting the dollar. In the early 'sixties central banks became willing to hold super-normal quantities of dollars, explicitly to help the Americans through their successive deficits. A further refinement was an arrangement by which some of these dollars were converted into medium term U.S. bonds (15 months or more). And in respect of *some* of these (commonly known as Roosa Bonds) the Americans guaranteed their value in terms of the currency of the holding country, in case the dollar might be devalued.

(a) 1963

By 1963 official circles were beginning to admit that there might in the future be a problem in relation to a shortage of world liquidity. The United Kingdom was temporarily in balance, and the downslide that was due to occur in the following year was not foreseen. But there was continuing doubt about the complete soundness of the United Kingdom balance of payments account and her general economic position seemed to the world to be rather weak. Thus, even if the United Kingdom had obligingly run some external deficits, there would be no great disposition on the part of the central banks to add permanently to their holdings of sterling. We have seen that at the time of the Basel agreement (February 1961), the central banks were unwilling to add to their sterling holdings permanently and requested the United Kingdom to transfer her indebtedness to the I.M.F., which was done in July. Sterling had not been contributing much to international liquidity since 1946. The external sterling balances had not increased, which means that their real value had declined considerably and their value in ratio to international trade had declined still more. Thus at this time sterling was not really in the picture as a contributor of additional international liquidity in the years to come.

Meanwhile, there was growing restiveness about the United States deficits. They meant that in effect the rest of the world was transferring real resources to the United States year by year, and it seemed wrong that other countries should thus pay what might be regarded as a tribute to the richest country in the world. In the preceding years, dollars had been making a much larger contribution to international liquidity than gold. Since 1957 the monetary gold stock of countries had been rising at an annual average rate of only 1·3%, while official dollar balances had been rising at 8·7%. Thus, if the United States did what it was strongly pressed to do and terminated or greatly reduced its deficits, there would be a future problem.

The central bankers have never been willing to allow the existence of a present problem. It is probable that this refusal was in main part due to the fear that any such admission could undermine confidence in currencies by suggesting that the price of gold might be raised. The ratio of reserves to international trade had greatly fallen, but the central bankers argued that one need not suppose that there should be a constant ratio of reserves to trade. Their judgement about the desirable level of world reserves may have been mixed up with the dislike on the part of non-Americans of the continuing United States deficits and the failure of the United States to 'adjust' its position. If there were too many reserves in the world this might lead to a similar weakening of discipline all round. Other countries might take a leaf out of the United States's book and run deficits without adopting proper methods of adjustment.

However, the probable occurrence of a problem in the future has been admitted, for some time.

At the meeting of the I.M.F. in Washington in 1963 the problem was referred to the Group of Ten. One may ask why it was not referred to the I.M.F. which was the official international agency for dealing with such matters. The inner core of central bankers lacked complete confidence in the I.M.F. for this purpose. By this time it had a large number of members, many of whom were countries with little experience in international financial problems. It was feared that these other countries might show some failure of responsibility, or at least put forward proposals which, owing to their lack of experience, were not practically viable. The I.M.F. staff consisted of men of high intellectual qualifications and great economic knowledge; but they too were lacking in experience of the day-by-day workings of international finance. The inner core of central bankers and officials wanted to retain consideration of these all-important matters in their own hands.

This development has an interesting relation to the ideas of

Keynes for the I.M.F. His proposal was that the board of management, which would have responsibility for the major decisions of the Fund, should not consist of full-time directors, but, on the contrary, should consist of the top authorities in each country, such as Finance Ministers and Heads of central banks, who would meet together every so often and themselves decide what had to be decided. The work of the permanent personnel of the Fund would be confined to the routine matters of day-to-day business. He was deeply grieved that his ideas on this topic were not adopted and that it was decided to have Executive Directors on permanent duty.

It is a little irony of history that the kind of mechanism that Keynes wanted to have for the Fund has actually been operated by the Group of Ten. What are known as the 'Deputies' are not in permanent session, but meet from time to time. They consist of top officials in the countries concerned. We have the result that what might be called the Governing Mind of the Group of Ten consists of men of higher standing and influence than those who compose the Executive Directors of the I.M.F. Thus, when it came to the need to reach decisions on the grave matters that have been under discussion since 1963, it was the Keynes type of mechanism, and not the type of mechanism wished on to the I.M.F. by the Americans, that operated. In retrospect accordingly it looks as if Keynes was right in his ideas about what sort of mechanism was needed, if the International Monetary Fund were to function effectively as an agency capable of important decisions, such as would be required if it were to play the kind of role in world monetary affairs that a central bank plays in national monetary affairs. This is not to imply that Keynes thought that the I.M.F. should be a 'world central bank' in the technical sense; but he did think of it as an agency which would have to take crucial decisions and strike out on new lines from time to time.

Human affairs somehow sort themselves out. When it came to the question of a big new development being possibly required, then it seemed essential that the mode of operation should be adapted to this. Instead of the Executive Directors of the Fund putting their heads together and reporting back to the top authorities in various countries what they had decided and what they wanted confirmed, the top authorities in the different countries took the matter into their own hands and devoted their own time to the consideration of what should be done.

This may be important for the future. It could happen that a scheme will be adopted on lines shortly to be described, which will work automatically and need no further policy decisions on the part of the inner core of wise heads. But the scheme proposed at Rio (see below) does not look quite like that. In its present form it will require important policy decisions from time to time. And who will make the decisions? Will it be the Executive Directors of the I.M.F.? The unwillingness of some to leave the last word to them has already been noted. Or will it be the Group of Ten?

On first appearance it looks as if someone who approves of Keynes's ideas should be quite happy that such issues should be left to the Group of Ten. But the matter is not quite so simple. The Group of Ten is an exclusive body, and its membership is somewhat fortuitous, springing, presumably, from the personal initiative of Per Jacobsson in 1961. The idea that it should rule the roost in world affairs from now onwards is not altogether satisfactory. The I.M.F. itself should rule the roost. But if it is really to fulfil that function, its mode of operation probably ought to be amended on the lines suggested by Keynes originally.

(b) To 1964

The Group of Ten presented a report before the annual meeting of the I.M.F. at Tokyo in 1964, consisting of a brief foreword by the Ministers and an 'annexe' by the Deputies. The report is a well-considered document, somewhat anodyne in tone, and without positive recommendations for action.

The Ministers, in their foreword, reaffirm their 'conviction' that 'a structure, based, as the present is, on fixed exchange rates and the established price of gold, has proved its value as a foundation on which to build for the future'. This 'conviction' is not deemed to need the support of analysis or argument, and the studies of the Deputies were made subject to these limitations. This is in itself profoundly unsatisfactory. The same limitation still continues (1968). No recommendations for some new system of international liquidity can be deemed valid until the merits of a rise in the price of gold and of flexible exchange rates have been fully considered. Such changes in our system might be effected either with or without the provision of an additional medium of liquidity of the kind that was discussed in the following years. If one is planning, not for two or three years but, hopefully, for twenty or fifty years, one cannot dismiss out of hand two recipes of major importance, raising the price of gold and introducing flexible exchange rates, one or other or both of which have recommended themselves to many minds. Furthermore, the merits or demerits of a scheme for a new medium of international liquidity will appear very different if that scheme is envisaged as being put into operation along with one or other of the aforementioned changes. The Ministers (and Governors) have not sufficient authority for the world to accept their 'conviction' without a statement of the reasons for that 'conviction' and the presentation of well-considered arguments against the many distinguished persons who have taken the opposite view.

The real reason why the Ministers did not call upon the Deputies to make a study in depth of these matters is quite simple. They feared that, if it were known that they were being given serious consideration, and that the price of gold might be altered, or the fixed exchange rates made flexible, this could give rise to vast movements of funds from precautionary or speculative motives, which could be disruptive of the existing system, in advance of a decision about what the new system should be. But the matter cannot be left there. If the world would indeed get on much better with gold at a higher price and/or exchange rates flexible, it is wrong that it should be denied the opportunity of enjoying this improvement, merely because the subject is too delicate to be discussed.

It is only fair to allow that there is a practical difficulty. The Ministers were doubtless right in thinking that discussion of the forbidden subject might lead to a breakdown of confidence in some currencies and disruptive movements of funds. It is to be noted, however, that the squeamish reticence of the Ministers, etc., has not prevented breakdowns in confidence in the following years, including large runs on sterling and on the dollar. Surely some expedient could have been devised, and can still be devised, to make discussion possible. Systems of mutual support for currencies already exist, to meet short-term movements of capital. What would be needed would be to enlarge the whole structure of mutual support, so that it was sufficient to look after still the greater 'runs' that might result from the discussion of the tabooed subjects. It may be said that these mutual supports might have to be on a heroic scale. But why not? What one country loses another will gain. Or, if there is a trek into gold, the extended holdings of foreign currencies due to these support operations will take the place of the gold thus lost to the monetary system. Actually the gold would probably come back again in due course and thus allow a tailoring down of the foreign currency holdings.

I would myself favour a large rise in the price of gold, say a doubling, as an expedient that could be put into effect right away, would cause a great easement, and give time for a deeper consideration – and a much deeper consideration is required than anything that we have yet had, of what would be the 'rational' basis of a world paper money system. In order to give support to the idea that this increase in the official price of gold was a once-over adjustment to the effects of the Second World War, one might agree upon, not a doubling of the dollar price, but a rise of the dollar price equal to the average rise in all other dollar prices since 1934. The rise in the price of gold could not possibly do any harm; and it could achieve in a very simple way an increased international liquidity, which is presumably desired. Objections have been raised on the grounds of equity since it would bring disproportionate benefit to those countries which happen to keep a high proportion of their reserves in the form of gold. This inequity would not be as great as is sometimes represented, since countries holding a high proportion of gold in their reserves have foregone the benefit of interest which the others have enjoyed. It could easily be rectified by a 'reshuffle' of the profit due to gold re-valuation among nations in proportion to the sizes of their reserves. But it is most unlikely that such a reshuffle would be agreed to by all countries, since it would injure the selfish interests of some. So long as this attitude continues, we are unlikely to get agreement for a 'rational' world monetary system.

The idea of flexible exchange rates has wide support, especially in academic circles. For reasons stated elsewhere I share the view of the bankers, who see far greater practical difficulties in such a system than the academics are prepared to allow. None the less I, on my side, am prepared to allow that, if and when means can be found for dealing with the said practical difficulties, it may in the end be the best system. It could accommodate, without imposing strains, the differences between the maximum rates of technical progress in practice achievable as between different countries, or, maybe, as between different regional groups of countries. But a principal condition would be that there must be a consensus about the underlying principles determining equilibrium rates; and also a consensus about how to deal with the practical difficulties. We are still far indeed removed from any such consensus, and a vast amount of thinking has still got to be done, both by theorists and practical men, before such a consensus can be obtained. We are all at sixes and sevens. But this whole problem should be actively discussed in the twenty years ahead; it is quite intolerable that discussion about flexible rates should be inhibited in official circles. Therefore an adequate shield – a far larger one than exists at present – is required against disturbances due to ephemeral movements of funds under precautionary and speculative influences.

The Ministers at this stage recognised that the continuing growth of world trade and payments was likely to entail a need for larger international liquidity in future. They added that 'this need may be met by an extension of credit facilities and in the longer run may possibly call for some new form of reserve asset'. Following the advice of the Deputies, they proposed the setting up of a study group to consider modes of creating a new reserve asset. This was done and the study group reported a year later. They also referred the question of the 'adjustment' process to Working Party No. 3 of the Economic Policy Committee of the O.E.C.D. Reference has already been made to the well-considered, but inconclusive, Report of that Working Party (1966).

They referred to 'multilateral surveillance' in relation to the financing of payments disequilibria. The United Kingdom has been subject to much multilateral surveillance in recent years, and it cannot be said that this has always, or even usually, led to recommendations conducive to the good health of the British economy. Before multilateral surveillance can become a useful institution, we need greater agreement on underlying principles.

The Ministers favoured a moderate increase in Fund quotas, which was subsequently put into effect (25%). The (rather brief) report of the Deputies contained a valuable description of the existing system and provides useful monetary statistics. It also called upon countries to furnish supplementary statistics, in addition to those published, for the guidance of the Bank for International Settlements and Working Party No. 3 of the O.E.C.D.

As regards the creation of additional reserve assets, the Deputies said that the choice was between a new type of asset on the one hand, and, on the other, the acceptance of gold tranches, or similar claims on the International Monetary Fund, as a form of international reserve, the volume of which could, if necessary, be enlarged to meet an agreed need.

Reference was made to the various inter-central bank short-term facilities (swaps, Roosa bonds, *ad hoc* support operations, etc.). There is also a reference to the Euro-currency market (see below, pp. 319–28), which includes a note of warning. There is a section on the possibilities of a long-term loan for dealing with a monetary disequilibrium. The implicit reference in this was doubtless to the United Kingdom. There is recurrent talk about the possibility of helping the United Kingdom to fund some of its foreign-held sterling balances. Such a funding would have been highly appropriate in 1946, when these balances were undoubtedly excessive and redundant to need. It is still (1968) not certain whether they were really redundant to need before the question of sterling devaluation came into the foreground. It is impossible to determine this matter until the United Kingdom brings its current and long-term capital account into balance. Reference will be made below to a recent measure for strengthening the position of some sterling balances.

(c) To 1965

The study group for considering possible types of new reserve asset was in due course set up, under the chairmanship of S. Ossola. It submitted a somewhat lengthier report before the I.M.F. meeting in 1965. It was an able document, as was to be expected. Three features may be noted. It may be added that, if these are to be regretted, the fault does not necessarily lie with the study group.

1. Differences of opinion stand out much more starkly in the Ossola Report than they do in the 1964 report of the Deputies. This is absolutely proper for the work of a sub-committee.

Unfortunately the differences are veiled in anonymity. It may be that those 'in the know' were able to identify countries subscribing to the various shades of difference. It is impossible, however, even for a well-informed outside reader to make the identification in all cases. While the anonymity may be regarded as diplomatic and genteel, there are reasons of substance against it. Positions taken are often influenced both by the different circumstances and the different viewpoints prevailing in different countries. It is expedient that, in assessing the weight and value of a given line taken, we should know the background circumstances and ideology of the member taking that line. Such knowledge could be important for a judgement on whether the line taken was sensible or not. It would be foolish to ignore the fact that different countries do have different circumstances and ideologies, and an ideal plan would have to take account of these. The reader who wants to form a considered judgement on a viewpoint set out needs to be able to relate it to the circumstances and ideology of the member concerned. It is unlikely that we shall get the final solution unless, not only those 'in the know', but other wiseheads also, can bring their thinking to bear upon the subject. This cannot be done without full revelation.

It may have been thought that, if the names of countries advocating or opposing something were mentioned, readers would align themselves according to their prejudices about each particular country. If this were fully valid, it would imply a criticism of the whole democratic process. The questions involved are most important matters for human welfare. There may be something in this idea, but not much. The majority of those well educated enough to read the Ossola Report are not likely to be the victims of narrow-minded prejudice. At least, so we hope.

2. The report has a somewhat scholastic form, with its classification of possibilities, and its arrangements and rearrangements into various orders of viewpoints taken. This was probably the best way of handling the matters in a report not destined to lead on to agreed conclusions.

3. The report is tortured both in its substance and in its language. The proposals considered are all of a complicated kind. One may contrast the complexity of the alternative plans with the great simplicity of the gold standard. With all its faults upon it, it had that outstanding merit. It is hard to believe that, in the case of something so very fundamental as the money that the whole world has to use, a very tortured scheme will have much longevity.

Some of the language is in the jargon of the inner circle of the Group of Ten and is not likely to be intelligible to those outside it. One of the alternative schemes is for 'Collective Reserve Units' (C.R.U.s). (The name C.R.U. is clearly a hang-over from Mr Bernstein's proposal in which, however, the 'C' stood for Composite.) It is assumed that the C.R.U. scheme would be available to, and managed by, a limited group of countries only, that the participating countries would maintain constant ratios of their C.R.U. holdings to their gold holdings (if necessary by 'reshuffling') and that voting would be by unanimity. One may perhaps infer that France was the originator of this scheme.

There is no reason, however, why a scheme of this general kind should necessarily have the attributes just listed. One ought to discuss such a scheme in a *general* way without being compelled to associate it with attributes that are not essential to its nature. It is understood that the sub-committee felt itself to be bound to consider various schemes in the form in which they were actually put up, and to be debarred from twisting them around and considering them without certain proposed attributes and with the addition of others. This seems a pity.

The C.R.U. scheme was to be managed outside the Fund. Schemes were also proposed that were to be in the sphere of the Fund's duties but with their management confined to a limited group within it. The whole question of whether the new reserve asset was to be of universal application or confined to a group was one of the main subjects at issue in the study group's deliberations.

The study group touches on a proposal, associated above all with the name of Mr Max Stamp, by which the new units would come into circulation via the World Bank, which would make them available *gratis* to less developed countries; these in turn would use them to buy capital goods from the industrial countries. It cautiously lays down that 'this technique would apply to only a modest fraction of the total reserves to be created'. In conclusion it states that 'the idea of combining asset creation with development finance was not widely favoured'.

There was an extensive setting out of pros and cons but no conclusion.

(d) To 1966

Thus two years had passed by the time that the report of the Ossola sub-committee was presented (1965), and an agreed-upon plan seemed to be no nearer attainment. There was growing impatience. Meanwhile the American deficits had not terminated, and the British had run into quite a formidable deficit (in 1964).

It was hoped at the 1965 meeting that a step forward had been taken there. The Group of Ten was asked to try to discover if there was an area of agreement for a new plan. It was understood at the time that this project would involve negotiation. If each country stood firmly in its own opinion, there would probably be no area of agreement at all; so the idea was that there might be some mutual concessions in order to create such an 'area'. The Americans, for instance, might give way on a point they favoured in return for the French giving way on some other point, and so on.

This step forward was made possible by the use of the expression 'contingency planning'; a country, which saw no need at all for any scheme of the kind under consideration, could yet be party to the formulation of such a scheme, provided it was understood that this planning was for a contingency only and for a contingency that might never arise.

But during the year it transpired that the French were not prepared to co-operate even in 'contingency planning'. The report presented on 25 August 1966 before the annual meeting of the I.M.F. states (p. 10) that

this member [i.e. France] considers that the drafting of an international agreement for the creation of reserves would, in present circumstances, give rise to an irresistible temptation to activate the agreement prematurely. He feels that the prevailing tendencies in both reserve currency countries and developing countries make it unlikely that the activation of an agreed scheme could in practice be deferred until a real need for additional reserves arose.

This member considers that the present difficulties of the international monetary system are due, not to the likelihood of a shortage of reserves in the near future, but to the persistent imbalances of the reserve currency countries ... Far from helping to reinforce confidence, contingency planning at this stage might further delay necessary adjustments and thus aggravate the insecurity and instability of international payments.

The 1966 report of the deputies of the Group of Ten went over the familiar ground and stated the advantages and disadvantages of various types of proposal. Five possible schemes were in fact presented, without, of course, the agreement of France, but these were set out with great brevity (less than a page each) and were extremely tortured.

An interesting point is to be found in the communiqué of the Ministers of the Group of Ten which prefaces the report of the Deputies. It is there stated that there should be a procedure whereby proposals for reserve creation would be considered both by the limited group (which would be something like the Group of Ten) and by the Fund. This in fact proposes a sort of bicameral constitution with the Fund as Lower House, and the Group of Ten as Second Chamber with veto power.

Matters thus having seemingly come to a standstill, it was proposed that the Deputies of the Group of Ten should enter into discussion with the Executive Directors of the International Monetary Fund. Hitherto, the Group of Ten had taken only the Managing Director of the Fund into consultation. The majority of well-informed persons were sceptical about this device. They envisaged a large amount of time-wasting, with the Deputies of the Group of Ten having to explain the intricacies of the problems and the disagreements of the last three years at large meetings. For quite some time it was thought that nothing could possibly come out of all this; but then, as the year wore on, before the forthcoming meeting of the I.M.F. at Rio de Janiero (September 1967), there was an insensible change of attitude. Impatience rose once more. Mr Callaghan, who was Chairman of the Ministers of the Group of Ten, may have put on some effective pressure. At the final meeting of the Deputies in Paris in June, there was still little hope that they could scratch together formulae that would find favour with all the Ministers. Later there was a meeting of the Ministers themselves in July in London. The matter again seemed hopeless; but at the eleventh hour some fresh ideas were mooted, which might conceivably be worked into acceptable form. The Deputies were asked to do their best in preparation for a final meeting in London on 26 August, to which the Ministers would be called back from their holidays. The matter still seemed uncertain, but on 26 August agreement was reached at long last in the late hours of an arduous day's session. It had taken four years to achieve this.

3. Rio de Janeiro (1967)

The fact that it was possible to present an agreed scheme at Rio (1967) was the subject of much rejoicing; speeches of welcome were made. It was said, rightly, that, although the plan might seem somewhat limited in scope, it could be made the basis of much larger developments as the years proceeded, and that a more extensive plan could gradually be evolved as the needs of the world became plain.

It was widely recognised, however, that underlying differences remained; the scheme was in some sense a 'papering over'. While these differences might not matter too much in relation to a simple and almost automatic system, they will inevitably be a serious drawback in the case of one that depends on the discretion and judgement of those who run it, and requires fresh fundamental policy decisions at intervals which might in fact be quite frequent. Further to this, the date of activation of the scheme and the amount of accommodation to be provided under it still (May 1969) remain unsettled.

On the whole, the points of dispute which had bedevilled the discussions over four years had been settled in a satisfactory way. Five points may be mentioned:

1. The basic problem had been in what way to supplement means of international settlement in the face of the diminishing role of gold, and the fact that it was believed, and by some hoped, that foreign-held dollar and sterling balances would not make any substantial additional contribution to the means of settlement in the years ahead. One important point at issue was whether the supplement to existing means should consist mainly of an extension of credit facilities or of a newly created 'reserve unit' in the form of a sort of international paper money, which, when issued, would pass into the ownership of the various countries and thus constitute an addition to 'owned reserves'. The parties to the final agreement changed sides during the course of the prolonged discussions, the Anglo-Saxon Group being inclined in the early stages to favour credit facilities, while the continentals sought for an addition to owned reserves. It appears that in the later stages these positions were reversed.

The medium that has long been provided by the I.M.F. is known as a 'Drawing Right'. If this had been usable without negotiations or conditions, as Keynes originally supposed, and as has been explained, it might have been regarded as an 'owned reserve' in the full sense, just as a citizen regards a deposit at his bank as his 'own'. In fact the I.M.F. insisted that, apart from the gold tranches, these were not drawable on without negotiations. In these circumstances they fall under the category of credit facilities.

The fact that the new instruments are called Special Drawing Rights might suggest that they belong to the same category. But this is deceptive, since the new rights are to be freely usable without conditions or negotiations. Their designation was probably a terminological concession to the opposite point of view.

This outcome is eminently satisfactory. The owned reserves in the form of Special Drawing Rights on the I.M.F. will exist concurrently with the old-type of Drawing Rights, which will continue to belong to the category of credit facilities.

2. When one obtains a credit facility, e.g. an overdraft facility at one's bank, one has to repay in due course; when one uses one's own deposit, one can 'reconstitute' it at a later date, but only if one wishes, according to the circumstances of the case. There is some vestige in the scheme of the idea of a repay-

ment obligation, but this plays a minor role in fact. To illustrate the survival of differences of outlook, it may be noted that Herr Schiller, the German representative at Rio, stated there that the scheme was based on the principle of repayability. It is difficult to interpret the scheme in this sense.

In the outline plan the word 'reconstitution' was used of the vestige of repayability that remains in the scheme. This was probably a terminological concession in a reverse direction to the one just cited. It suggests rebuilding one's own deposit position, rather than repaying a debt.

The scheme provides that the average amount of the S.D.R.s used by a country over a five-year period must not exceed 70% of the total amount of those assigned to the country; it must accordingly be vigilant to reconstitute its holding in such a way as to bring down the average to 70% for the period as a whole. Thus if a country has used 100% of the S.D.R.s assigned to it for the first three and a half years of the five-year period, it would have to reconstitute fully at the end of the three and a half years, so as to bring its average use during the five years as a whole down to 70%. Any country will probably think it wise never to use more than brings its average use up to date to 70%, and then it will have no repayment obligation. In fact, the plan may best be thought of as providing owned reserves up to an amount equal to 70% of the S.D.R.s assigned. One might think that it would have been simpler to assign only 70% of the amount of S.D.R.s to be decided upon, whatever that may be, and thus eliminate all repayment obligation; a simpler plan is better. But this would not have suited the ideology of those who wish to insist that there is a repayment obligation implicit in the scheme (cf. Herr Schiller).

3. It has already been explained how the I.M.F. is always in principle insolvent in the event of the international balance being lop-sided, in the sense that the sum total of the quotas of the credit countries can fall short of the sum total of the quotas of the countries that happen temporarily to be in debit, assuming that the 'scarce currency clause' is a dead letter, and how the General Arrangements to Borrow were introduced as a make-shift device to overcome this difficulty. The new plan does not go to the full length of the original Keynes plan for Bancor, by which Bancor would have to be accepted as legal

tender in unlimited amounts. There is still a limit to the amount of payment by way of S.D.R.s that creditor countries are bound to accept; but the plan is more generous than that of the I.M.F. whereby creditors are obliged to accept payments via the I.M.F. machinery only up to the amount of their quotas. Under the Rio plan they are obliged to accept in payment S.D.R.s up to *twice* the amount assigned to them to date. This is not a logical solution of the problem, but it may well be a sufficiently good pragmatic solution. It was probably decided that a world balance of payments position is not likely to become so very lop-sided that the issues of S.D.R.s to the countries in debit exceed twice the issues of S.D.R.s to the countries in credit. Thus it is to be hoped that the S.D.R. scheme will be able to remain quite independent of any such plan as the G.A.B., to which exception may be taken. It is to be noted that this limitation on the obligation of countries to receive S.D.R.s in payment shows that gold is still held in higher esteem than S.D.R.s (cf. page 271).

4. The benefits and responsibilities accruing under the new scheme are to be universal; thus the stubborn resistance of those who wished to confine these to a limited group was eventually overcome. Doubtless the I.M.F. played its part in bringing about this happy result. And behind the I.M.F. was world opinion. Whatever a limited group may do among themselves for mutual support on an *ad hoc* basis, it would not have been feasible to secure the passage of a formal scheme, declared to be an important step forward in international monetary arrangements and requiring ratification by legislatures, if the benefits of this scheme were to be confined to a limited group of rich countries.

5. It will be recalled that of the proposals classified in the Ossola Report, one was for the creation of new reserve units through an agency right outside the I.M.F., while another proposed that the scheme, although administered under the I.M.F. umbrella, should be kept quite separate from the general I.M.F. organisation and have its own special decision-making procedures. Even as late as 1966 the Ministers were still proposing a bi-cameral constitution. All this has now been swept away; responsibility for the administration of the proposed scheme will be placed fairly and squarely on the general

authorities (Governors and Executive Directors) of the I.M.F. The operations under the scheme will be kept separate from other I.M.F. operations through the existence of separate accounts.

So far so good. There remain outstanding questions (May 1969) about ratification, the date of activation and the amounts of S.D.R.s to be issued.

It is officially hoped that ratification by the various legislatures will be effected at an early date. Strong differences of opinion remain about the appropriate date for the activation of the scheme, i.e. the initial issue of S.D.R.s. While the authorities, and probably the main mass of opinion, are favourable to early ratification, doubt about the wisdom of this could be raised. Prior to ratification, a decision about the date of activation could be embodied in the 'amendment' that has to be ratified; there would be nothing abnormal in such a procedure. It is true that when the I.M.F. itself was ratified no date for activation was inserted in the articles. But the position in that regard was entirely different; everyone then assumed and hoped that the I.M.F. would be activated on the earliest date practically feasible. This is not so in relation to the S.D.R. scheme. There are some who will seek to impose delays before it is activated.

Before the new scheme is ratified, an 80% majority in the Fund would suffice to determine the date of the activation. But once the amendment is ratified, an 85% majority will be required to determine the date of activation. Thus ratification in advance of any date of activation being inserted, will give greater power to those who want to delay activation.[1]

There is a further point about voting that needs clearing up, and ought really to be cleared up in very precise terms before ratification. For such an important decision as the date of activation of the new scheme, would the E.E.C. countries act

[1] The author, when testifying to the relevant sub-committee of the Joint Economic Committee of Congress (22 November 1967), ventured to use an expression that was reminiscent of a famous American slogan, when the British were seeking to impose new taxes on the American 'colonies', namely 'no ratification without activation'. More precisely, but less epigrammatically, this should have been, 'no ratification without the date of activation being embodied in the amendment'.

collectively or in accordance with the individual choice of each one? At the meeting of the Group of Ten in Stockholm (April 1968), when the finished draft of the scheme agreed to at Rio was presented by the I.M.F. to the Group of Ten, the *latter* procedure was adopted, France dissenting while the other countries agreed. It is not possible to build much on this. In due course the E.E.C. may decide to vote as a collective unit on such matters. We then go over to the voting machinery within the E.E.C. itself. Would a unanimity rule be required? In this case one member of the E.E.C. could effectively block activation, or some further development, of the scheme, even if the whole of the rest of the world wanted it. It is true that under the existing arrangements the United States could block any scheme requiring an 80% majority. Maybe this ought to be changed. But the United States remains in a position in which the rest of the world would not wish to flout it on a very important matter relating to the international monetary system. The same cannot be said of each separate country in the E.E.C. This is another reason for a delay in ratification, which puts the E.E.C. group into a power position, until it is made crystal clear that the E.E.C. will not vote collectively about activation (and subsequent crucial decisions), or, at least, that, if it does vote collectively, this will be based on a well-defined majority rule within the E.E.C., and not on unanimity there.

We may go over to the question of activation. At the Rio meeting M. Debré, the French Minister, stated categorically that the French were agreeing to the scheme only on three conditions. These were: (1) that there must be a collective agreement that an actual shortage of international liquidity obtained; (2) that there must be an improvement in the adjustment process by which countries rectified imbalances of payments; (3) that the external deficits of the reserve currency countries, viz. the United States and the United Kingdom, should be terminated. Even at Rio, and still more since developments subsequent to Rio, the third of these conditions has seemed likely to involve considerable delay before activation.[1] But the first two conditions are not easy ones either. 'Collective' agreement on the first point presumably covers at least the

---

[1] It is to be noted that the U.S. external 'surplus' of $156 m. in 1968 was due to window-dressing. The true U.S. balance in that year was a deficit of $2.144 billion.

industrial powers. This is one of the matters on which great differences of opinion have existed and continue to exist between them. On the second point also, there remain profound differences of opinion, namely about what the appropriate adjustment processes are. Thus, in this respect, the position is not satisfactory. The German Finance Minister also stipulated that the deficits of the reserve currency countries must be reduced.

Reasons for delay have been put more moderately by others. It has been stated that the scheme cannot be activated as long as existing uncertainties remain. These have been intensified in 1968.

As of 1969 the uncertainties in question may be classified under three heads. The reference is to the five-year period following activation. It is proposed that the initial decision to activate would state how many S.D.R.s were to be issued in each of the five following years, but this would be subject to revision in the course of those years.

1. It is uncertain how much gold will come into official monetary holdings in the next five years.

2. It is uncertain how many dollars will be added to the official external holdings in that period.

3. It is uncertain how large the structural changes, causing changes in international balances of payments, will be during the five-year period.

The third of the foregoing grounds for delay is not valid. There is not likely to be any year in the foreseeable future in which uncertainties about future structural changes in the following five years will be any less than they are at present. It is an illusion to suppose that, whereas uncertainties on this head are very great now, all will become clear and plain-sailing within the foreseeable future. This third argument would lie against an immediate activation at *any* future date.

The first two grounds for delay could have been modified by a technical change in the scheme, and it is difficult to see why the Group of Ten, who pondered on it for so long, did not propose it. The scheme at present stipulates that X units of S.D.R.s shall be issued in each of the five years following activation, subject to revision during the course of those years.

In place of that, one might decide that world monetary reserves should be increased by X units each year for five years, and that an amount of S.D.R.s should be issued each year equal to X minus the number of units of gold that had accrued to official stocks in the preceding year (or plus any depletion in official gold stocks) and minus any accretions of dollars or sterling during that year (or plus any depletions). This would fully eliminate the first two uncertainties referred to.

While no official decision had been reached at Rio (or Stockholm) about the amount of issue, it was said in the corridors that some such sum as $1 billion worth per annum, or $2 billion worth, were in contemplation, probably with a preference for the former amount. On the face of it, this looks inadequate. We may assume that there are no further accretions of dollar holdings; but, if there were, the amount could be modified in accordance with the formula suggested above. Gold accretions have played a very small part in recent years. At the end of 1962, the gold holdings of countries listed in the I.M.F. statistics amounted to $39,280 million, and at the end of 1967 to $39,480 million. This is a very minute increase over a five-year period. If, instead, we include all official holdings of gold (i.e. including I.M.F., B.I.S., etc.), we find an increase from $41,480 million to $41,580 million. Further to this, we note that the United States holding of gold fell by $1,362 million in the first quarter of 1968, and most of this is not likely to have gone into other official holdings.

Between 1962 and 1968, the dollar value of world imports rose from $132,400 million to $224,800 million, an average annual rate of increase of 9·2%. Only about 1% per annum is to be attributable to price increase.

At the end of 1967 the total reserve of countries stood at $73,405 million. Thus an issuance of $1 billion worth of S.D.R.s per annum would increase total reserves only by 1·35% per annum, and an issuance of $2 billions only by 2·7% per annum. This must be compared with the 9·2% increase in the value of international trade, or about 8% increase in volume. International investment, to meet chance variations in which reserves are also required, has been growing strongly too.

Further to this, there is the question of the adequacy of the present amount of reserves. This has been a matter tabooed from discussion for reasons stated in an earlier section. In 1937–38 – the average of the two years has been taken as the world went into recession in the second of these years – world reserves were equal to 107% of world imports; in 1967 they stood at 34·8% only. Experts argue that the pre-war period may not furnish a good yardstick. It is to be stressed that no experts at that time held the reserves to be redundant; and it was not a period of inflation. Keynes asked for an international issue of gold notes in 1933. It is true that the position was somewhat eased by the devaluation of the dollar in 1933–34, but not, in the judgement of any responsible authority, to such an extent as to create a redundancy of reserves. It is further argued that there is no principle requiring reserves to move in proportion to turnover. This may have some validity if we are striving to get a very precise proportion. But there must be some truth in the idea of a rough proportion of reserves to trade; otherwise a very large country would not need any more reserve than a very small one. Furthermore, a reduction of the proportion to less than one-third is a very *spectacular* event, and gives a *prima facie* ground for thinking reserves now inadequate. Indeed, one may hold that it is not surprising, in view of this event, that the international machinery for settlement is creaking, as it notoriously is.

It is often argued, quite correctly, that the shortage of reserves in particular countries is no sign of world shortage. Some countries that have been running deficits must expect, on any system, to have a period of temporary shortage. The implication of this argument is that the present shortages in some countries are offset by surpluses in others, and it is true that some countries may at present be deemed to have some redundancy of reserves. But in this case, as in others, it is expedient to look at *quantities*. Presumably the United States and the United Kingdom will, over the years, seek to achieve surpluses in order to make their reserve positions more comfortable. We may suppose, that, to be comfortable, the United States would like to see an extra $10 billion in its reserve, while the United Kingdom might like to see an extra $7 billion. (It is not always remembered that United Kingdom merchandise trade is still running at about half the level of United States merchandise trade.) Japan is also short of reserves, having about $2 billion worth against

imports worth about $12 billion a year. Canada has a reserve
of about $2·2 billion against about $11 billion worth of imports.
The total reserves of Germany, France and Italy in March 1968
were as follows:

Million Dollars' Worth of Reserves

France	6,906
Germany	8,539
Italy	5,298
Total	20,743

If these reserves fell to zero, which is a *fantastic* hypothesis,
there still would not be enough reserves released to render the
United States, the United Kingdom, Japan and Canada all
comfortable. This seems to settle the issue.

4. Devaluation of Sterling (1967)

The devaluation of sterling in November 1967, which was described in Chapter 10, Section 5, from the British point of view,
followed rather quickly on the heels of the agreement for
Special Drawing Rights at Rio. It was there doubtless hoped
that sufficiently calm water would prevail in the international
monetary scene until the time was ripe to activate the Special
Drawing Rights plan. From the point of view of operators in
the international capital market, that plan still seemed rather
remote. Furthermore, it was clearly understood by all parties,
by its ardent advocates as well as by those more doubtful, that
the new facilities were not intended for use by the United States
or the United Kingdom to finance their under-lying deficits,
the more gloomy continuing to hold that they should not be
made available until those deficits were terminated.

Meanwhile the United Kingdom ran into special troubles in
1967, which have already been described. The deficit in the
balance of payments increased by consequence, contrary to the
hopes and promises of the British authorities. It is to be noted,
however, that the deficit on current account was not very large.
If two adjustments are made, it stood at only £158,000,000,
which is about the same as the average deficit in the preceding

three years. (The actual current account deficit in 1967 was £404,000,000.)

One adjustment would be to credit the export account with those exports that were held back in the last quarter of the year owing to the dock strikes. This amount may be put at about £150,000,000. The other adjustment would be in relation to the payments for United States military aircraft, which amounted to £98,000,000 in 1967, an upward jump of over £50,000,000. These imports are financed on credit. While they clearly should not be excluded altogether, since in the long run the credits will have to be repaid, there is something to be said for providing a separate account, as the British do in some of their publications, showing the balance free of this item. If the advisers to international corporations had a somewhat larger perspective, they might have judged that there was nothing especially wrong with the British position in 1967, although the United Kingdom had had tiresome knocks in respect of Suez and Rhodesia. But the advisers did not take this view.

The chain of events terminating in the devaluation has already been described. Its effect was not confined to the British economy or to the status of sterling. It seemed to many to put the dollar into the first line of defence, since the American deficits were continuing unabated. This led to the major crisis of March 1968, which is described in the next section.

It also had a more far-reaching effect – it undermined confidence in the principal currencies generally. If the British, with their great banking traditions and still powerful international connections, could be knocked off their perch by dockers' strikes and some other untoward events which, in the overall position, were minor, one must expect that other currencies also, even of countries eminent enough to be members of the Group of Ten, might be jeopardised by events which, on the long haul, ought not to be considered of very great importance. Thus student and other disturbances in France, in May and June, led to a crisis of the French franc in November 1968, despite the fact that the French had for a long time had a very massive reserve, sufficient to cover the losses due to the disturbances, and that the recovery from them seemed to be proceeding well. These matters will be discussed in Section 6 (below).

5. *Two-tier Gold* (*1968*)

In 1934 it was made illegal for United States citizens, other than goldsmiths, etc., to hold bar gold. Consequently they were no longer able to obtain gold at will in exchange for a dollar bill. People of an old-fashioned cast of mind said that the dollar had been made 'inconvertible', but the majority did not adopt this linguistic usage, since the American authorities were still willing to give gold on demand in unlimited quantities in exchange for dollars held by the monetary authorities of foreign countries. This was generally held to entitle the dollar still to be called convertible. Most other countries that at that time remained on the gold standard still gave citizens the right of converting their notes into gold. The maintenance by arbitrage of fixed exchange rates between the currencies of these countries and the dollar kept the market price of gold, in terms of the dollars, fixed at the same level as the official dollar price of gold, as it was established in February 1934 after the devaluations of President Roosevelt. The willingness of the Americans to convert dollars, held by other central banks into gold at a fixed rate, would not have sustained the gold value of the dollar in free markets had it not been for arbitrage undertaken by members of other gold standard countries.

During the war most currencies became inconvertible and remained so for some time after it. In this period the market price of gold in terms of the dollar, as fixed in places like Beirut, Cairo and Macao, rose far above the official price.

This situation was terminated by the reopening of the gold bullion market in London in April 1954. The British had a fixed gold value for the pound established with the International Monetary Fund, and, accordingly, the British authorities operated to ensure that the sterling price of gold was kept within the proper margins of its official parity by dealing in the market. Prices in other markets in due course fell into line with the London price, except in countries like India, where the import of gold was illegal and its price continued to stand at a premium. The fixing of the sterling market price of gold in London, combined with the arrangement by which the sterling/dollar exchange rate was kept within the prescribed limits, ensured that the dollar market price of gold also remained fixed.

In 1954 sterling had not yet become convertible. The fixed sterling price of gold, referred to above, was the price in terms of official sterling. Holders of transferable account sterling could get gold for it only at a premium, which varied with the discount on transferable account sterling compared with official sterling. In February 1955 the British authorities began intervening in the transferable account market, to keep the discount on transferable sterling within about 1% of official sterling. In December 1958 all sterling was made officially convertible and transferable account sterling was abolished.

The new system worked smoothly for a time, but in the autumn of 1960 a crisis arose. The cause of this was the continuance of heavy deficits in the United States balance of payments for more than two years. There were some who thought that, as a result of these deficits, the American authorities might think of devaluing the dollar. It was a year of Presidential Election. Some wondered whether, if the Democrats won, they might embark on unorthodox economic experiments, just as President Roosevelt had done twenty-eight years earlier. Mr Kennedy was known to be a man of independent views, who had progressive advisers. Such experiments might include the devaluation of the dollar, as had been done in 1933, although, of course, the circumstances were entirely different. In 1933 there was intense domestic depression and a financial crisis of a most violent kind, while in 1961 the only important trouble was the American deficit. Mr Kennedy had not yet made his firm statement that he would in no event contemplate changing the dollar price of gold.

In anticipation of these possibilities there was very heavy buying of gold in the London market in the autumn of 1960, and the British authorities allowed its price to rise substantially above the parity. The reason for this was that the British were not sure how the Americans would interpret their obligations under the International Monetary Fund in respect of the purchase of dollars for gold from other central banks. There is a reference in Article VIII, Section 4, to the 'balances having recently been acquired in respect to current transactions'. The line between capital transactions and current transactions originally intended by the draftsmen of the Fund had already become very blurred, but this purchase of gold for dollars on a large scale might be thought by the American authorities to be something quite exceptional and of a purely speculative character. It would not suit the British to buy large quantities of dollars in support of the dollar and then find that the Americans were not willing to convert them into gold. There had to be some trans-Atlantic telephoning. After a few days the British got agreement that the Americans would repurchase dollars acquired by the British through operations in support of the dollar in the London market. The British then resumed normal operations there, and the premium on gold rapidly disappeared.

This episode produced a further effect. It was not only dollar holders, but holders of other currencies also, who might from time to time feel inclined to sell currencies for gold. It might not be easy to determine in what proportions the various currencies had been tendered, as the dollar would probably be used as the currency of intermediation. To meet these difficulties, an arrangement was made known as the 'gold pool'.[1] Seven countries agreed that, whenever gold had to be sold in London to prevent its price from rising, they would pool the cost by providing gold from their own reserves in certain fixed proportions. From time to time gold was acquired by the pool, when it was possible to do this within the prescribed limits, and this gold was redistributed to the members of the pool by way of repayment. It is understood that, taking one period with another and setting repurchases through the pool against out-payments by it, the operations of the pool were not very expensive to its members. A number of years passed without there being another major crisis.

But a very large one occurred in March 1968. Gold was bought in enormous quantities. The cause of the crisis was the devaluation of sterling in November 1967. The question arose in the minds of many advisers whether the dollar would have to follow suit. The average United States deficit had in recent years been greater than the British even when taken in proportion to the value of the exports of those two countries. The

[1] Cf. p. 74 above.

devaluation of sterling might further weaken the dollar on the external side, by giving British producers an edge on their price quotations when competing with American producers.

If one was an adviser, one had to think how to protect one's corporation's interests in relation to its liquid assets. The word 'speculation' has been much too freely used in relation to the March crisis. The adviser has to rack his brains to think how he can protect his employers against loss. In view of the question-mark over the dollar he might think it expedient to move, anyhow, some moderate part of the liquid assets out of dollars into some other currency. But what currency? Many thought that the British might have to devalue for a second time, so that sterling would not be appropriate. As late as April 1968, the authorities of Japan and mainland China decided to go over to the French franc as the medium for invoicing and settling their mutual trade. This would presumably entail their building up some French franc reserves in due course. But owing to the events in France during May and June it became clear that this agreement had been unwise, and it was temporarily res-cinded. The Deutschemark had been very strong for some time, but the Germans do not like the idea of its becoming a reserve currency in too important a degree, and from time to time take action towards preventing this, e.g. by regulations about interest payable to foreigners, regulations about reserve requirements in respect of foreign deposits and by operations in the forward market for Deutschemarks. The yen is not yet quite mature enough. If one takes a currency of small dimensions, however excellent it may be, it is clear that any big movement into it for reserve purposes would weaken it and make it less excellent.

And so some advisers thought that gold would be a good idea. The origin of the movement into gold was precautionary rather than speculative, although there was doubtless a good deal of speculation during the last few days of the crisis. The operations of the gold pool accelerated violently and became greater than was to the taste of the Americans, who were such heavy con-tributors to it, and were thereby losing gold from their reserves, which had already dwindled, at a great rate. At their request the operations of the gold pool were suspended on 15 March. There was a meeting of the members in Washington on the next day. There had originally been seven, but France had dropped out during 1967. Thus they became the Group of Six, which has quite different functions from the Group of Ten.

On 17 March they issued a pronunciamento. They announced that they would continue to remit gold at the previous official rate of $35 to the ounce to other central banks in exchange for their own currencies. But they would no longer contribute to the gold pool, so that the market price of gold would be permitted to rise. They added that they would not be willing to remit gold to other central banks if those in turn proceeded to sell their gold at a premium in the market. This was probably a necessary restriction; but it does entail that the currencies of all who join in the system can no longer be called gold-convertible in any meaningful sense; they are convertible only into inconvertible gold. The idea is that the gold held in official reserves shall move round in a closed circuit, its value being detached from that of gold in the world at large. The internal gold has really become the equivalent of a counter, or indeed of a paper note. Some have even suggested that the central banks might just as well sell all their gold and print bits of paper to take its place in mutual settlement. It is true that such action might reduce the price that they could get for their gold to a low level; but something is better than nothing. But the real objection is not that. What currencies would they receive in return for the gold? Such action would cause great confusion in the mutual liabilities of countries. And, to go still deeper, there remains great uncertainty about what the future of the world monetary system is to be. Pending clarification, the central banks, as a group, will think it wise to hang on to their gold.

The communiqué of the Group of Six also stated that there seemed to be no good reason for them to buy gold from the market, since there was already enough gold in the internal 'circuit'. This was doubtless intended to create a bearish sentiment in relation to open market gold, since it would not have the support of official purchases. If this decision is to be taken seriously, it surely does imply that ideas about the quantity of S.D.R.s that will be required are in need of revision. It is true that gold had been making hardly any contribution to monetary stocks for some years before the meeting at Rio. But people there did not take the view that it would make no contribution at all in the years to come. Rather the idea was that, when the S.D.R. system had got going and people had gained confidence that it was a workable system and would continue, this would lead to a dishoarding of gold by those who had previously thought that the whole international monetary system, including the role of the dollar, was likely to break down; or, if not a dishoarding, at least an abatement in the rate of hoarding, so that some substantial fraction of world production would be added each year to monetary stocks.

After the Washington communiqué the market price of gold rose. For most of the time since then, it has stood above $40. The Americans would probably like to see it return to the level of $35, which would give some meaning to the idea that the dollar was still a gold standard currency. Some might like to see it go below the official level, which would suggest that people thought more highly of the dollar than they did of gold.

Some Americans, indeed, would like to see the dollar functioning as the world currency. There is much to be said in favour of that outcome; it would simplify the whole problem. Despite a certain British sentimental attitude to sterling, I should not oppose such a project, if it were feasible. But it is not feasible. There is quite a lot of prejudice against it, even if we confine ourselves to the free market world. But, when we think of a world currency, despite the postponement of any rapprochement that the recent events in Czechoslovakia will doubtless cause, we have to think of a world monetary system as eventually embracing the communist world, for purposes of interchange between that world and the rest. For that purpose gold would be acceptable; or international paper money, if the rules governing its issue were sufficiently automatic, and not in effect subject to the discretion of bodies like the Group of Ten or the Group of Six. But the dollar would not be acceptable.

Further to mere prejudice, there is a substantial point (cf. above). The United States is the richest country in the world. It does not seem quite right that to the wealth that it gains by its great productive powers there should be added 100% seigniorage profit on all the new money that the whole world needs each year. It must be remembered that the rest of the world would have to buy its dollars, which cost the Americans

L

next to nothing to print, by remitting to the United States goods and services of an equivalent value, which would cost the rest of the world very much to produce. It would be a sort of tribute, and a very large one, paid to the United States by the rest of the world for no particular reason.

There is a general feeling that the two-tier system will not be a permanent one. If the United States balance of payments becomes favourable in the near future, then it might last for a substantial time. But if it does not become favourable, then further crises are likely to arise, anyhow in the medium-term future. In July 1968 the United States enacted a 10% surcharge on income tax and corporation tax. The proposal to have such a tax had for quite a long time had a symbolic significance in most official international circles and some unofficial circles. There was a twofold idea, namely, first, that the passage of the tax would show that the Americans really meant business and were prepared to make sacrifices in order to get their balance of payments straight and, secondly, that that tax would have an actual effect in improving the balance. The second point is, however, doubtful. The passage of the tax caused a weakening in the market price of gold.

If, as things turn out, the United States balance of payments is not greatly affected by the tax, the 'advisers' will begin worrying again about the future of the dollar, and suggest to their employers or clients a diversification of the currency denomination in which they hold their assets. If the pressure becomes sufficiently great, the United States might have to suspend gold payments. That would be the end of the two-tier system.

We may start with the peripheral central banks. Under the two-tier system they must be under some temptation to sell their gold at a higher price in the free market. But, so long as the dollar is convertible into gold among central banks, on the lines of the Washington statement, they will argue that, by selling gold for a profit at its market price, they will deprive themselves of the chance of buying gold for dollars below its market price. That might not be a good trade-off. But once the opportunity of buying gold for dollars below the market price were denied them, they would begin to act like international corporations and diversify their holdings at the expense of the dollar.

If the dollar became no longer convertible for central banks, difficulties might arise even among the inner circle. They would presumably continue to fulfil their obligation under the International Monetary Fund to maintain fixed rates of exchange in their own markets, whether using the dollar as a currency of intermediation or not. But what would happen if, in sustaining the dollar in their own markets, they acquired considerable quantities of dollars which the Americans were no longer willing to convert into gold? Would they grin and bear it? Or would they apply to the I.M.F. to be relieved of their obligation to maintain an irredeemable dollar at its official value in their own markets. If they did the latter, the dollar would begin to float. Then we should need another pooling of ideas among the high authorities, but on this occasion in quick time and not proceeding over four years. Great questions would then have to be decided – about the role of gold, about proper rules for the issue of an international paper money, and about the role, if any, of flexible foreign exchange rates.

6. Currency Crisis (November 1968)

The two-tier gold system, established in March, made for increased uncertainty, as regards currencies, during 1968. People raised the question whether this new-fangled system for gold was really viable. If it broke down, then there would almost inevitably have to be currency adjustments. The S.D.R.s were still beyond the visible horizon in that year.

Then in May occurred the student/labour troubles in France. The country was thrown into great disorder for two months. Subsequently it seemed to snap out of them well, and things returned to normal. There were losses from the reserves, but the French reserves had been very large, so that the drain could be tolerated. The authorities put a brave face on the matter and proposed that the planned growth rate should be put up to 7% in 1969, to make good the ground lost owing to the troubles. The external balance of payments was restored to equilibrium. There remained, however, uneasiness in the minds of some, who feared that the adverse effects of the troubles on the external balance had not yet been fully felt.

Also, what about the 7% growth rate in 1969 in relation to that balance?

Meanwhile the British balance was not showing the improvement that had been hoped for in consequence of the devaluation of sterling. Exports were rising well, but the volume of imports of manufactures, instead of falling, as it should in accordance with the theory of devaluation, were also rising at a quite abnormal rate.

It was generally agreed among experts that, if the November devaluation proved a failure, or a partial one, another devaluation was not the right answer. (The financial 'advisers', however, thought that the United Kingdom might be forced into one.) In some quarters there was talk of the need for temporary import controls.

But those with faith in automatic systems were not receptive to this idea. They pinned the blame, not only for the British difficulties but also for the wider international monetary malaise, on a wrong alignment of the currencies. There must, according to their view, which is not necessarily correct, be *some* realignment which would bring things to rights immediately. Sterling had been readjusted. What was next to be done? The German mark should be valued upwards.

In the later part of August there was quite a campaign in influential sections of the British Press to this effect. It triggered off a large movement of funds out of sterling into Deutschemarks. History was repeating itself. Exactly the same thing had happened in the summer of 1957, but with this difference. In 1957 the British external balance was in good shape and improving; there was a reverse flow of funds into sterling later in the year.

The crisis of late August 1968 did not at once gather momentum. It became known that, despite what might be urged in the British Press, the Germans were determined not to countenance an upward valuation. There was a return flow into sterling in the later part of September. But some background of uneasiness remained. Although the Germans did not have an overall surplus, they had a very large merchandise surplus, which was offset by large foreign investment. Some held that the Germans were unlikely to continue to export capital at so great a rate, while the large merchandise surplus might remain. Then there would be trouble.

Meanwhile attention returned to France. There seemed to be some weakening in the government stance, and economy measures were introduced. It was inferred that the authorities must know things to be worse than they seemed to be on the surface. When there is underlying uncertainty in the field of currency, it seems to be difficult to do the right thing! If one does not deflate, one is asking for trouble. If one does deflate, then things must be worse than they seem.

The November currency crisis, which was an extremely severe one, was centred on the French franc and the Deutschemark. There was a double force behind the great flow out of French francs into Deutschemarks. The reasons why the French might devalue or the Germans might value upwards were really quite independent of one another. But they led to a flow of funds in the same direction.

Sterling was also involved. If it seemed likely that the Germans would be forced to value upwards, that was a good reason for going out of sterling into Deutschemarks. The British would certainly not join in an upward valuation. If, on the other hand, the French devalued, that would put additional pressure on sterling, bringing it, so to speak, into the front line of defence.

The dollar was largely exempt from trouble in this crisis. If there was some movement out of dollars into Deutschemarks, this was offset by larger movements out of other currencies into dollars – if anything happened to the French franc or sterling, other currencies also might be in trouble. The imposition of a 10% surtax by Congress in July, after prolonged deadlock, gave the world the idea that the Americans were prepared to make sacrifices in order to restore their external balance. The United States merchandise balance had deteriorated substantially in 1968; but there was a large gain on the side of capital inflow. There is a paradox about the third quarter figures, which gave good cheer. The overall balance, *including* errors and omissions, improved by $237 million, but errors and omissions improved by $902 million, so that the overall balance, excluding errors and omissions, actually declined by $665 million. The good figure for errors and omissions doubtless represented confidence in the dollar during the troubled summer months. They are at all times volatile. Strictly interpreted, the third quarter figures for the United States were not in themselves encouraging;

rather the other way. The figure for errors and omissions was not known in November; had it been, it is likely that the dollar would have been heavily involved in the November crisis.

The grave crisis was discussed at the routine meeting of the Governors of Central Banks at Basel on 16–17 November. It was decided to summon an emergency meeting of the Group of Ten at Bonn (20–22 November).

Germany stood firm against an upward valuation of the Deutschemark, but promised two courses of action and adumbrated a third: (1) it would reduce its border taxes on imports and its rebates on exports, both offsets to its domestic value added tax, by 4%; (2) it would impose a 100% 'reserve requirement' on any additional foreign deposits at German commercial banks; (3) it adumbrated a positive restriction on foreign deposits, which, in fact, was executed very promptly.

Comments may be made on these three items:

1. The 4% adjustment should not be considered as a *de facto* upward valuation, although it was so described in an official German publication. It was not comprehensive, since agricultural products were not affected; nor were capital movements or other non-merchandise transactions. More important, if the flow of events proves it to have been needless, and even injurious, it can easily be reversed. That would not be true of a variation in the currency parity. Once valued upwards, the Deutschemark could probably not be revalued downwards without a major currency crisis occurring.

Changes in the offsets to a value added tax are thus a more flexible instrument than use of the 'adjustable peg'. Would it be desirable to regard such changes as a regular weapon for adjusting imbalances? This would add something to our armoury, or at least to those of the countries that have value added taxes. If the changes became frequent, what would be the attitude of the G.A.T.T.? The weapon would not be available for a country the currency of which was tending to over-valuation, unless it had previously been used in a reverse sense, since a country would not be entitled to impose a border tax in excess of its value added tax.

2. The imposition of the 100% reserve requirement may be regarded as a normal weapon of monetary policy. But it is

different, in that it discriminates against the foreigner. It thus has to be regarded as a sort of trammel on the international flow of capital.

3. The third measure is openly so. It is a striking manifestation, since it has been applied by a country which had for a number of years been very liberal in its policy as regards capital movements. One may take the matter light-heartedly, on the ground that the objective of a free international flow of capital is all nonsense anyway. That would not be the last word. If there are to be restrictions, they should be subject to agreed criteria and imposed after due consideration and not in consequence of pressure from the 'gnomes' (financial advisers).

These various phenomena suggest that there is something seriously wrong with the international system, as it is functioning at present.

It was supposed at the Bonn meeting that the French would devalue, and a large credit was provided to see them through their difficulties. Some of those concerned were doubtful if the evidence was clear that the French franc was in fundamental disequilibrium at its existing parity. But the 'gnomes' were at work, and it was supposed that something must be done. Wise heads considered that a 5% devaluation, if any, would be about right. But then what is known as the 'credibility gap' came into consideration. Would the 'gnomes' consider 5% sufficient? If they did not, it might be expedient to meet their views and have 10% right away. No figure was agreed upon at Bonn and no undertaking given that there would be a devaluation. But the belief among top officials that the French would, in fact, devalue continued into the morning of 23 November, namely after the meeting had broken up.

But in the afternoon of that day the French decided not to devalue.

It is still too early (May 1969), to form a judgement whether confidence in the existing parity will last for a reasonable length of time. If it does, the French will have made a very valuable contribution. If a change of parity is to be made, it should be decided on by those who know the facts and are responsible for general economic policy. It is intolerable that their hands should be forced and the course of events determined by financial advisers to private corporations, whose knowledge about the underlying facts is often quite superficial.

This crisis had an aftermath. In many circles it was considered that the mutual support arrangements should be strengthened and regularised. These matters have since been discussed at later Basel meetings with a result that may be set down as on the whole negative.

It has been suggested that the support credits should be: (1) larger; (2) multilateral; (3) automatic, i.e. not subject to conditions; (4) of longer-term, even to the extent of leaving the date of repayment undefined; and that (5) the whole system should be quasi-permanent, i.e. due to continue *sine die* pending some radical change in the general monetary system.

The idea behind such proposals is that, if these conditions were fulfilled on an adequate scale, the private financial advisers would be convinced that a country just could not be forced to devalue (or value upwards) against its own better judgement. That, in turn, would on a number of occasions prevent the private precautionary movements of funds from occurring, and thus, in the event, the standby credits, so generously provided, would not have to be used.

This kind of situation must strike anyone versed in monetary history as extremely familiar. It has occurred over and over again in various forms. For example, in the quarter-century after Peel's Bank Act, the Bank of England was on occasions down to its last penny and on the brink of having to close its doors. Then the Act was suspended, which made the gold previously locked up behind the note issue available for its use. But then it no longer needed to use the gold! The fears of people, once they knew that it had these extra funds at its disposal, were allayed, and the run on the Bank ceased.

But although a strengthened mutual support system might prevent massive movements of funds on many occasions, it would not necessarily do so on all occasions. The 'gnomes' would know that the authorities could not be forced to change a parity against this better judgement. But it would still be open to them to believe that the authorities would presently *desire* to change the parity. And they might believe this, even when it was not in fact true. It is impossible for the financial advisers – or for others! – to read the inner minds of those responsible for these matters in each country. In such cases massive funds would be moved and the support credits would have to be called into play.

There are two reasons why the Basel group refuses to establish an adequate automatic system.

The more important relates to the question of discipline. The creditor countries – and all countries are potentially creditor – fear that ready and unconditional access to massive support funds would remove an impelling motive for the debtor countries to take unpleasant steps as needed to terminate their deficits. Of course the credits could be made conditional on the receiving countries taking such steps, or, anyhow, some steps in that direction, as indeed they have been on occasions under the existing system. But that at once undermines the confidence of the 'gnomes'. It is open to them to argue, 'we are sure that, say, the British can get all the credit they need subject to conditions, since no one wants to see sterling devalued again; but we are not sure that they will accept the conditions'. That is probably a partial description of the course of events as regards sterling in November 1967. The 'gnomes' were proved right then, and they can argue that they will probably be proved right again. *Un*conditionality is of the essence of a sound system. Some *other* method should be found for nations to assure each other, and not near times of crisis only, that they are managing their respective economies on sound agreed-upon lines.

The second point is the difficulty of distinguishing flows of funds due to an underlying deficit from these due to precautionary movements. It is agreed that the support credits are provided to finance the latter kind of flows only. To finance underlying deficits resort must be had to owned reserves or to drawing rights, including Special Drawing Rights, if any, on the I.M.F. This second difficulty has been stressed by spokesmen. It is probably exaggerated.

It is true that a current overall deficit may be larger than the country running it believes, and that this will only show up later in the statistics. But such discrepancies are not likely to be large by comparison with the movements of precautionary funds. If a country underestimates its own underlying deficit and inadvertently draws on the support credits to finance a part of it, the error can be rectified later. The amounts involved will be small. On the other hand, it is fairly obvious when precautionary funds are flowing; it could be made even more so by continuous statistical co-operation in assessing balances of payments, with the I.M.F. lending a helping hand. This statistical point should not therefore be taken too seriously. Incidentally, it may be noted that it has been discovered (June 1969) that the U.K. has recently been *underestimating* its true position by some £120 million a year.

It can hardly be denied that to date we have a fairly ramshackle international monetary system. There is the stock of gold dwindling rapidly in proportion to trade, and even absolutely somewhat; there is the two-tier system which bears the hall-mark of something makeshift; there are dollars, the stock of which will not be replenished if the Americans are 'virtuous' and terminate their deficits; there is sterling, the use of which will not be increased much, unless and until the British position gets considerably stronger; there are the supergold tranches in the I.M.F. which vary very much in quantity and increase only if some countries run substantial deficits; there is hope for some S.D.R.s, but of inadequate amount, the activation of which is not yet agreed upon; and there are the mutual support credits, which have had some success in tiding over crises, but which have not yet been welded into a regular system. Those countries which have value added taxes may (or may not?) be allowed to vary the offsets from time to time in order to affect their balances of payments.

No further comment is needed.

12

EURO-DOLLARS

WHILE the official world was moving forward in a rather
fumbling way towards a tentative scheme, not on the face of it
very satisfactory, for supplementing international liquidity,
private enterprise was proceeding swiftly to establish an international short-term capital market. This event will surely rank
as a great landmark in monetary history. From time to time the
author of this volume has shown that he has no prejudice in
favour of private enterprise as such, e.g. in his recommendation
of indicative planning, even on a world scale, of an incomes
policy, possibly with legal sanctions, of quantitative import
controls, to cite some instances only. But in this matter of an
international capital market, hats must be taken off to the
marvellous achievement of private enterprise. Economists have
not yet succeeded in relating its functions and effects to a
theoretical framework. What follows can, therefore, be tentative
only. The primary function of this market, as in the case of any
market, is to bring supply into contact with demand. On the
one side monetary balances which might otherwise have
remained idle are activated or, alternatively, are put to more
fruitful uses, and, on the other, projects that might have been
impeded by lack of finance are enabled to go forward. This
bringing together of demand and supply is mainly across
national frontiers and therefore transcends what is done by
national commercial banks in the ordinary course of their
business.

The greater part of the deals in this international market are
effectuated in dollars, and the dollars that are lent in this
market are known as Euro-dollars. But there are operations in
other currencies also, of which sterling is the most important.
There are also operations in Swiss francs, Deutschemarks, lire,
Dutch guilders and French francs. In each case the prefix
'Euro-' is used, and the generic name for the whole market is

the Euro-currency market. This prefix is not altogether appropriate, since, although the market is mainly based on Europe, it is in fact world-wide. Japan has at times been a heavy borrower in the market and the Middle Eastern oil states large lenders.

It must be stressed at the outset that Euro-dollars are not a separate species of dollars; they are just plain dollars. Similarly with the other currencies. Euro-dollars consist of deposits at some commercial bank located in the United States. The fact that they are just ordinary dollars, and nothing other than ordinary dollars, is evidenced by the fact that there is no foreign exchange quotation for them. By contrast there is an exchange quotation for what are known in the United Kingdom as 'investment dollars', these being the dollars that come into existence when a British resident, subject to British exchange control, sells dollar securities for dollars, which are inconvertible by him but can then be purchased by other British residents with a view to buying American securities or for other purposes. These investment dollars have an exchange quotation. At times this has run close to the quotation for official dollars, but at other times there has been a very large premium indeed on investment dollars. Similarly in the days of sterling inconvertibility, transferable sterling had its own foreign exchange quotation, which was different from that of official sterling. Dealings in these species of currencies consist of purchase and sale. Dealings in Euro-dollars, by contrast, consist in loan and repayment. They have no foreign exchange quotation. The quotation for Euro-dollars in an interest rate.

When does a dollar become a Euro-dollar? The definition is not an altogether easy matter. To begin with, it would normally be the case that, when a non-resident of the United States lends dollars to another non-resident on the condition of being repaid in dollars, these would be Euro-dollars. But Americans resident in the United States also deal heavily in the Euro-dollar market, both as lenders to it and borrowers from it. In these cases one of the parties to the loan transaction is a non-resident of the United States. But it is also possible for resident Americans to lend Euro-dollars to each other. Clearly the vast mass of lending by resident Americans to other resident Americans does not consist of Euro-dollar loans. It may be possible to distinguish one sort of lending from the other by saying that dollars lent by an American resident A to an American resident B (and possibly onwards to C), are Euro-dollars, if there is a tag on them by which A has eventually to repay to a non-resident.

It cannot be stated that all borrowings of dollars by resident Americans from non-residents are Euro-dollar loans, or conversely. Americans may have all sorts of special arrangements of their own, whether of lending or borrowing, with outside corporations. In the last resort I believe that a loan can be defined as a Euro-dollar loan only by reference to the fact that it is made at the Euro-dollar interest rate. This might seem to be a circular definition. But perhaps it can be rescued. The fact is that day by day there is a vast amount of lending of dollars by non-residents to each other and that day by day a common interest rate is quoted for such lending. Then if an American borrows from the outside world or lends to the outside world *at this rate*, and by explicit reference to the going rate, he is operating in the Euro-dollar market.

A notable characteristic of the market is that it has no headquarters or buildings of its own, no committee supervising it, no official code of behaviour and no legal constraint. Physically it consists merely of a network of telephones and telex machines around the world, telephones which may be used also for purposes other than Euro-dollar deals.

Operations of this sort have doubtless existed for a long time, and, to discover the ultimate origins, one might have to delve a long way back into remote history. But the market only began to be of primary importance in the late 1950s. Two specific origins are worthy of mention. One was a Russian attitude. A Russian agency might acquire dollars and believe that they might come in useful at a later date. But the agency in question might dislike being on the books of a bank in New York as a client. So the agency might lend the dollars at short-term to some bank in Europe. The dollars would then stand in the books of, say, the Chase Manhattan Bank, as a liability, not to a Russian agency but to a Western European bank. The Russian agency would recapture the dollars only when it wanted to use them, and thus would be on the Chase Manhattan record as an intermediary only. If a Western European bank had taken over the dollars merely to oblige its Russian client, and had no immediate use for them, it might relend them on short term to another bank in its own country or in some other country. That other bank might do the same. And so a chain of lending might be set up until the dollars passed into the hands of a bank or corporation which had an immediate end-use for the dollars.

Another 'origin' of the market was the imposition of additional exchange restrictions by the United Kingdom authorities in 1957, to meet difficulties arising from the large flow of funds out of sterling into the Deutschemark in anticipation of an expected upward revaluation of the Deutschemark. London had traditionally been, and still is, a centre of international dealing in short-term capital. The frustration due to the new restrictions could be in part avoided if the banks, instead of arranging for sterling loans, borrowed some dollars and lent them. London has been throughout the most important centre for Euro-dollar dealings. That has doubtless been due to the *expertise* in such operations in London, which has been perfected over many generations.

Passing from these special factors, we have to explain why this international loan market rapidly acquired a great popularity and established itself as what may well be the most important financial institution in the world. The *expertise* just mentioned, which was not, of course, confined to London, but existed in a number of other places, such as Zürich, enabled the market to establish very fine margins between its borrowing and lending rates. The parties to Euro-dollar deals crossing national frontiers are usually, but not exclusively, as has sometimes been said, banks. These banks could be expected to have more detailed knowledge of the credit worthiness of numerous corporations or other would-be borrowers in their own country than of that of companies abroad. One may compare the Euro-dollar market with the international short-term capital market that was traditionally centred on London. The latter depended on the world-wide knowledge of the credit-worthiness of short-term borrowers that existed in the merchant banks in London.[1] The international network of telephones that constitutes the Euro-dollar market has made possible a devolution of the business of judging credit-worthiness. Thus a London merchant bank may lend dollars to a German bank, which in turn wants

[1] Cf. p. 49 above.

to lend them to a client resident in Germany. The London merchant bank no longer has to know anything about the credit-worthiness of the borrower from the German bank; the London bank's asset is a liability of the German bank, which it knows; it does not have to bother any further. Much, although not of course all, of the long-established type of lending was based on documents, such as bills of exchange, accepted by a merchant bank, which represented actual goods in transit; these constituted the ultimate security behind the loan. It is understood that the Euro-dollar market has a much more relaxed attitude in relation to security. That is possible because the end-user usually borrows from a bank in his own country on the strength of a good customer relation with that bank.

There is sometimes a very long chain of lending and relending before the dollars reach their end-use. Fears have been expressed that there is a precarious element in the Euro-dollar market, on the ground that if the end-user went bankrupt that would have an ill effect on a long chain of intermediaries. These fears are probably exaggerated. But there might be widespread international trouble if a whole country, which was a net borrower of Euro-dollars of substantial importance, had to declare a moratorium.

The popularity of the market depends on the fine margin between borrowing and lending rates, which in its turn depends on the *expertise* aforementioned. The lender can get a better rate of interest on his liquid funds than he could get on a time deposit in a commercial bank. Incidentally, Regulation Q of the Federal Reserve System, which restricts the power of member banks in the United States to bid up the rates they offer on time deposits, is said to have been an important cause of the growth of the market. Likewise a borrower can get his loan at a rate below the prime lending rate of a bank in the United States. Thus the existence of the Euro-dollar market brings advantage both to lenders and borrowers in it.

The question may be asked why commercial banks – the London merchant banks are in a rather different position – are willing to have a smaller spread in their Euro-dollar dealings than they have between the general run of their ordinary deposits and of their ordinary lending. Why should it make all the difference that the lending and borrowing are denominated in a foreign currency? I believe that the true answer to this question is a subtle one. Banks have to have a spread between their deposit rate and their lending rate of substantial size, in order to cover their running expenses, the upkeep of their buildings, and a profit. (The London discount houses, which have less overhead expenses, do in fact work to much finer margins.) While the spread of the commercial banks on their ordinary business has to be of substantial size for the reasons given, it might be profitable for them to do marginal business with a smaller spread. And doubtless they sometimes do such marginal business, charging favoured customers rates below their regular rates. But there is a limit to this; if they carried it too far embarrassments could arise. The denomination of the borrowing and lending in a different currency puts the Euro-dollar business into a separate category. If an ordinary borrower A complained to his bank that it had discriminated against him, because it had given B a loan at a lower rate, the bank can reply – 'but that was a Euro-dollar loan; that is an entirely different matter'. And it is a different matter, even if B wants to use the loan to make payment for local costs – perhaps in competition with A! B will have to carry out a dollar-swap transaction, which will cost him something, or, if he does not do so, run an exchange risk, since he is committed to repay his bank in dollars. The Euro-dollar market, in fine, enables banks to do what may be a very great deal of marginal business that, despite its narrow spread, is profitable to them. The lower spread between the Euro-currency borrowing and lending rates gives leverage for a discrimination between rates on average and on marginal business.

End-borrowers in the Euro-dollar market must be sharply divided into two categories, whom we may call class A and class B. Class A consists of those who want dollars as such, whether to make an immediate payment to a United States resident or to a resident in some other country his trade with whom is denominated in dollars. Class A borrowers might also consist of banks or other corporations which have some reason for wanting to show dollars in their books.

Class B borrowers consist of those who do not want dollars at all, but simply immediate cash. A very good example of these is the British Local Authorities who from time to time have borrowed heavily in the Euro-dollar market, simply because that was the cheapest way by which they could obtain funds on short-term. They had no use for dollars as such, and probably never even saw the dollars. They would normally carry out a swap operation, authorising the lending bank to sell the dollars spot and buy them forward.

This distinction is relevant to the question that has been raised whether the Euro-dollar market has the effect of 'creating' credit, like the collection of commercial banks dependent on one national central bank. When the borrowed dollars are used to pay debts denominated in dollars, there does not seem to be a possibility of any such creation, although of course the existence of the market performs the valuable function of bringing someone who has dollars going begging for the time being into contact with someone who has an immediate need for them.

The dollars borrowed by class B borrowers are likely to go back into the Euro-dollar circuit. It is in this connection that the question of the 'creation of credit' must be considered. If all borrowers were class A borrowers it does not appear that there could be any multiplication. If the dollars borrowed by class B borrowers go back into the system, they do so *via* a swap operation. For the sake of argument, we can assume that the same dealer bought dollars spot from the class B borrower and sold him dollars forward. Actually this borrower might use two deals. But the effect on dealers as a class would be the same, and therefore we may assume that the same dealer that bought dollars spot from him also sold them to him forward.

In analysis one should always assume that a given operation is marginal, namely that prior to it, or, better, in its absence, all would-be buyers and sellers at existing exchange rates in both spot and forward markets have been able to satisfy their needs.

The buyer of class B borrower's dollars is in an admirable position to go into the Euro-dollar market. He has dollars in hand and a forward commitment by which he will have to provide dollars in three months time, or whatever the period may be. What better than to lend his dollars for that period? I have no doubt that the self-same dollars that were used by the United Kingdom Local Authorities could be used to finance

M

another end-use. Indeed, if the second borrower is a class B borrower, they can be used to finance a third end-use, and so on. This proposition has been challenged by one eminent authority. But I do not believe that it can be refuted, provided that one strictly adheres to the rule, mentioned in the last paragraph, of regarding a given operation as a marginal operation. Actually the dollars used to finance the British Local Authority expenditure and thereafter to finance, say, a warehouse in Germany could in principle be identical dollars, e.g. a deposit at the Chase Manhattan, New York, put into circulation by the Sheik of X and destined after a given time period to return to the Sheik of X's account at the Chase Manhattan.

If I am correct in this, the quantity of dollars lent for *end-uses*, i.e. excluding mere bank to bank relending, exceeds the number of dollars initially placed in the market, provided that some of the borrowers are class B borrowers. The difference between the two totals is exactly equal to the number of dollars entering into swap operations in consequence of the disposal of them by class B borrowers. It does not directly follow from the foregoing that the Euro-dollar market is capable of 'creating' credit. The dealer who does the swap operation in class B borrower's dollars, or the bank for whom he acts, if he acts for a bank, must have liquid resources in hand in order to be able to engage in the swap. A swap of this kind necessarily involves locking up liquid resources. The dealer in question has got to hold spot dollars against a forward commitment. If he does not like this burden, viz. locking up his resources in this way – but they can earn interest in the Euro-dollar market – he can transfer the burden to someone else. But *some* resources have to be locked up for the duration of the swap. The key question then is – would the bank or dealer have found some other method for lending out these liquid resources in the absence of the Euro-dollar market? In fine, does the Euro-dollar market activate idle balances or merely deflect them from other lending channels? I would suppose that deflection is much more important than activation, taking the aggregate of dealings. But, even if all the funds put into the Euro-market were merely deflected from other uses, the Euro-market can add to the short-term funds available in a *particular* country, to the extent that that country is a net borrower in the Euro-dollar market.

Thus one understands the uneasiness on the part of some central banks, on the ground that the existence of the market might frustrate policies of credit restraint that they wished to pursue at a particular time. The employment of purchasing power acquired by class B borrowers through the Euro-dollar market adds to the total purchasing power in the country in question, provided that that country is a net borrower.

A very interesting question is how the Euro-dollar market affects the dollar and the balance of payments of the United States. The same question applies, of course, to other Euro-currencies. The analysis of this is very intricate. I have reached the following provisional conclusions.

All lendings in the Euro-dollar market are equal to all borrowings in it. Let p be the fraction of all lending constituted by (i) the lendings of those lenders who in the absence of the market would have sold their dollars spot, without forward purchase, and by (ii) the lendings of those who buy dollars spot, without forward resale, in order to lend them into the market. Let q consist of the fraction of all borrowings constituted by (i) class A borrowers, who, in the absence of the Euro-dollar market, would have rustled up enough local currency to buy the dollars that they needed for immediate settlement and by (ii) class B borrowers who do not cover their commitment to repay by buying forward. The existence (and growth) of the Euro-dollar market is beneficial to the dollar if p is greater than q, and conversely.

Its effect on the 'Commerce Balance' (official balance published by the United States Department of Commerce) is somewhat different. Let r be the fraction of all borrowing from the market constituted by (i) all those sums borrowed from it to make payments to United States residents which, in the absence of the Euro-dollar market, would have been financed temporarily by loans by United States residents or deferred, and by (ii) borrowings by United States residents from the Euro-dollar market, and let s be the fraction of all lendings constituted by lendings by United States residents into the market. If r is greater than s the Commerce Balance gains from the existence of the market, and conversely.

It is not possible to say *a priori* whether $(p - q)$ or $(r - s)$ are likely to be positive or negative or which is likely to be algebraically greater than the other.

The reverse question is also interesting. What effect does the United States deficit have on the size of the Euro-dollar market? We may suppose that this deficit contributed to the growth of the market in the early stages. But the market, having proved its usefulness, may survive if the United States deficit is terminated or even turned into a surplus. If its usefulness is well established, sufficient funds to keep it growing can be obtained from the United States itself. In accordance with the $(p - q)$ formula given above, United States lending into the market would have no effect, one way or the other, on the status of the dollar or therefore on the United States gold reserve. But it would affect the Commerce Balance adversely. In conditions in which the status of the dollar was not under pressure, the United States authorities would probably not give much thought to the Commerce Balance being adverse, provided that they were at the time suffering no loss of gold reserve nor increase in dollars officially held abroad. In that case the adverse Commerce Balance would present no threat to them. The adverse figure in the Commerce Balance might, it is true, have a bad psychological effect, causing leads and lags in trade payments. But, if the underlying position was one of equal balance or United States surplus, the leads and lags effect would be likely to be of minor importance only. In these conditions there seems to be no reason why the Euro-dollar market should not continue to be replenished by borrowings from United States residents.

The position would be different if the United States was in substantial deficit. But in that case the Euro-dollar market would get replenishments through the United States deficit itself. So, either way, so long as the market continues to prove useful, it is likely to get the replenishments that it requires.

Subject to the maintenance of sufficient confidence in the currencies concerned, other Euro-currency markets are likely to continue to grow.

PART FOUR

Principles of Policy for the Future

13

PRINCIPLES OF POLICY FOR
THE FUTURE: DOMESTIC

AT the opening of this book it was suggested that the centre-piece of monetary policy should be the maintenance of a stable value for money. It seems right in principle that the 'measuring rod' should itself have absolute constancy of value. Historically, over many generations, it was held that the best approximation we could get to this was to give our unit of account a constant value in terms of some fairly reliable commodity, like gold. And the primary method for attaining this was to establish a two-way convertibility between bars of gold and the bank-notes and bank deposits that were in active circulation. Of course it was recognised that this was not a perfect system, because gold itself does not have perfect stability of value.

The theorists of bimetallism held that the rupture of the bimetallic parity (1873) was a step backwards. They held that, if the value of the domestic monetary unit depended on the joint abundance or scarcity of two metals, the abundance or scarcity of each of which varied *independently*, this unit would be likely to have greater stability than if it depended on the abundance or scarcity of one of the metals only. It is true that the maintenance of the bimetallic parity had at times presented certain administrative difficulties; and we have seen that Alfred Marshall proposed to overcome this by his system of 'symmetal-lism', under which the currency unit would be convertible into a certain weight of gold plus a certain weight of silver, the silver price of gold being allowed to fluctuate freely in the market.

One could carry that idea a great deal further by making the currency unit convertible into certain quantities, not merely of two commodities, but also of quite a wide range of commodities. Thus one gets to the idea of having what is sometimes known as a 'commodity standard'. It was assumed that the principle of convertibility would be kept in play, as the only known method of maintaining the 'standard' *de facto*. To meet the objection that it might be difficult for arbitrage dealers to handle a wide range of commodities, it was suggested that one could use one commodity, such as gold, for purposes of intermediation. But the owner of the monetary unit would be guaranteed that he had in hand the power to purchase specified quantities of a specified list of commodities.

One might argue that the idea of such a 'commodity standard' never came within our horizon of what was practicable, but remained rather a remote ideal. None the less, one could urge that it was the ideal towards which monetary reformers should continually be striving. It was generally agreed at that time that the maxim for maintaining such a standard must be the same as it was under the gold standard, namely *convertibility*.

Less has been heard of a commodity standard of this type in recent decades. Thinking has moved in a different direction. The maintenance of stable prices is indeed still held to be a primary objective; but the idea that this should or could be obtained by making the unit legally convertible into commodities has tended to fade out. In its place we have the idea, largely due to the thinking of Keynes, that stable prices should be achieved, not by making a unit of money directly convertible into a basketful of commodities, but by ensuring that the aggregate demand for goods and services is so regulated by the authorities, by means of monetary and fiscal policies, that the price level of goods and services remains stable in consequence.

But then we have the intrusion of a somewhat different idea, namely that these same weapons of monetary and fiscal policy should be used to maintain full employment, or, by more advanced thinking, to ensure that the demand for goods and services grows at a rate equal to the growth of the supply potential of the economy. This raises the question of a possible conflict between the age-old historic objective of stable prices and the objective of full employment and growth. Is it possible that, if monetary and fiscal policies cause demand to grow at the rate required for the new objectives, this will in itself cause prices not to remain stable but to rise progressively? We may recall the Tinbergen requirement that we must have as many instruments of policy as we have objectives.

One way out of the difficulty might be to ensure full employ-ment and growth, not by using the impersonal weapons of monetary and fiscal policies operating through market forces, but by state planning and centrally determined prices. It is to be noted, however, that communist régimes have not always succeeded in avoiding inflation. Presumably the free market world will prefer not to choose that way out of the difficulty.

One next asks the question why it is that, if demand is maintained at a level equal to no more nor less than the amount of goods and services that the economy is able to produce from time to time, there should be any tendency for prices to rise. That brings us right up against the wages question. Wage rates are not in fact fixed in a market in which dealers are responsible for establishing a price that will make supply equal to demand. It is held that the maintenance of full employment will inevitably in any free market economy cause wages to increase at a greater rate than productivity increases. There is a certain amount of controversy on this point. Some hold that quite a moderate and tolerable amount of unemployment would suffice to prevent wages rising faster than productivity. Others argue that to bring this result about, very heavy un-employment would be required, such as would, by general agreement now, be held to be socially intolerable. Others again argue that, owing to unemployment being so great a social evil, it is not morally justifiable deliberately to create any un-employment *at all* – although in a free market economy some frictional unemployment can hardly be prevented.

So finally we come, in order to comply with Tinbergen's dictum, to a new instrument of policy, known as incomes policy. The idea is to prevent an excessive upward surge of wages by influencing what is done in collective bargaining by education, persuasion, and even, possibly, legal restraints. It is not yet known if an incomes policy is workable as a *permanent* procedure in a free society.

And thus, paradoxically, incomes policy has become a part of what has to be considered as monetary theory. The present idea is, anyhow in forward-looking circles, that monetary policy, aided by fiscal policy, shall be used, not, as by ancient historic tradition, to maintain a stable value of money, but to ensure that the level of aggregate demand for goods and services matches the supply potential of the economy, while the ancient role of monetary policy in maintaining stable prices is to be taken over by an incomes policy. The role of 'convertibility', anyhow so far as the domestic scene is concerned, has been very much diminished.

Towards the close of a volume one may be permitted to state one's own normative views. I would affirm that maximum economic growth in accordance with the potential supply capacity of the country is the primary objective and that all other objectives are subordinate to this. Indeed, the other objectives are to be aimed at precisely because they are deemed to contribute to growth. If they do not so contribute, then they should be cast aside. I do not think that this is merely a personal view. I hold that it expresses what economics has always been thought to be about. That subject has been deemed to constitute a body of systematic thinking about how maximum economic welfare can be obtained. Economic welfare has been defined as that part of the total welfare which springs from the provision of goods and services that can be exchanged. This definition is too narrow, because it implies a system in which exchange takes place. In a fully communist system, as distinct from the socialist systems now obtaining in what are incorrectly called the communist countries, there would presumably be no exchange. But the concept of economic welfare would still apply, as also the distinction between economic welfare and general welfare. We may accordingly redefine the goods and services that contribute to economic welfare as being those that are alternatively allocable to different persons.

Maximising growth is not an alternative to maximising economic welfare. The word 'growth' is used as a reminder that the maximisation of economic welfare has to be considered through time. There is nothing new in this, when regarded as an objective; what is new is the recognition that the tools of thought that are appropriate for the analysis of how economic welfare can be maximised at a given point of time are not by themselves adequate for analysing how economic welfare can be maximised through time.

Maximising economic growth is not to be identified with maximising growth of the Gross National Product for two reasons:

1. Leisure is an economic good. One can buy leisure in exchange for money income forgone. Leisure is not included in measures of the G.N.P.; accordingly the latter needs to be modified so that the amount of voluntary leisure achieved in the community is allowed for.

2. Maximum economic growth means the maximum growth of the goods and services that people desire. In the G.N.P. the various goods and services have to be given weights at a certain point of time. Through time technological progress may allow a higher increase in output per person in the case of some goods than that in the case of others. It is presumably a correct generalisation that technological advances cannot yield as high a growth rate in the output of services per person employed as in the output of material goods. Having regard to the initial weighting, one would presumably get a higher growth of the total G.N.P. if productive endeavour was more concentrated on the output of material goods than on that of services, and a lower G.N.P. if it were more concentrated on services. It does not follow that the former kind of concentration is to be preferred because it yields a higher G.N.P. It all depends on what people want! If they want to take out a greater part of their higher potential income in the form of services, economic welfare is more advanced if they are allowed to do so, although the G.N.P. grows less. There appears to be a tendency for people to desire to take out a larger part of their increase of income in the form of services as they grow richer. This may even be a characteristic of a higher degree of civilisation.

It has been argued in favour of the Selective Employment Tax, recently adopted in the United Kingdom, which discriminates against employment in the services industries, that, by so doing, it tends to divert labour into the production of material goods and thereby renders the growth of the G.N.P. greater than it would otherwise have been. No argument could be more topsy-turvy. While rendering the growth of G.N.P. greater it renders the growth of economic welfare less.

We must revert to the possible conflict between securing a maximum growth of economic welfare and containing price inflation. If this conflict is unavoidable, maximising growth should be unequivocally preferred. A good monetary system, which implies stable prices, is desirable because on the whole it is likely to contribute to growth. For instance, it facilitates accurate forward planning and thereby greater growth, since growth is likely to be greater if forward planning is accurate than if it is inaccurate. But, if it can be demonstrated, which is not yet certain, that stable prices can be achieved only by sacrificing maximum growth, e.g. by allowing the aggregate demand for goods and services to grow at a slower rate than the supply potential of the economy, then the objective of stable prices must be thrown overboard. Or, more strictly, we should still seek for stability of prices to the greatest possible extent, but only use instruments to achieve it that can be clearly shown not to interfere with maximum economic growth.

Much depends on the feasibility of a successful incomes policy. This situation arises if we are no longer content to hold down the aggregate demand for goods and services to a level that leaves the economy underemployed. Being deprived of that weapon for preserving price stability, a weapon which has not always been altogether effective, we have to have resort to the novel weapon of an incomes policy. We do not know whether this weapon will be completely successful; but, even if it is not, we must persevere with it, and try to make it as successful as we can. This may seem to some to be a dreary prospect, namely having to struggle year after year in the implementation of a very complicated policy, without perhaps complete success. Some have thought of the incomes policy as being a temporary expedient only, for example to see the United States and the United Kingdom through a transitional period in which they are adjusting their external balances of payment. This is a wrong view. The need for an incomes policy will be permanently with us, until some alternative device is thought of.

To some this may seem retrogressive. It substitutes a complex and awkward mechanism for the much simpler device that had been relied on in the past for ensuring stable prices, namely convertibility into gold. Even convertibility into a basketful of commodities, on the lines of the idealist reformers, would be a far simpler method of maintaining price stability than an incomes policy. In general, one would think it undesirable to proceed from the simple to the complex. In this case we seem to have no choice. It is the consequence of setting our sights higher, namely making it a matter of public policy that full employment and full growth should be maintained.

It might be objected that the foregoing account has omitted an important element, namely the equitable distribution of income. It might be considered desirable to accept a lower rate of overall growth, if that was needed to get a more equitable distribution of the fruits of growth. And it could further be argued that stable prices should be given parity of esteem as an objective because inflation leads to inequities. I would suggest that this point can be met in two ways:

1. Once again we have to look at the matter in quantitative terms. Doubtless it is very difficult, if not impossible, to do that with absolute precision. I would suggest that the loss of welfare through growth being held below potential over a number of years would be greater than the loss due to inequities caused by inflation.

2. If inflation proves to be unpreventable, there are means of preventing inequities arising, e.g. by putting pensions and the incomes of those in a weak bargaining position on to sliding scales based on the cost of living. Incidentally, it is to be observed that the United Kingdom, which had policies that clamped down on growth for most of the period from 1955 to 1968, did not thereby escape the evil of inflation.

Finally, we come to the question of the external balance of payments. According to earlier ways of thinking, convertibility would suffice to look after this. Convertibility would automatically regulate the quantity of the domestic money supply and thereby the level of domestic prices and thereby ensure that price quotations of domestic products would be at the level required to make imports and exports balance. This reduces the matter to its simplest terms and ignores the question of capital movements which have already been fully discussed. The problems connected with having a floating exchange rate as an alternative to convertibility have also been discussed. I would suggest that the recipe of import controls has not received sufficient attention among those who in recent years have been debating the problems of the correct adjustment mechanism for imbalances of external payments. There has been a strong tendency for countries with deficits on external account to adopt monetary and fiscal policies that are inimical to growth. The loss due to cutting out marginal items from the schedule of goods entering international trade must surely be small indeed compared with the loss due to holding growth even by as little as 1% below its potential. I would suggest that dis-inflationary monetary and fiscal policies should not be regarded as appropriate weapons for correcting an external imbalance unless they are required for purely domestic reasons.

To recapitulate. Monetary and fiscal policies should be used to ensure that the aggregate demand for goods and services increases by no more and no less than the supply potential of the economy. We have to rely upon the admittedly precarious incomes policy to maintain stability of prices to the greatest possible extent. This will also help the external balance. In regard to that balance there are the possibilities of floating exchange rates or of occasional readjustments of a fixed rate. Neither should not be assumed to be a quick-working remedy when there has been a structural change. Import controls should not be frowned upon as a bridge device for periods of uncertainty, and should always be preferred to deflation.

14

PRINCIPLES OF POLICY FOR
THE FUTURE: INTERNATIONAL

THE main feature of the international scene recently has been the shortage of reserves available for international settlement. This has been becoming progressively more severe, and they are probably now at the lowest level since the precious metals ceased to be the main medium of domestic circulation in the leading countries.

The problem is made more acute by the fact that there are two methods for correcting an external imbalance, and thereby lessening the need for reserves that are no longer available. National policy makers tend to be unwilling to let unemployment build up to a great extent; this was one process by which an external deficit used to be corrected. Secondly, there has been a manful effort since the war, especially by the more advanced countries, to avoid the use of restrictions on trade. These had become more severe before the Second World War; although they were not so manifest in earlier times, there was a fairly free resort to increased tariff protection, when this seemed expedient.

At the conference at Bretton Woods there was general agreement that it would be desirable after the war to have less resort to restrictive international commercial policies, especially those of a discriminatory kind, and there was also general agreement that it would be desirable to supplement the amount of reserves available for international settlement as a condition for implementing a policy of greater freedom of trade. Having this supplementary medium to hand, policy-makers would not have to watch the day to day balance of payments so closely; they would thereby be relieved from having to have quick resort to restrictive commercial measures. It was supposed that the institution of quotas at the International Monetary Fund would achieve this object.

In the event all has turned out differently. Instead of reserves being more ample, they have dwindled, even if we count in quotas with the I.M.F., to much less than half what they were before the war.

The situation would have become worse but for the emergence of the dollar as an important medium of reserve and settlement. This, while helpful in itself, has given rise to a somewhat tangled situation in relation to the consideration of these matters. The growth of externally held dollar balances was a reflection of the continuing deficits of the United States. In the earlier days these were welcomed, precisely because they lead to a wider diffusion of world reserves, which had previously been highly concentrated in the United States. This was partly constituted by a wider diffusion of gold itself. But the deficits were also financed in part by the willingness of other countries to hold dollars in lieu of gold. It is rather curious that in international book-keeping foreign currencies held by monetary authorities count as assets, when they estimate the size of their reserves, while the liabilities that are the counterpart of these assets are not subtracted in the computation of the size of the reserve that each country has. This applies, for instance, to the statements of the reserve position of each country provided in International Finance Statistics (I.M.F.). In the reference above to the recent shortage of reserves, no subtraction of liabilities was made. If the external liabilities of the monetary authorities were debited, the shortage mentioned would be far greater. Indeed if the United States and the United Kingdom had based their policies on the size of their *net* reserves, the system would have broken down completely.

From this point of view the United States deficits have been a very helpful factor in easing the world monetary situation. But, after they became more severe (1958) and continued to be so, the attitude to them in a number of countries changed. Criticisms began to be levelled at this important feature in the situation that alone allowed the system to continue to tick over. Thus a severe contradiction arose. The criticisms must be considered under two main heads.

1. There developed in certain quarters what may be called a prejudice against what was coming to be the predominant

position of the dollar in international finance. Some regarded it as a sort of neo-imperialism. If people around the world came more and more to do their business in terms of the American currency, this seemed to imply, however mistakenly, that the United States was ruling the roost around the world, apart from, of course, the communist countries. In the old days peoples might do obeisance to a crowned head, even if the amount of interference in their affairs that was involved thereby was fairly light. The use of the dollar in day-to-day business seemed to some to involve a greater degree of dependence. It entered more intimately into the lives of people. And what would happen if the dollar came to be mismanaged? Its history has not been altogether unchequered.

2. More important was the idea, which has already been discussed, that there seemed to be something wrong with a system, the essential working of which involved the rendering by other countries of real goods and services to the United States, year by year, in exchange for bits of paper which had cost that country very little to print. The issuer of paper money gets 100% seigniorage profit, which is far more than the *grands seigneurs* got in medieval times.

In due course the Americans themselves, at least the more responsible of their number, became convinced that the American external deficits ought to be terminated at a fairly early date and officials became committed to doing their best to secure that. But then what would happen to the international monetary system? Its main source of replenishment would dry up. This dilemma led to the discussions described in Chapter 11.

The use of sterling as a reserve currency has not been increasing in ratio to British trade. Owing to the devaluation of 1967, and also to the fact that in the months that followed this seemed to be having no good effect on the external U.K. deficit, holders of sterling as a reserve began considering whether they ought not substantially to reduce their holdings. Had this happened, it would have further exacerbated the international liquidity problem.

Accordingly, with the backing of the major central banks, the U.K. made a new arrangement with sterling area members in the later part of 1968. 90% of their sterling holdings received a dollar guarantee, while they agreed to continue to hold sterling in roughly the customary proportion of their total reserves. The position of sterling was underpinned by the granting by the twelve participating countries of a standby credit of $2,000 million to meet cases when the use of sterling by the sterling area countries to finance non-sterling deficits – reserves are there to be used! – might cause embarrassment to the U.K. The credit was to be employed for this purpose only. ('Basel facility'.)

It is to be noted that the use of sterling as a reserve currency has *not* contributed to the successive 'runs' on sterling, which have arisen for the kind of reasons described on pp. 79–85, and been effectuated by the non-central bank world. There have been recurrent misconceptions about this.

The upshot is that, as things stand at present, there is no prospect of sterling making a substantial contribution in the near future to the further replenishment of world reserves.

The consequence of this tangle and this contradiction was the agreement at Rio de Janeiro for the scheme for the issuance of international paper money. If the quantity of the issue is of the order of magnitude mentioned in the discussions, the scheme can have peripheral influence only on the central problem.

At the heart of the matter is the question of what should be considered to be the correct 'adjustment process', when a country has an external imbalance. Reference has already been made to the distinguished, but inconclusive, report of the Working Party No. 3 of the O.E.C.D. Certain principles may be agreed on in the official world. But these principles will have no authority, unless it is understood that correct action in any particular case must be based on a deep analysis of the situation. The thinking that recommends deflation whenever there is an external deficit is hardly more advanced than the medicine of an earlier age which, when a high temperature was recorded, recommended blood-letting.

Reference can be made here only to a few aspects.

In the first place, in analysing the trend of a country's imports, it is necessary to distinguish those which are necessary to the country's economic life and cannot be produced at home, from those which could be produced at home but are imported because the foreign goods are superior in price, quality, etc. There cannot be a sharp border-line, because some raw materials may be substituted by synthetic products; but in most cases there could probably be a provisional and pragmatic border-line that would help. The necessary imports would be expected to grow as a function of the growth of the economic activity of the country. For balance to be maintained it is needful that exports *minus* unnecessary imports (to be called hereafter net exports) should grow at a rate equal to the rate of growth of the necessary imports. Statistical analysis is necessary to determine whether this balance is being maintained from year to year.[1]

Then we have to go deeper. If the growth of net exports is tending to fall short of the growth of necessary imports, we may distinguish two main possibilities. I am not entering at this point into discrepancies arising, whether through demand inflation or cost-push inflation, which have already been fully discussed. One possibility is that the adverse trend is due to the failure of the real productivity of the country to grow at the same rate as those of foreign competitors. This might consist in an across-the-board failure or failures in particular sectors. The other possibility is that, if the contents of imports and exports are determined on the classical principle of comparative advantage, the failing country may have advantage in the production of goods the income elasticity of the demand for which is less than that of the goods for which she is at a disadvantage. The latter case is, of course, very important in relation to the less developed countries. It is not clear that the correct adjustment mechanism is the same in these two cases, and, if it is not the same, it is necessary to have an analysis to determine to which class a country belongs. Of course a given country may fail in both respects. On the other hand, it is possible to have a case in which overall productivity is growing more rapidly in a given country and yet for that country to have a declining balance of net exports against necessary imports because of the elasticity position. Where the difficulty arises from elasticity conditions, then it is arguable that the deficit country should be encouraged, by international consensus, to

[1] Cf. R. F. Harrod, *Economic Journal*, 1967, and Ronald McKinnon, *American Economic Review*, 1963.

give discriminatory subsidies (or perhaps impose import restrictions) in favour of domestic products the world demands for which are more elastic. Doubtless commodities should be chosen, from the whole spectrum, in which the initial comparative disadvantage of the country is least.

Another very vital matter is whether there is an inflection in the growth curve. The classic example of such an inflection was when American enterprise began to be much more interested in foreign opportunities for investment in 1956 and the following years. It is by no means clear that the proper treatment of an imbalance arising from an inflection is the same as that arising in consequence of a continuing trend. An inflection suggests the need for special bridging measures. It also has to be considered whether there is likely to be an inflection in the reverse direction at a later date.

Then we have to consider the case where there is an existing gap that is not due to any current events at all, but is a hangover from events already passed. Here again it would seem that the correct remedy for a 'hangover' gap is not the same as that for a process that is continuing.

The foregoing does not profess to set out any principles, but only to give pointers to the kind of subjects requiring deep analysis before any authoritative statements can be made about appropriate adjustment mechanisms.

The theory of monetary policy of the future will be concerned, not only with the discovery of appropriate principles, but also with the methods by which they are defined and actuated both at the official national level and by way of international consensus. So far as the United Kingdom economy is concerned, which is the one that I know most about, I am convinced that to date 'multilateral surveillance' has been perverse.

We have to be concerned not only with the actual 'economics' of the matter but also with the organisation of the administration which is responsible for the day-to-day decisions. I would not make high claims for the present condition of economics itself, but there is also lack of adequate communication in most countries between the economists and the administrators, whether in governments or central banks; and politicians have also to be brought into the picture. If one could get the right kind of set up in a few important countries, that would have great value by way of example, and would probably lead to an international consensus in quite a short period.

In the free market world France should probably be regarded as the leader in putting growth in the forefront of policy. This should be said in fairness whatever *other* grounds there may be for criticising France. Deliberate policy may not be necessary in all cases. Germany may have overtopped France on the basis of a largely *laissez-faire* policy. Nothing can be inferred from this without going deeply into economic causation in the post-war period. Furthermore, surpluses, as well as deficits, call for the right kind of adjustment mechanisms, and it is not clear that Germany has been markedly successful in this. In spite of Keynes and his followers, the United Kingdom authorities, which have not hesitated to depart far from *laissez-faire*, have none the less been ideologically backward in relation to growth. The situation in the United States has been mixed, but with on the whole a good record since the advent to power of President Kennedy. This statement *may* have to be modified (1969)!

The United Kingdom authorities set a fine example to the world in basing themselves on the thinking of economists in the decades following 1830. She has slipped back since then. Unhappily there is a large difference between the requirements of the thinking of that period and requirements now. Much of what the Free Traders required could be done by an administrative stroke of the pen; tariffs had to be reduced or eliminated. The methods of implementing a growth policy, even when properly understood, would be likely to be complex, and somewhat different in each country. It is very important, indeed indispensable, to obtain an international consensus; but this would have to take account of the fact that the adjustment mechanisms appropriate to each country might vary much, although based on the same underlying principles.

If the idea that all should be done to promote economic 'growth', that is a progressive increase in human welfare, could capture the minds of men, in the way that Free Trade did in the mid-nineteenth century, that would be of vast benefit to mankind.

But it does not seem likely to do so in the near future.

INDEX

INDEX